Understanding Families

SAGE has been part of the global academic community since 1965, supporting high quality research and learning that transforms society and our understanding of individuals, groups, and cultures. SAGE is the independent, innovative, natural home for authors, editors and societies who share our commitment and passion for the social sciences.

Find out more at: **www.sagepublications.com**

LINDA McKIE = SAMANTHA CALLAN

Understanding Families

A Global Introduction

Los Angeles | London | New Delhi
Singapore | Washington DC

SAGE Publications Ltd
1 Oliver's Yard
55 City Road
London EC1Y 1SP

SAGE Publications Inc.
2455 Teller Road
Thousand Oaks, California 91320

SAGE Publications India Pvt Ltd
B 1/I 1 Mohan Cooperative Industrial Area
Mathura Road, Post Bag 7
New Delhi 110 044

SAGE Publications Asia-Pacific Pte Ltd
3 Church Street
#10-04 Samsung Hub
Singapore 049483

Library of Congress Control Number: 2011927607

British Library Cataloguing in Publication data

A catalogue record for this book is available from the British Library

ISBN 978-1-84787-931-8
ISBN 978-1-84787-932-5 (pbk)

Typeset by C&M Digitals (P) Ltd, Chennai, India
Printed and bound by CPI Group (UK) Ltd, Croydon, CR0 4YY
Printed on paper from sustainable resources

This book is dedicated to:

My daughter Laura, mother Irene, father James, sister Ann and her family Glenn, Scott and Katie – for your energy, enthusiasm and pursuit of the important things in life!

Linda

My husband Paul, children Elizabeth and Daniel, father Frank, sister Catrina, stepmother Moira, brother Peter and mother-in-law Anita – for all they have done and said to help me understand families.

Samantha

To colleagues at the Centre for Research in Families and Relationships (www.crfr.ac.uk) for their support during the writing and production of this book. As the Centre celebrates its tenth anniversary we look forward to future collaborations.

Linda and Samantha

Contents

PART III: FAMILIES IN ACTION

Chapter 5: Relationships and Sexualities

Chapter 6: Families and Work

About the Authors

Linda McKie is Professor of Sociology, Glasgow Caledonian University and Associate Director, Centre for Research on Families and Relationships, University of Edinburgh. In 2004 she was elected to the Academy of Social Sciences. In addition to teaching courses on families, social theory, work, and research methods she co-ordinates a research programme on organizations, work and care (see www.organisationsworkan-dcare.org). Linda has strong links with a range of charities and is currently a trustee for Evaluation Support Scotland, the Institute of Rural Health and a co-opted trustee for the veterans charity, Erskine. In 2009 she qualified as a Certified Member of the Institute of Fundraising. Linda has published widely on the topics of families, gender, work and organizations. Recent relevant publications include *Interdependency and Care Over the Lifecourse*, with Sophia Bowlby, Susan Gregory and Isobel MacPherson (Routledge, 2010), *Families in Society: Relationships and Boundaries*, with Sarah Cunningham-Burley (Policy Press, 2005) and *Families, Violence and Social Change* (Open University Press, 2005).

Samantha Callan is a published academic and honorary research fellow at Edinburgh University, based at the Centre for Research on Families and Relationships. She works with a broad spectrum of UK and international non-governmental family organizations and academics in her current role as a family policy specialist. She chairs major policy reviews for the Westminster-based Centre for Social Justice and advises government and opposition parties on issues concerning family life, children's early years and mental health. She is a frequent contributor to media, parliamentary and policy debates on these subjects. She is first author of the family volumes of *Breakdown Britain* (Centre for Social Justice, 2006) and *Breakthrough Britain: Ending the Costs of Social Breakdown* (Centre for Social Justice, 2007) and of *Breakthrough Britain: The Next Generation* (Centre for Social Justice, 2008). She also co-edited, with Harry Benson, *What Works in Relationship Education?* (Doha International Institute for Family Studies and Development, 2009).

Acknowledgements

This book is intended to be as accessible as possible given that it aims to be an introductory text for students from a wide range of disciplines. With this in mind it was essential that fresh eyes scoured every page to check that ideas and material were clearly expressed and that we had not assumed prior knowledge of the field. Our 'critical readers' Ingrid Biese and Anita Callan, from Finland and England, respectively, performed this role superbly and provided many helpful comments within very tight timescales. The anonymous peer reviewer offered useful insights and ideas on clarity and content. We adopted and adapted most of their suggestions and thank them very much.

Laura Keeler and Cheryl Hobbs worked with us closely in the editing stages of the manuscript. Both ensured we were kept on 'our toes' in this process, reminded us of the goal when the journey seemed long and tortuous, and offered practical and positive support in numerous ways. In the final stages Maria Breslin got us through to submission. Many thanks!

We have both found the encouragement and practical support of staff at the Centre for Research on Families and Relationships (CRFR) based at the University of Edinburgh (where Linda is an associate director and Samantha is an honorary fellow) to be invaluable. In this centre of excellence for family studies, many insightful comments are made in everyday interactions. These have served to enrich a publication as wide ranging as this one intended to be.

Similarly, many stimulating discussions have taken place with colleagues at the Westminster thinktank, the Centre for Social Justice, where Samantha is a Chairman-in-Residence. She has also benefited from many conversations with politicians and policy makers across the political spectrum, and from (Westminster) Houses of Parliament, devolved assemblies and local authorities. Interaction over several years with academic and political colleagues from Australia, the USA, Europe, the Nordic countries and the Arab world have all helped to prevent parochialism from creeping into her work.

The Department of Social Sciences, Glasgow Caledonian University, funded a sabbatical semester for Linda and the School of Health in Social Science, University of Edinburgh, co-hosted Linda's sabbatical time at CRFR. While there, Isobel MacPherson ably covered her teaching and along with colleagues in social sciences, Glasgow Caledonian University took up any slack. We would like to thank the Department of Social Sciences for support throughout the production of the book.

A book is a team effort. Many of those engaged in this process are not fully aware of their membership of the said team and the academic, practical and everyday support they provided. We would like to thank Allan Alstead, Ella Anderson, Rocco Conforti, Liz Jagger, Marjut Jyrkinen, Adrian Kidd, Lydia Lewis, Nancy Lombard, Tim May, Gavin Moreton and the many colleagues, friends and family members who supported us while completing this book. You can rest easy now; we are done! Until the next time …

Last, but not least, a heartfelt thanks to Katherine Haw and Jai Seaman of Sage, who kept us going through thick and thin. Their energy and support helped us to continue when the whole task seemed a chore and kept us focused on the final output of this book.

All errors remain those of the authors but there would have been many more without the input of the colleagues and friends noted above.

List of Figures and Tables

FIGURE

TABLES

List of Acronyms

AAHMI	African American Healthy Marriage Initiative
AIDS	acquired immune deficiency syndrome
ART	assisted reproductive technology
ESRC	Economic and Social Research Council
ESS	European Social Survey
EU	European Union
GDP	gross domestic product
GUS	Growing up in Scotland
HIV	human immunodeficiency virus
ILO	International Labour Organization
IMF	International Monetary Fund
LAT	living apart together
LGBT	lesbian, gay, bisexual, transgender
MDG	Millennium Development Goals, UN
MMR	maternal mortality rate
NGO	non-governmental organization
ODI	Overseas Development Institute
OECD	Organisation for Economic Co-operation and Development
TSOL	total social organization of labour
UN	United Nations
UNHRC	United Nations Human Rights Commission
WB	World Bank
WHO	World Health Organization

How to Use this Book

We have written a book with content and in a format we hope will be amenable to readers new to the topic. To ease the reader's progress through the book we have used visual aids as well as an accessible writing style.

Illustrations of the subjects and concepts introduced in the main body of the text and material to which we want to give prominence, so that it is less easily glanced over in the reading, are pulled out into several types of boxes.

Where themes are revisited elsewhere in the book we have made interconnections explicit using 'signposting arrows' as illustrated below.

> ➜ When describing earlier how one of the authors of this book travels and communicates across the UK and the Netherlands and has day-to-day experience of how families work over distances, we introduced the theme of 'transnational' families. The growing numbers of such families and the personal and policy consequences arising from difficulties in continuity of care and maintenance of relationships are looked at closely in Chapters 4 and 6.

When we think the reader could benefit from pausing and reflecting on the material under discussion we have inserted a 'stop and think' question mark:

> **?** Have you ever finished reading a whole book and realized that you have not at any point considered either the implications of what it has said for your own life and situations you are familiar with or the wider application to other areas of study and interest? To help the reader engage more consistently with the subject matter we have punctuated the text with opportunities to reflect on what they have just read.

A summary is provided at the end of each chapter with a short section titled 'Explore Further', which offers recommendations for further reading and the links to relevant websites.

In addition, the glossary at the end of the book gives brief definitions of all the key terms and ideas.

We have consciously avoided a 'formulaic' approach, the presentation of a compendium of facts or a generalized commentary that tends towards the simplification of social phenomena, and does not require critical thinking on the part of the reader.

Paradoxically the familiarity with the subject that we have been trying to foster can challenge this aspiration because our very experiences of families and relationships can make these social phenomena as an academic subject appear 'commonsense' and straightforward and can lead to them being interpreted and discussed in simplistic ways.

We have sought at all points to draw the reader into the subject in ways which stimulate ideas and internal debate, employing facts and commentary to serve that purpose.

Introduction

- Structures, Processes and Strategies
- Family or Families?
- Families in History
- The Families We Live With, the Families We Live By
- The Contents of the Book
- Summary
- Explore Further

Keywords: family structures, process, global strategies, history, idealizations, realties

Welcome to *Understanding Families: A Global Introduction*. Our subject matter is one all readers have experiences to draw upon and many will do so with a range of powerful and often conflicting emotions. All of us are, to a greater or lesser extent, saturated in the implications of families. Popular culture provides a seemingly endless stream of commentary and critique about families, such as that found on the pages of celebrity and human interest magazines and in online blogs. Soap opera storylines allow us to partake, voyeuristically, of other people's family dramas with only a faint whiff of the pain such misadventures would bring if we were actually caught up in the tugging emotions as flesh and blood participants.

'Zeitgeist' films and other manifestations of popular culture which chart the relational landscape of society have enduring appeal. The fact that we find films, plays, musicals and books that attend to the ordinariness of messy family life utterly compelling is evident in their box office successes, DVD sales and literary ratings. Similarly there has been a surge of interest in family lineage, a leisure activity which, according to the sociologist Carol Smart (2007), uses the past to make sense of the present. Also, for example, there has been a rash of television programmes where a range of celebrities go back to their roots.

A key aim for us is to address diversity by looking across the world at the range of challenges families face and how they are met. Given this global perspective, we ask the reader to note we use the terms *majority world* and *minority world*. These acknowledge that those living in more affluent societies, including those in North America, Europe, Australia, New Zealand and parts of Latin America are in the statistical minority. What has often been called the 'Third World' is the majority world with most of the global population and landmass (Punch, 2003). Using these terms promotes an appreciation of global inequalities and encourages us to scrutinize commonly held ways of reflecting on the world and turn these – quite literally – upside down.

STRUCTURES, PROCESSES AND STRATEGIES

This book aims to employ all the mental and personal 'hooks' students will already have as they come to this subject. We do not assume familiarity with prior social science studies on families. Our guiding objective is to provide an accessible treatment of key trends, explanations, policies and ideas on and about families to our main audiences. Given that we are all instinctively drawn to and implicated in the subject matter of family studies, we want to make it accessible to students not just in mainstream social studies but also in subjects ranging across education, social work, business and nursing.

One important distinction we make at the outset and return to throughout the book is between family structure and family process. These are distinctive dimensions to the study of families and we offer definitions for both in Boxes I and II.

Box I Families' structures

Family structure refers to family composition or how families are formed. A family might be an elderly grandmother and her orphaned grandchildren, the vast majority of whose other relatives have succumbed to acquired immune deficiency syndrome (AIDS)-related deaths. Or it might be a same-sex couple who have adopted or conceived children through assisted reproductive technology (ART). Equally it might be a mother, a father and their biological children in what tends to be referred to (especially if the parents are married) as the traditional nuclear family.

Having defined how a family is formed or composed – the family structure – we turn to what happens day in day out. For example, who cares for whom in the grandmother and grandchild family? Which parent tends to administer first aid in the 'traditional' or in the same-sex family, and in whose diary do dental appointments tend to be entered? Are disagreements resolved through discussion or are members coerced into consensus by threats of, or actual violence? These are aspects of family processes.

Box II Family processes

Family processes refer to the functions carried out by family members, or the dynamics of the relationships in the family structure. The way families are composed and the processes that occur within a family vary enormously within and between societies. The student of family studies must appreciate how structures and processes interweave, and how these impact on, and are affected by, wider contexts of paid work, education, health services and so on.

If family processes is the term used to describe the dynamics of what goes on in families then the term family 'practices' offers a way to identify and examine the 'little fragments of daily life which are part of the normal, taken for granted existence of the practitioners' (Morgan, 1996: 190). Not only do family practices shape and organize time and its use but they are also highly meaningful in personal or moral terms. At the same time what people do with and for their children or elderly dependants and why they do those things have huge ramifications for, among other things, the human resources policies of businesses, hospital admissions procedures and social work protocols.

→ In Chapter 2 we discuss a range of explanations of family structures and processes. The idea of family practices offers insights to family processes and the work of David Morgan is discussed in more detail in Box 2.2 on page 59.

An important debate running through subsequent chapters is the extent to which families are shaped by what is external to them, most notably large-scale (or macro-) economic processes. Sociological accounts that emphasize how families take on distinct forms in particular economic systems such as capitalism (Fine, 1992) are examples of economic determinism. These are contrasted by Cheal (2002) with accounts that suggest that family life is less determined by large-scale economic shifts than might be supposed and he argues for paying closer attention to family processes and how these are evident in family strategies (see Box III).

Box III Family strategies and household strategies

Families 'create and shape their responses to change, through adaptive *family strategies*' (Cheal, 2002: 14, emphasis in original). Wallace proposes the term *household strategies*. She describes how the idea of strategies has assumed relevance in studies in Latin America, Ireland, Italy, in developing countries where there is no state support and in post-communist countries in Eastern and Central Europe (such as Hungary, the Czech Republic and the Ukraine) (Wallace, 2002). Here we note that Cheal uses the term family and Wallace uses household. The former encourages us to consider members of families whether in the context of their relationships which may be through kin, cohabitation or the law, whereas the latter term is broader, including all those who live in the same dwelling regardless of their relationships.

➜ In Chapter 1 we consider how the terms family and household differ. All key terms are also defined in the glossary at the end of the book.

Throughout the seven chapters that follow we return to family structures and strategies, processes and practices to aid understandings and explanations of families. We also note how differences and similarities in these aspects are evident when we look at families from a global perspective.

?   Consider how ideas of family strategies and household strategies differ. Can you identify examples of how these ideas overlap and differ?

FAMILY OR FAMILIES?

In almost every occupation in which it is possible to work, or any course we study, the implications of 'family' are hard to ignore, and essential to be aware of. This is why this book imparts tools for the building of an understanding of the family and an appreciation of all the richness of social experience implied in that term. By introducing readers to a wide range of transdisciplinary and international social science work, we hope to provide some conceptual starting points for constructing a framework of understanding about family relationships. How do these relationships affect what motivates people? To what extent are these their most pressing and personal concerns? What are the barriers thrown up in people's lives by the intergenerational transmission of disadvantage? What determines if these become insuperable or hurdles which, when crossed, lead to the transformation of life chances?

The people we relate to as teachers, students, clients, line managers, workers, patients, and friends are also caught up in the complex web of family membership. Their roles as mothers, fathers, sisters, brothers, daughters and all other possible permutations impact on their occupational roles and are themselves affected by the demands of what might be termed the non-domestic sphere. Family dynamics often strongly determine how people engage with other aspects of life and we consider this in more detail in Box IV.

Box IV   The family as a reference point

Research by Jordan et al. (1994) into middle-class couples with children reveals the extent to which people's accounts of who they are and what they are trying to achieve use 'family' as a reference point. For example, actions are framed in terms of prioritizing family responsibilities in such a way that individuals constantly and consciously place limits on what is reasonable for them to seek for themselves. One interpretation of their conclusions is that 'the sense of self which an individual has is frequently hard to separate from their sense of the family unit to which they belong' (Allan and Crow, 2001: 11). Yet this need not lead to the presumption that family and individual interests always coincide. The contested nature of family membership is most clearly seen when family interests and individual interests diverge (Allan and Crow, 2001).

It is important to consider how family dynamics play out in families in different cultures or groups. One example is in certain religious communities where gender roles may be more tightly ascribed as well as obligations to family and kin. However, what actually happens in the home and at family gatherings may be more relaxed and less ascribed.

Today there is general acceptance of the diverse nature of families. Debates and research have emphasized the need to rethink how we define and consider families. One example is parenting and ethnicity. Phoenix and Husain (2007) note how in Britain, Black and Asian parents have come under scrutiny. Differences in culture and in approaches to parenting can be viewed as unacceptable or even deviant. They argue that how we construct and understand 'race' and 'ethnicity' has a bearing on family policies and services. Race is a term used to describe 'people who belong to the same human stock' (Phoenix and Husain, 2007: 5) and ethnicity refers to a community or grouping which shares common cultural practices and history. Not fully appreciating what goes to make up a family's ethnicity can and does impact on the relationships between families and service providers such as teachers, nurses and social workers, and neighbours. As we discuss across the book, social class, gender, religion, sexuality and impairment will also differentiate experiences of race and ethnicity. Nevertheless, it remains the case that race and ethnicity can result in stereotyped views and assumptions about parenting, caring and familial relationships. Sometimes these assumptions are contradictory. For example, South Asian families can be considered too narrow and traditional in their parenting styles, especially in their upbringing of girls, and yet can be supportive and proud of education and training, resulting in notable attainments in qualifications for children of both sexes.

A constant theme running through the literature is the extent to which, in recent decades, families and the way people live their lives in households and relationships have become more varied. In response to this variation, core concepts in social science literature, such as that of 'family cycle' with its implication that discrete, easily discernible family units pass through routine stages, 'each one tidily following the last' (Allan and Crow, 2001: 3), have undergone revision. Adopting instead the term 'family course' (Finch, 1987) permits the exploration of diversity in how individuals' family lives and commitments develop over time. Even those people who seem to be following fairly 'conventional' pathways are caught up in the more complex family lives of their friends, children, siblings and colleagues. Relationship formation patterns such as living apart together (LAT), cohabitation, and remarriage go alongside the parenting of 'his', 'her' and 'our' children, the possibility of several different pairs of grandparents, and parenting alone for some or all of a child's lifecourse.

Yet in spite of this growing complexity, the term 'family' continues to have a meaning that is recognizable across the globe. Moreover, we all tend to hold assumptions about family life whether they relate to typical structures or forms or to what individuals can expect or demand from other family members and relatives, in other words about the typical processes that go on inside families.

> **?** What are the differences between the terms family and families? Why do these matter?

FAMILIES IN HISTORY

One unsubstantiated impression is that before the industrial revolution many or most people lived in extended, multigenerational families, which could accommodate those unable to work, including the younger, weaker members and older members. Peter Laslett studied the size and shape of families over the centuries by gathering large amounts of statistical evidence and was obliged to demolish what he regarded as a romantic myth: 'the wish to believe in the large, kin-enfolding, multigenerational, welfare- and support-providing household in the world we have lost' (2005: 92).

The 'lost world' he refers to is typically considered to belong to the pre-industrialization phase in socioeconomic development. Yet, considering how common early death was prior to industrialization, the image of a three-generational family typically co-operating and caring for each other is flawed, not least by the fact that very few people lived long enough to become grandparents. Allan (1985) also makes the point that most families were materially ill-equipped to meet extensive health and welfare needs effectively and usually had scant medical information.

Following a review of historical evidence in the UK, Thane (2010) concluded that those who speak of a golden age for families are ignoring the large bodies of evidence demonstrating that conception outside marriage, extramarital sex and violence in families are not recent phenomena. But although trends from the past continue, the causes of these differ. For example, divorce has replaced death as the major reason for the premature ending of a marriage. Sons growing up without resident male 'role models' and complex stepfamilies were not uncommon for centuries, but this was caused largely by early death, especially among younger men. High death rates, driven by diseases, accidents and wars, resulted in high rates of lone motherhood in the past.

Poor families have always struggled and inequality is a key factor in how families manage and cope with stresses and tensions. In summary, Thane's position is that politicians, policy makers and people who reminisce about a golden era when most of the population lived in stable two-parent nuclear families without extramarital sex and family violence are misinformed (Thane, 2010). Probert and Callan (2011) offer a critique of Thane's review of historical evidence on families and family life. They argue that marriage remains a dominant type of relationship although there are diverse forms of families today. As the process of ending of a marriage is different now, having shifted from being caused by death to being initiated through divorce law, so too is the nature of suffering. Cohabitation has increased as a family type and the legal standing of these relationships varies between countries. Probert and Callan (2011) note that contemporary changes in families reflect longevity, new family law, changes in social and gender norms and economic transformations. To look back is not the best approach as we are not comparing like with like. We can, however, note and assess the trends and how changes come about.

Smart (2007) describes the need to understand the 'iconic' nature of the family and the cultural impact of that right across society. In spite of most people's proximity to, and intimacy with, the subject of family, there are many idealizations and myths illuminated in family studies and the related literature. The social historian John Gillis (2004), for example, draws a distinction between the two family systems he argues that we now have in contemporary Europe and North America: the families we live 'with' and those we live 'by'. We can, he says, access much information about the former from statistics describing what types of families people are living in, the entry and exit rates into and from various relationship statuses and future projections of trends. However, in order to understand the families we live 'by', we need the output of a different kind of research, associated with social anthropology and a school of thought in sociology based upon the idea that people act based upon their definitions of situations (known as symbolic interactionism). The mental images, rituals and stories around family are the subject matter of these disciplines in their exploitation of the family's iconic character, and to what we aspire to, even against personal and social odds.

THE FAMILIES WE LIVE WITH, THE FAMILIES WE LIVE BY

Divorce rates are high and marriage rates have fallen by two-thirds in countries such as the UK and New Zealand. However, an analysis of surveys such as the British Household Panel Study found that when asked about their future intentions, three-quarters of men and women reported that they were either planning, or expected, to get married. In Sweden, the data reveal similar attitudes, which might be surprising given its perceived progressiveness illustrated through familial and gender policies that claim to promote equality (Bernhardt, 2004). Nevertheless, an analysis of couples' attitudes to marriage led the sociologist Eva Bernhardt to conclude that 'an overwhelming majority of young cohabiting couples in Sweden expect to get married' (2004: 8). Given the high rates of relationship breakdown, mental health difficulties and the negative effect of poverty on family functioning, Gillis (2004) concludes that the families we live *with* may encounter multiple difficulties. The idealizations we hold and the high hopes we have for these same families, however, mean that the families we live *by* seem to be flourishing through what Smart describes as 'an investment in the cultural imaginary' (2007: 34). The kind of research that provides insights into how people experience family life and how they *feel* about it, adopts a sentiments approach. Chapter 3 compares and contrasts this with demographic and economic approaches to the study of family.

> **?** Consider the distinction Gillis makes above. Can you think of examples of family ideals that people might subscribe to regardless of the experiences of those around them and the 'track record' of their own family?

It is not just shared biology or romantic possibilities that exert a pull on our heart-strings: many adoptive parents agonize over the children they are raising as profoundly as if those children carried their genes; same-sex and opposite-sex friendships can engage our emotions as powerfully as relationships with those normatively considered to be part of the family. Indeed a large body of sociological work is building up around the concept of 'families of choice', which are contrasted with 'families of fate'. This literature, which we discuss more extensively in Chapter 5, examines differences between those relationships that are *chosen* and which can include both kin and non-kin, and those relationships that are *given* primarily, but not necessarily exclusively, through kinship ties.

Other writers instead draw attention to the blurring of boundaries between friendship and family relationships (McKie and Cunningham-Burley, 2005). They problematize other distinctions, hitherto considered to be clear-cut, such as notions of the public and the private where the realm of family is treated as part of the latter. Citing theorists like Bourdieu (1996: 25), who stated that

> the public vision … is deeply involved in our vision of domestic things, and our most private behaviours themselves depend on public actions, such as housing policy or, more directly, family policy

McKie and Cunningham-Burley emphasize that public and private spheres are not isolated but are rather separated by a permeable boundary 'which shapes and is shaped by our personal lives' (2005: 8).

Morgan (1996) draws attention to a trend in sociology that ended in the 1960s, which conjoined family and community studies and to think about family relationships in the wider frame of overlapping ties of family, kin, friends and neighbours. This recognized the continuities between work and non-work, domestic and occupational spheres and, again, the public and the private. However, more recently the study of family relationships has become separate from other sets of relationships, concentrating on marital or couple relationships, on parenting and socialization and, in short, on treating family relationships more systematically. Morgan (1996) goes on to describe how feminist studies moved the field of family relationships to a new level of integration with other sociological sites of interest. This was, he said, achieved by replacing the link between family and community with a link between family and gender, where gender acted as something of a code word for women, their lives, their work and ultimately their long-neglected significance in sociological analysis. In Chapter 2 we look in depth at the contribution made by feminist theory and site it in the context of other major strands of social theory that have had a particularly strong influence on the study of families.

It is worth noting that coming to the fore at present is a concern with the new and multiple ways in which people feel that they can belong. As well as wanting freedom and mobility, people also need a sense of tradition (perhaps better expressed as a connection with the past, as we said earlier) and belonging (Eagleton, 2003). There is also a growing interest in the morality of family life, with writers such as Williams (2004) exploring how commitment and care might be changing in shape rather than in quality. More prosaically, there is a discernible movement back towards seeing the primacy of economics, raising one of sociology's key issues of the extent to which people are free actors or are unduly constrained by external, 'structural' forces beyond their control.

There is also a strong link between most governments' social policies and their economic policies, reflected in a concern with how paid work articulates with family life across the income spectrum. Supranational organizations, including the United Nations (UN), the International Labour Organization (ILO) and the European Union (EU), address the role of families, recognizing the work of nurturing the next generation, caring for those who cannot be in paid work, and enabling others to participate in education, training and employment.

> ➜ The interweaving of families and economy may be taken for granted but is important and we devote much attention to such issues in Chapters 4 (on policy) and 6 (on work and families).

THE CONTENTS OF THE BOOK

As we noted in the section 'How to Use this Book', throughout the book we have used the signposting mechanisms of an arrow to note a connection between topics or issues across chapters, a question mark for reflective and think points, and boxes to draw out definitions and highlight relevant pieces of research. The intention in using this structure and approach is to provide as many connecting and reflective points as possible in the hope that this enhances the reader's ability to be engaged. As the sociologist Arlie Hochschild (2003b: 6) has noted

> The self is an instrument of enquiry. Every time we see we compare …
> so our subjectivity, with the wealth of comparisons it implants in us
> transplants us into tourists of ourselves, visitors of the odd sights of eve-
> ryday life. It removes the dull sense that anything is at all obvious.

The signposts appear in all seven chapters of the book and below we outline the contents of each of these.

In Chapter 1 we pose the question 'What is the family?' by looking at what is considered mainstream and what is marginal, and the shifting nature of that distinction in many societies. The overarching aim of this chapter is to provide factual information in ways that illustrate and illuminate trends. We also consider how families 'mesh' with wider kinship networks in terms of how individuals identify themselves, and in terms of the nature of obligations, responsibilities and expectations towards and regarding kin. In the second half of the chapter we present two case studies of welfare policies on families in France, Russia, former East and West Germany, and subsequently Asia, noting trends in China, Japan, Singapore and South Korea.

Chapter 2 outlines how key theoretical perspectives aim to explain families. Without attempting to address theoretical frameworks in depth, we concentrate on exploring why we have theories by treating them under a limited number of broad headings (economic systems and perspectives; gender and identities and political).

Chapter 3 shows how we research families by presenting for consideration some of the dilemmas, data and debates tackled by seminal, earlier studies. It also contrasts quantitative data available in national and international surveys, which provide information on broad trends over time but offer few insights to the everyday workings of families and relationships. Qualitative methods are often used to explore the 'practices' of families, but in order to chart and mesh trends and practices there would seem to be a notable shift to multimethod projects. This trend brings a range of challenges and opportunities to family research.

This review of how we might best address the complexities of familial and human relationships provides a framework for Chapter 4, which considers politics, policies and practices, the evidence base on which politicians, policy makers and practitioners draw or ignore and how the relationship between these three groups of agents plays out differently according to context.

In Chapter 5 we chart and address the dynamic nature of relationships and of family formation, dissolution and re-formation. Most of us will marry or cohabit at some points during our lifetime. We are likely to forge a range of relationships in and around our family. These may focus on the creation of children and become blood ties, or include step-parenting and thus a growth in immediate family membership. Intimate and sexual relationships, care roles and interdependencies underpin family life. Insufficient access to material and emotional resources poses significant challenges for families and relationships, often leading to tensions, abuse and violence. Friends, neighbours, churches, charities and welfare services also engage with families to offer support in general and at critical points.

Chapter 6 explores the interweaving of employment, work and care, as families strive to achieve a balance between economic necessities and social and emotional needs. Although changes in care facilities and services, backed by policies, have improved the potential for parents (especially mothers) to enter or increase their participation in the workforce, these developments mask a connection between women and caring that enduringly underpins policy-oriented notions of 'the family' and what women and men are expected to do.

The themes of marriage and cohabitation, solo living, friendships, social networks and communities recur throughout the book, and in the final chapter, Chapter 7, we draw these threads together. We not only revisit differing ways of explaining and researching families in the global context but also explore the future of families. The wider policy agendas and the significant role many states have assumed in areas formerly considered to fall outside their purview are examined. Global economic and demographic trends continue to impact on families and relationships to varying degrees in what continues to be a world of inequalities and challenges.

At the end of each chapter we offer suggestions for further reading and a list of websites of relevance. The glossary at the back of the book offers brief definitions of key terms and concepts.

SUMMARY

Debates about families are lively and achieve a high profile in media, policy and politics. Relevant social issues include parenting, longevity, solo living, crime, religion and how family life plays out in developing societies. Politicians utilize (at best) and manipulate (at worst) meanings and understandings about 'the family' for the purposes of making policy, often in ways that are advantageous to public institutions rather than to private individuals. For example, particular family structures may be assumed such as the male breadwinner and female home-based carer, even in societies where it is not uncommon for one parent to raise a child on their own. Or, when assessing how adult individuals' health and social care needs are to be met, assumptions are often made about the level of provision families are capable of and willing to deliver: in other words about ideal family processes. Family issues are not just of universal *personal* relevance. The study of families draws attention to profound changes as well as to continuities in contemporary societies across the globe. It also illuminates the relevance of families for all aspects of social life.

Physically or mentally, directly or indirectly, our families influence almost every waking moment of our lives. Our aim within this book is to take the reader beyond that truism and to anatomize the ways in which family relationships, past, present and anticipated, shape and may even ultimately determine the meanings of other aspects of our existence. We do this by drawing on the organizing themes of family structure and family process, how families form and how they function. We look across the world, adopting a global perspective rather than restricting the subject matter to what would be immediately familiar to readers in the minority world. Given the introductory nature of this text, the aim was to build incrementally on the basic foundation of commonly held understandings of the family, to provide something akin to a mezzanine floor from where the reader could explore unfamiliar concepts. It is our hope that such a text will encourage many to move further up the family studies building, and that those not tempted will still have come away with a much improved framework for understanding their own and others' family lives.

EXPLORE FURTHER

Graham Allan and Graham Crow's *Families, Households and Society* (2001) is well-respected in the area of family studies. These authors have addressed most of the areas essential to the field. The content is largely minority world and mostly UK based.

Jon Bernardes' *Family Studies. An Introduction* (1997) remains an excellent introduction and, before the publication of *Understanding Families: A Global Introduction*, the only real resource book aimed specifically at students new to family studies.

David Cheal's *Sociology of Family Life* (2002) provides a more introductory tone to material. The book has a useful glossary and each chapter begins with a signpost paragraph of chapter content and ends with a summarizing discussion.

Jane Ribbens McCarthy and Rosalind Edwards' *Key Concepts in Family Studies* (2010) comprises 48 short essays on major themes significant to the study of families. It is a reference book as well as offering insights to the analysis of families.

David Morgan's *Family Connections: An Introduction to Family Studies* (1996) remains an influential book in which he introduces the notion of family practices.

USEFUL WEBSITES

Centre for Research on Families, Life Course and Generations, University of Leeds: www.sociology.leeds.ac.uk/flag/about

Centre for Research on Families and Relationships, University of Edinburgh: www.crfr.ac.uk.

Clearing House on International Developments in Child, Youth and Family Policies at Columbia University in New York City: www.childpolicyintl.org.

The Morgan Centre for the Study of Relationships and Personal Life. Available at www.socialsciences.manchester.ac.uk/morgancentre.

The Weeks Centre, South Bank University, London: www.lsbu.ac.uk/ahs/research/weeks.shtml.

PART I

INTRODUCING FAMILIES

1

Families and Relationships

Keywords: characteristics, trends, values, kinship, global perspectives, eastern European families, Asian families

INTRODUCTION

Families are the oldest and most enduring form of social grouping. The depth of debates and feeling engendered by the subject of families reflects our personal investment in familial relationships. During our lifetimes we experience a range of intimate experiences which may include cohabitation, marriage and parenting, divorce, caring for a sick spouse or child, and bereavement. Families are a source of strength, groupings in which we experience enjoyment and emotional fulfilment. Families may become destabilized, dissolve and re-form. Unhappiness, tensions and conflict may be evident at times.

Regardless of our strength of feeling on family arrangements, most of us, at every age and stage of our lives, think of ourselves as part of one or more families. These are formed, dissolved and reconfigured in the light of many factors, not least of which is the need for some sense of stability and unity to ensure day-to-day survival and sustenance and, in the longer term, growth and flourishing. Personal experiences and views on, for example, intimate relationships, working and parenting or elder care are continually revised as we mature, grow older and engage with others.

> **?**   Families change all the time. To illustrate this point, write down the name of anyone you consider members of your family.
>
> • What is the age range of the members?
> • Where do they live?
> • What changes in family structures and family processes have taken place in the past decade?
> • What future changes do you anticipate and why might these happen?

Over the course of history, families have taken many forms and they continue to provide the context in which we experience many of our most intimate and caring relationships. The topic of families has been one of heated debates, especially around the question of what constitutes 'a family'? Ideas about families traverse a spectrum from those in which there is one dominant form of 'the family' to others which passionately support diverse forms of family arrangements. People can hold strong views about what a family should be and the experiences they have had in families. Comment, debates and policies bring families into the spotlight: how can families be supported, monitored, adapted and encouraged?

Julia Brannen (2003) has asserted the UK is entering a period of what is termed 'beanpole' families. As people live longer but have fewer children, and so each generation has fewer siblings, the family trees of living relatives are becoming longer and thinner, sometimes extending to four generations – hence the analogy of the beanpole. Same-sex relationships, solo living and the choice to remain childless do not exclude people from family or household membership. In some societies these types of families are on the increase.

Before we go further we note the difference and overlap between the terms household and family. These can be used interchangeably but are distinct. A household consists of a person or group of people living together in a specific dwelling. This group may or may not consider themselves to be a family. A household of two generations, generally parents and children, is commonly referred to as the nuclear family. An extended family household incorporates three or more generations. These can include great-grandparents, grandparents, parents and children, commonly referred to as vertical generations. Aunts and uncles may also be extended members of families and form what are known as horizontal generations. However, whether we talk of a family or household, this is the social grouping in which we learn about health and hygiene, physical and emotional care, leisure and social engagement, and prepare for key life stages, including primary and secondary education, working life, retirement and death.

Sociology offers ways of examining families and relationships, and sociological studies on families consider, among other topics, family formation, breakdown, democratization and continuity. Commentators and researchers may be optimistic, pessimistic or ambivalent about families and family life. Whatever the perspective taken, Gillies comments that much sociological work on families 'revolves around the theme of social change' (2003: 2). A focus on change, sometimes referred to as 'families in flux' (Giddens, 1992) is not new; and you will have explored this in response to the exercise above.

> **?**   Sociology is, among other things, the study of groups in societies and how these interact. Above we noted that sociology often examines changes in families. What other topics or issues might sociologists concerned with families study?

FAMILIES: A CONSTANT STATE OF FLUX

Changes in living arrangements and family formations have encouraged ever more complex networks of current and former families to exist alongside continuities (Hunt, 2010). Historical research, however, demonstrates that families are in a constant state of flux. For example, parenting types include grandparents, single parents, extended family groupings, and heterosexual and homosexual couples. The reasons for diverse parenting arrangements vary. Events and circumstances which lead to differing arrangements include death, illness, relationship breakdown, opportunities for work elsewhere, and the impact of wars and civil conflict (Blaikie, 1998). Likewise, care arrangements for sick or older relatives have also varied from the multiple generation household in which care is provided for children and elders, to the adult child living with frail parents and more recently to the adult child supporting the move of a parent into sheltered housing or a nursing home. As with all care arrangements family members and family needs are at the forefront of the planning and day-to-day delivery of care (Hareven, 2000).

Today in the UK, half of all births are registered to unmarried parents, although, in most cases the mother and father provide the same address for the birth certificate. To register a birth to unmarried parents 50 years ago would have been considered unacceptable and potentially stigmatizing for the child. Cohabiting parents in, for example, western Europe or North America are rarely considered worthy of note. Contrast this with Japan, where births outside marriage are relatively rare at around 8% and single parenthood is strongly associated with people in their 30s and 40s, who have been widowed or divorced.

A further contrast is offered through the example of care for older relatives provided by paid carers. In the UK, this is no longer considered a poor reflection on the capabilities of families. With changes in employment and in economic aspirations and opportunities, family members might live many miles from each other. Distance may make the physical delivery of care impossible but communication technologies enable emotional support and allow for practical inputs as care and support can be organized over phone and email. By contrast, in Singapore it is rare for older people to live alone (less that 20% of those over 65) and care is predominately provided by family members.

Historical studies and debates have demonstrated how families across the world are always changing in response to a range of opportunities and challenges (Hareven, 1994). Furthermore, historical work has illuminated how debates about families have considered social breakdown, social cohesion, and the development and role of family networks and relationships. These changes may seem to be of greater relevance for some countries and continents than others, but changes, alongside continuities are evident in all families.

CONTINUITIES AND PRESUMPTIONS

Alongside change, there are numerous continuities evident in families and family life. In times of crisis most people look to their family for practical, financial and emotional support. Generally the presumption that support will be forthcoming is borne out. Further, the continued and strong association of all forms of nurturing and care with families serves to constantly ignite and reinforce familial obligations and duties. The workings of families and society's responses to them reflect a range of ideas. These can include gender roles, age-specific behaviours, ethnicity and cultural norms (Bowlby et al., 2010).

?   Thinking about your family are there assumptions made about who will be the main person to:

- Take children to the dentist for a regular check-up?
- Cook a meal for family members to share on an evening?
- Do the gardening?
- Press the button on the television remote control during the weekend
- Organize a holiday?
- Pay utility bills?

Write down the sex and age of the person(s) for each of above tasks. Are these roles openly discussed? Are these negotiated? Have roles and tasks changed in recent years?

Changes and continuities can collide. The increase in men's involvement in formal and informal types of care in northern Europe is noteworthy and welcomed by many. Regardless of this change most care work remains 'gender coded' in so far as it is work associated with feminine skills and attributes and is largely undertaken by women as family members or as care workers (Crompton, 2001). Where there are no or limited welfare or healthcare regimes the family is the main provider of health-care, as in for example, rural communities in sub-Saharan Africa. In communities or societies where services do exist, these are based on presumptions about the role and availability of family members. For example, the convalescence of an older rela-tive after medical care is generally undertaken by family and friends who may shop, cook, clean and work in many practical and emotional ways to aid recovery. Families are commonly viewed as units in which, and through which, members, friends and sometimes neighbours receive various forms of psychological and physical support and care.

This chapter, and the book as a whole, are organized around three main topics.

- **Structures: identifying and talking about families**. Family arrangements vary across countries and communities reflecting a range of social and economic arrangements. What we understand by a family is under constant review and reflects a range of beliefs, values and legally or socially sanctioned living arrangements. Legal definitions form the basis for collecting statistical data on living arrangements through, for example, census surveys. The data inform the policy and service responses of governments and international organizations, and thus the 'snap shot' taken every decade through a census survey provides important information about policy efficacy and which services might be expanded or contracted. Other definitions and experiences evolve through personal, group and community ideas on what are acceptable living arrangements for men and women, for the young and old and for the healthy and sick. Whatever the definition we choose to use, it reflects ideas about sexual relationships, care arrangements and resource exchanges among people drawn to each other through intimate and blood relationships.

- **Processes: families, kinship and activities**. Those related through blood lines are automatically given membership to a family which is enshrined in the law starting with the registration of births and including the recording of marriages and deaths. Others achieve membership through intimate relationships such as cohabitation or long-term friendships when family friends become accepted as members. The words and emotions people use to discuss who is in 'their family' illuminate what families mean to them. The word kin is a particularly important and emotive word, which can be defined as 'of the same kind or nature'. Kinship is an important organizing concept, especially at times of bereavement, serious illness and crisis, when the idea of 'next of kin' comes to the fore. This is laden with responsibilities and powers: for example, to give consent for emergency medical treatment, or in the event of death for organ donation. The term kin-keeping, however, describes the various day-to-day and longer-term activities associated with sustaining family networks and connections, such as remembering birthdays, organizing family get-togethers and sustaining flows of information on family members.

- **Global families**. It is easy to think of families and family life largely through the lens of our own social experiences. Family formations differ from community to community across the world. The examining of global differences and trends at the outset of any study of families draws our attention to the many ways in which differences emerge and change takes place. Social, political and economic contexts, religious or other belief systems, conflicts, natural disasters and diseases impact on families, living arrangements and relationships, resulting in changes. There is also the 'global family', through which we are drawn together by interconnected problems such as wars, climate change and economic interdependencies. Thus family life is also a major topic for governments and international organizations, including the UN, the World Health Organization (WHO) and the International Monetary Fund (IMF). In this section of the chapter we identify trends in health and illness in families across the world. Subsequently, we examine how welfare policies impact on families in the countries of France, East and West Germany and the Russian Federation (Topic 1) and the impact of religious and cultural beliefs on family types in China, Japan, Singapore and South Korea (Topic 2).

Throughout this book we use the terms *majority world* and *minority world*. To reiterate what we said in the Introduction, these terms acknowledge that those who live in more affluent societies, including those in North America, Europe, Australia, New Zealand and parts of Latin America are in the statistical minority. What has often been called the 'Third World' is the majority world with most of the global population and land-mass (Punch, 2003). Many find these terms counterintuitive, assuming that the majority world is associated with affluence rather than vice versa. We maintain that the adoption of the terms minority world and majority world reminds us of the disproportionate role of the few affluent economies on global economics, health and well-being, and climate change.

STRUCTURES: IDENTIFYING AND TALKING ABOUT FAMILIES

The aim of this section is to provide the building bricks to aid the reader to critically examine families. These include the:

- common characteristics of families
- principles underpinning families and relationships
- statistical information on contemporary trends in families and family life.

Before we offer ideas and information to aid the identification of families we alert readers to the work of Carol Smart (2007). In her discussion of families and personal life, Smart places emphasis on the affection and emotions evident in family relationships and asserts that definitions can downplay 'emotional connectedness' (2007: 189). This matters when we talk of our family – the conversation will be illustrated by the many types of relationship and emotion we experience, including concern, anxiety, love, sexual feelings, frustration, excitement, fear and friendship.

In addition, we draw attention to Therborn's statement of the obvious in so far as most of us arrive as the result of sexual activity: 'A family is always an outcome of sexual relations past or current: no sex, no family' (2004: 1). However, with the growth of fertility treatments and technologies, family members may result from the wish to reproduce assisted by medical intervention. Therborn also notes how the family is a 'regulator of sexual relations', for it sets unwritten but understood guidelines for who can and cannot engage in sexual relations without sanction or stigma. Thus familial relationships and networks provide a range of intimate, emotional, physical and economic experiences.

DEFINING FAMILIES 1: COMMON CHARACTERISTICS

With the proviso that definitions and studies of families may underplay the role of emotion and sex, what characteristics of families might we consider?

- **A common identity**. This refers to an individual's comprehension of themselves as a discrete, separate entity through being part of their family grouping. The common identity of families can flourish over distance and time. This includes returning to participate in family gatherings such as birthdays, weddings or funerals and family-focused celebrations including Christmas or the Hindu festival of Diwali. Family memories are recalled, challenged, discussed and forged through new experiences, and such memories are critical to identities.

- **Economic co-operation and ownership**. This refers to the creation and allocation of resources across families, and may include money from earned income, money from investments, benefits from governments (such as tax allowances to help with the care of children), benefits in kind from employers achieved through the employment of family members (for example, health insurance that includes the employee and their family), goods and services including gifts of furniture, and the provision of no cost care or support through advice and skills. Economic co-operation is core to most families and interweaves members across generations and locations through everyday exchanges and legacies on the death of members.

- **Reproduction of the next generation**. The birth of children is generally a cause for celebration in most families. Coupled with celebrations are concerns about the health and well-being of children. Families make a major investment in the development and futures of children, including those who join families through adoption or marriage. When children arrive into a family the work of rearing the next generation to adulthood becomes a core focus. Relatives and friends also play a part and this can include periods of co-residence to help with childcare during periods of particular stress or the provision of short-term practical support, such as helping with the costs of a child's clothes or activities. Thus rearing the next generation involves a range of family members, friends and neighbours, who can play a key role through informal care such as babysitting or transport, support with homework, sports activities or other leisure pursuits.

  Today, many more people are childless out of choice in comparison with a century ago. Households are also becoming childless as a result of children growing up, moving away or being estranged.

- **Care work and domestic labour**. People need certain basics to flourish, not least of which are the provision of food and a location in which to sleep and to manage basic hygiene. In times of illness and dependency, the interdependencies of families come to the fore. As noted earlier, these forms of work are gendered in so far as they are considered to be labour associated with feminine skills. Thus it is predominately adult women and girl children who are the family members and workers who provide physical and emotional care and domestic labour. That said, a vocal and notable minority of men and men's groups express concerns that they are edged out of care as a result of the gender coding of childcare. Furthermore, concerns about the potential for the physical and sexual abuse of children by male relatives also pose barriers to a greater engagement of men in care work. In many households the negotiation of responsibility for domestic and familial-related tasks can be a sensitive process, and men and women struggle to achieve a greater sense of justice and fairness while ensuring that family members are thriving. The sometimes blurred identities of, for example, man/father and of woman/mother lead to tensions and struggles between the individual and the myriad roles they can inhabit.

- **Co-residence**. Living under the same roof is a qualification for immediate family membership, but as the next generation of family members grow up and move out some of them may subsequently move back in. This trend, notable in middle-class households in parts of Europe is referred to as the boomerang generation. In countries that overall may be considered better off, a notable trend in recent decades is solo living – for example, a third of all households in Scotland in 2006 were classified as a one-person household. By 2031 this is predicted to be two-fifths (44%) with more men than women living alone in the under-55 age group (General Register Office for Scotland, 2008; Office for National Statistics, 2009b). Whilst co-residence is a fluid characteristic, prone to changes over time, there is generally one residence which is considered the family home. This tends to change as new generations emerge, and in some societies this is the home in which the oldest members reside and in others it is where future generations live.

Further characteristics and issues that come to mind when we think of families include childcare and working parents, solo childrearing, care for sick or older relatives, the legal and social implications of cohabitation, life after divorce for parents and children, and home-based care for the terminally ill (Leeder, 2004; Williams, 2004; Hennon and Wilson, 2008). Migration and extended families also demonstrate the ways in which cultures, traditions and rituals cross continents and localities. Some Asian families and communities in the UK, for example, may continue to arrange marriages and organize these according to caste or other categories. For some communities there is also the impact of war, civil strife and natural disasters (Kilmer et al., 2009).

? Who is a member of a family is open to debate. For example, is someone a blood relative, or have they joined a family through cohabitation, family formation, dissolution and re-formation, or friendship? The many ways in which people can join, leave and return to families ensure we are always changing how we view family life. Nevertheless there are aspects of family life we speak of as unique to 'our family' and there are everyday activities we find familiar. How would you describe the common identity of your family?

- Are there particular family 'practices' or things you do together which you consider to be unusual or even unique?
- Do you share common attitudes to money, politics, religion or care within the family?
- Or is the variation across your family part of what you think makes your family distinctive? (Some people say 'parts of my family are like chalk and cheese' and emphasize difference rather than sameness.)

DEFINING FAMILIES 2: VALUES, MEMORIES, AND SPACES AND PLACES

Underpinning the characteristics described above are a number of principles and ideas which can further define families. These include:

- **Values**. What is acceptable in one family may not be acceptable in another. Personal values are principles that define you as an individual and can include honesty, reliability and trust. These can determine how individuals relate to others and what they consider to be appropriate behaviour. Family values, such as disapproval of divorce or acceptance of cohabitation are formed among members but need not necessarily be adhered to by individual members. Substance misuse of parents raises contradictions; the levels of alcohol consumption considered acceptable in one household may not be acceptable across the family. Children and parents can tolerate extreme behaviours, such as long-term drug addiction, in their respective drive to retain the valued status of family membership. This raises issues of when intervention in families by other members and welfare services is necessary and desirable (Forrester, 2010).

- **Memories**. A shared history exchanged through words, photographs or possessions is a core element of family membership. There may also be family secrets, familial forms of speech or specific terms of endearment and family traditions. When members challenge memories or lose items associated with family histories tensions and arguments can emerge. People in families can demonstrate strong commitment to memories, regardless of how partisan or flawed these may be. The range of people talked about as being 'in' a family can be vast and include long-dead relatives, distant cousins, siblings living overseas and friends who are invited to join family events as 'honorary' members. Some members may never be met in the flesh, others are distant memories. But without people – and not just immediate family members – there would not be extended families and the networks of families and friends that infuse much of our lives.

- **Spaces and places**. The place in which members of families co-reside or think about as home may range from a tent in a refugee camp in sub-Saharan Africa, to a four-bedroom, detached house in a middle-class community in California. The ability to be a group of people with connections and some sense of common identity comes together around a place. Family spaces are often called the family home and become a focus for key family activities such as the celebration of festivals and events. What is considered an acceptable family home differs between countries, societies and communities. It is also determined by income, costs and availability.

STATISTICAL TRENDS AND FAMILY STRUCTURES

Demographic trends describe changes in a population over time. As people set up and sustain families, demographic trends are crucial to any understanding of families. In societies that have experienced stability, narrowing inequalities and relative peace, there have been marked decreases in mortality rates, particularly among infants, over the past century. Assumptions can now be made in these societies about common patterns of parenting and childcare responsibilities as well as the expectations associated with age-related illness and growing to old age.

Life expectancy in the EU continues to increase. Someone born in 2007 can reasonably expect to live for over 78 years. Overall, the USA shows a similar trend. Regional averages, however, do tend to mask variations in life expectancy. For example, in 2005 the highest life expectancies in Europe were in Spain (80.7) and in Sweden (80.6) (World Bank, 2008). (It should also be noted that health improvements, and concomitantly longer life expectancies, are distributed unevenly across the classes and subcultures of individual countries.) In contrast, the lowest life expectancies were in Latvia and Lithuania, at 65 for men and 77 for women. Indeed, the majority of the lower life expectancies were to be found within the 12 countries that joined the EU in 2004, the majority of which are post-communist states which, from the 1990s, experienced notable changes in welfare services and benefits. These changes included the extent to which governments provide for citizens' material and social needs. While this variation in life expectancy is significant, the EU is largely a success story for longevity in all countries. In 2007 in sub-Saharan Africa the life expectancy at birth was 50 for women and 48 for men; five countries within this geographical zone (Swaziland, Botswana, Lesotho, Zimbabwe, Zambia) had the lowest average life expectancies in the world with a range of 33–38 years (World Bank, 2008). Despite evidence of improved survival rates in some African countries, only 3% of the population survives to reach the age of 65 or older.

? What are the implications of these patterns of life expectancy for families in, for example, Botswana and Belgium? What might be the impact in terms of

- economics
- patterns of care
- living arrangements
- intergenerational support, for example, between grandparents and grandchildren?

Growth in the overall world population has slowed down in the past decade. Population growth, however, remains higher in countries that are often termed 'developing'. Over 80% of the world's population lives in such countries, and over half of the world's population lives in urban areas. In sub-Saharan Africa only a third (34%) of its population resides in urban areas while in Europe three-quarters of people live in cities. It should be noted that almost half of those who live in urban areas, regardless of the continent, live in cities of 500,000 or fewer inhabitants and cities vary not just in size but in socioeconomic composition. Moreover, their history, environment, economic, migration and demographic trends differ. Life for low-income households in France may share some broad similarities to a family in a shanty town on the outskirts of Durban, South Africa, but the experience of everyday living is quite different.

For those who live in remote and sparsely populated regions there are specific pressures related to the costs of transport and communication that can affect support for individuals, families, social networks, and access to services. However, in poor urban areas families face a range of barriers and pressures not dissimilar to those facing rural populations. Poor families may have, for example, limited access to affordable transport, higher food costs and struggle to access health and welfare services regardless of where they reside.

Most children continue to be born into a household where their parents live as a married or cohabiting couple. Patterns of marriage, cohabitation and other couple relationships leading to the formation and break-up of families are examined in greater detail in Chapter 5. Here we offer an overview of trends.

Although many argue that marriage is now not as popular as it once was, Table 1.1 demonstrates that between 1998 and 2008 this was not the case. There have been dips and rises but overall the rate of marriage has remained relatively stable.

Changes in family types are evident too. In Table 1.2, the example of families in the UK between 2001and 2009 illustrates the growth in cohabitation. Table 1.2 also charts the influence of migration and immigration and the growth in ethnic groups. Beliefs about marriage, cohabitation and childrearing can differ between ethnic groups. The tradition of marrying or cohabiting 'for love' is not necessarily pursued among all groups and cultures. Arranged marriages, predicated on the idea that love will grow in a marriage in which husband and wife share similar customs, backgrounds and aspirations, are evident in some religious and ethnic groups from, for example, the Asian Sub Continent.

> **?**   Think about the last wedding you attended. How did the couple meet? Had they lived together before marriage? What religious or belief system was evident in the ceremony?

There are two notable trends to draw attention to. First, over 44 years divorce rates have changed in all countries (see Table 1.1). These points of change have been generally triggered by the introduction of new or revised legislation. Other factors in promoting change include shifts in political and economic systems. For example the rise in divorce in the Czech Republic in 1995 came five years after major upheaval in the political system and resultant economic constraints. The other post-communist countries of Lithuania and Poland, likewise, continue to experience economic challenges and the resultant financial constraints due to unemployment and low salaries have placed strain on marriages. The second notable trend is the difference in rates between countries. This reflects legislation and access to support during and after divorce from welfare benefits and services. Trends also illuminate varied attitudes to divorce; for example the Catholic religion which does not recognize divorce may play a role in the rates documented in Poland and Italy (see Figure 1.1, page 29).

Rates of divorce do not include people who are separated but not legally divorced. Moreover, people who are unhappily married may choose to stay together for a host of reasons. These may include a belief in the sanctity of marriage, financial constraints, concern about the emotional consequences of a break-up, or wish to remain with one another to give their children a 'family' home. People who have been married are more likely to marry again than those never married in their age group. That said, divorce rates in subsequent marriages are higher than among first marriages and this may be due to raised expectations of marriage or having survived a previous divorce. Marriage and re-marriage may generate reconstituted families in which children may find themselves living with one biological parent and another adult. Many reconstituted families work well but for some the tensions become evident, for instance, the other biological parent may exert a negative

TABLE 1.1 The 27 EU Member States: marriages per 1,000 population, 1998–2008 (Eurostat, 2010: 183)

	1998	1999	2000	2001	2002	2003	2004	2005	2006	2007	2008
EU-27	5.1	5.2	5.2	4.9	4.9	4.9	4.9	4.9	:	4.9	:
Euro area	5.0	5.0	5.1	4.8	4.8	4.7	4.7	4.6	4.5	4.5	:
Belgium	4.4	4.3	4.4	4.1	3.9	4.0	4.2	4.1	4.3	4.3	4.4
Bulgaria	4.3	4.3	4.3	4.0	3.7	3.9	4.0	4.3	4.3	3.9	3.6
Czech Republic	5.4	5.2	5.4	5.1	5.2	4.8	5.0	5.1	5.2	5.5	5.0
Denmark	6.6	6.7	7.2	6.8	6.9	6.5	7.0	6.7	6.7	6.7	6.8
Germany	5.1	5.3	5.1	4.7	4.8	4.6	4.8	4.7	4.5	4.5	4.6
Estonia	3.9	4.1	4.0	4.1	4.3	4.2	4.5	4.6	5.2	5.2	4.6
Ireland	4.5	4.9	5.0	5.0	5.2	5.1	5.1	5.1	5.1	5.2	:
Greece	5.1	5.6	4.5	5.2	5.3	5.5	4.6	5.5	5.2	5.5	4.6
Spain	5.2	5.2	5.4	5.1	5.1	5.1	5.1	4.8	4.6	4.5	:
France	4.6	4.9	5.0	4.8	4.7	4.6	4.5	4.5	4.3	4.3	4.3
Italy	4.9	4.9	5.0	4.6	4.7	4.5	4.3	4.2	4.1	4.2	4.1
Cyprus[1]	11.4	13.2	14.1	15.1	14.5	7.7	7.2	7.8	6.8	7.5	:
Latvia	4.0	3.9	3.9	3.9	4.2	4.3	4.5	5.5	6.4	6.8	5.7
Lithuania	5.2	5.1	4.8	4.5	4.7	4.9	5.6	5.8	6.3	6.8	7.2
Luxembourg	4.8	4.9	4.9	4.5	4.5	4.4	4.4	4.4	4.2	4.1	3.9
Hungary	4.4	4.4	4.7	4.3	4.5	4.5	4.3	4.4	4.4	4.1	4.0
Malta	6.5	6.4	6.6	5.6	5.7	5.9	6.0	5.9	6.3	6.1	6.0
Netherlands	5.5	5.7	5.5	5.0	5.2	4.9	4.5	4.5	4.4	4.3	4.6
Austria	4.9	4.9	4.9	4.3	4.5	4.6	4.7	4.8	4.5	4.3	4.2
Poland	5.4	5.7	5.5	5.1	5.0	5.1	5.0	5.4	5.9	6.5	6.8
Portugal	6.6	6.8	6.2	5.7	5.5	5.2	4.7	4.6	4.5	4.4	4.1
Romania	6.5	6.2	6.1	5.9	5.9	6.2	6.6	6.6	6.8	8.8	7.0
Slovenia	3.8	3.9	3.6	3.5	3.5	3.4	3.3	2.9	3.2	3.2	3.1
Slovakia	5.1	5.1	4.8	4.4	4.7	4.8	5.2	4.9	4.8	5.1	5.2
Finland	4.7	4.7	5.1	4.8	5.2	5.0	5.6	5.6	5.4	5.6	5.8
Sweden	3.6	4.0	4.5	4.0	4.3	4.4	4.8	4.9	5.0	5.2	5.5
United Kingdom	5.2	5.1	5.2	4.8	4.9	5.1	5.2	5.2	:	4.4	:

1. Up to an including 2002, data refer to total marriages contracted in the country, including marriages between non-residents. From 2003 onwards data refer to marriages in which at least one spouse is a resident in the country.

TABLE 1.2   British families with dependent children,[1] 2001–09: by ethnic group (Office for National Statistics, 2010: 18)

Dependent children:[1] by family type and ethnic group[2][3]

	2001	2003	2005	2007	2009
Married couple[4]					
White	7,863	7,637	7,313	7,061	6,717
Mixed	125	126	151	167	188
Asian or Asian British	620	659	693	752	894
Black or Black British	131	148	152	215	196
Chinese	33	23	33	36	25
Other ethnic group	45	108	142	148	181
Total dependent children with married parents[5]	8,997	8,772	8,577	8,441	8,290
Cohabiting couple[6]					
White	1,256	1,300	1,383	1,492	1,567
Mixed	27	26	29	50	55
Asian or Asian British	3	7	2	5	7
Black or Black British	26	19	24	26	22
Chinese	2	*	*	2	3
Other ethnic group	*	4	5	7	12
Total dependent children with cohabiting parents[5]	1,339	1,366	1,455	1,597	1,682
Lone parent					
White	2,418	2,557	2,474	2,424	2,496
Mixed	127	128	133	134	150
Asian or Asian British	94	81	107	134	143
Black or Black British	198	206	206	240	279
Chinese	12	9	6	10	6
Other ethnic group	5	24	47	73	40
Total dependent children with lone parents[5]	2,900	3,020	2,995	3,028	3,146

1. Children aged under 16 and those aged 16 to 18 who have never married and are in full-time education.
2. See Appendix, Part 1: Classification of ethnic groups
3. Data are collected between April and June each year and not seasonally adjusted. See Appendix, Part 4.
4. Data for 2007 onwards include civil partnerships.
5. Includes those who did not know or state their ethnicity.
6. Data for 2007 onwards include same-sex couples.

influence. Further, merging families from different backgrounds with varied expectations may result in a clash of lifestyles and expectations of familial roles (Allan et al. 2011).

> **?**   Thinking about the trends in family structures and formation identified above, which of these are evident in your family?

PROCESSES: FAMILIES, KINSHIP AND ACTIVITIES

Family members engage in activities with each other, and may do so in preference to friends, colleagues or neighbours. People may talk to their family and communicate on

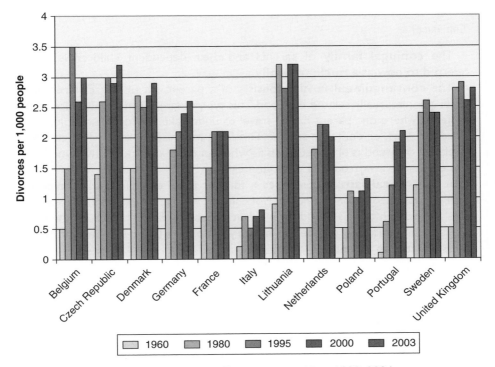

FIGURE 1.1   Divorce rates in selected European countries, 1960–2004
(Eurostat, 2007: 70)

a regular basis, or do so for specific events or life stages, such as birthdays, religious festivals, illness and death. The memberships of families constantly change with births, deaths and the development or cessation of relationships that offer various forms of sexual, emotional and economic support. The recall of major family events, such as births, marriages, relationship break-ups and deaths, as well as other less momentous shared experiences evokes a sense of membership. So too do memories of historical and religious events, including festivals and rituals, which also contribute to a distinct sense of identity. Blood ties (see Box 1.1) or biological membership, while not critical to family membership, are relevant to medical history and heritable diseases.

Box 1.1   Describing blood ties

Family members are generally, but not exclusively, linked through blood or intimate relationships. Immediate family members, most often parents and children, and in some cultures grandparents and grandchildren, are likely to live together or nearby.

(Continued)

(*Continued*)

The **conjugal family** of parents and their dependent children is often referred to now as a **nuclear family**.

The **consanguineal family** consists of a parent, his or her children, and other people usually related by blood. This type of family can be often found in societies where one parent has to travel to undertake work, for example, construction work or domestic service. This form may also be seen when care for a relative or friend is provided, such as when an older or sick relative who lives some distance away requires dedicated care.

A **matrifocal family** comprises a mother and her children. This type of family is not uncommon in a number of cultures where, for example, it is acceptable for women to raise children without cohabiting fathers, because the men migrate for work, are engaged in military action, or there is a separation or divorce between parents.

Just as families are constantly changing, so too are the meanings we attribute to them. Sometimes we refer to previous generations and our genealogy gives us meaning. For some, families only have meaning if there are children present; for example, the question 'Do you have a family?' is often interpreted as, 'Are you a parent?'. On other occasions or at certain times of life it is affection and love that is important; when medical or social service providers ask 'Is your family able to offer care and support?' this generally means, is there a family member who can contribute to physical, practical and emotional tasks associated with sick care and elder care. Families also have meanings we attribute to ownership. For example, the terms 'my husband', 'my mother' or 'my child' are interpreted as us having a say over aspects of the life of the person to whom we refer. While laws can reinforce the social sense of ownership there are also family traditions and memories that may be talked about in ways such as 'Our family celebrates birthdays with a homemade cake' or 'We don't do glum funerals and never will!' But recourse to family meanings can also involve taking the moral high ground with comments meant to place some families above others; for example, consider the assertion made by an individual using a disdainful attitude and tone that 'Members of my family wouldn't behave like that'.

?   How would you describe your family role(s) and relationships? Son, daughter, mother, father, sister, brother, cousin, aunt, etc.

Coltrane notes 'we can never be quite sure what family means unless we can understand the context in which it is used' (1998: 5). One starting point or context is to reflect on the legal basis for setting up and changing families. The word 'affinity' describes how relationships and memberships may be perceived and labelled. In Box 1.2 we outline the terms associated with the concept of affinity.

Box 1.2   Membership through legal arrangements

Affinal kinship describes the relationship that a person has to the blood relatives of a spouse by virtue of marriage or a civil partnership. The core relationship is the legal one established between two adults, albeit that in many societies cohabitation can offer a not dissimilar basis to kinship where there is social recognition of a durable relationship. There are three types of affinity.

Direct affinity exists when two people are married or are in a legally recognized relationship. **Secondary affinity** exists between a spouse and the other spouse's relatives by marriage and **collateral affinity** between a spouse and the relatives of the other spouse's relatives; for example, brother or sister-in-law. Affinity is important in various legal matters, such as deciding whether to prosecute a person for incest or whether to disqualify someone for jury service due to familial relationships and obligations.

In describing kinship relationships the terms employed in many societies include:

- mother: a female parent
- daughter: a female child of a parent
- sister: a female child of the same parent
- grandmother: mother of a father or mother.

The pattern is the same for the male lineage of father, son, brother and grandfather. A common assumption in this system is that biological lines are adhered to and a lineal format follows; descent from one person to another is in a direct line. In some families a woman, for example, may have children with more than one man and the siblings may be referred to as half-brother or half-sister. Further, same-sex civil partnerships create fuzzy boundaries in biological lines as children may be adopted or created through reproductive technologies. A step-brother or step-sister refers to a child related by remarriage of a spouse or parent.

Attempts to offer fixed definitions of families are tricky. Legal definitions capture something of the importance of the institutional focus of families, including legally sanctioned adult sexual and parenting relationships. The legal dimension also comes to the fore when we consider families that break up or re-form, but these definitions cannot completely capture the breadth of possible family arrangements (see Boxes 1.1, 1.2 and 1.3). Single parents, solo households, and intergenerational households with grandchildren and grandparents are among the many forms of families recognized in policies and services with varying degrees of support. These families can, however, struggle to achieve the same legal and social recognition afforded to those headed by the parenting heterosexual adult couple.

Box 1.3   Coexisting members of families

Collateral refers to a relative descended from the same biological pool but in a different line. Collateral relatives form an important grouping in many families and members include the following: uncle (father's brother, mother's brother, father's/mother's sister's husband) and nephew (sister's son, brother's son, wife's brother's son, wife's sister's son, husband's sister's son). In most societies cousins are classified as first, second or third cousins.

Additional generations can be identified with prefixes that vary across cultures and languages. In North America and in the UK the prefixes are 'great' or 'grand', in French it is 'beau'. Two people of the same generation who share a grandparent are related by **one degree of collaterality**; they are first cousins. If they share a great-grandparent they are second cousins, and so on.

Relationships through marriage can be denoted by the term 'in-law' and upon marriage the mother of a spouse becomes known as mother-in-law. The term half-brother or half-sister indicates siblings with one common biological or adoptive parent. Sometimes close family friends are referred to as aunts or uncles or sisters or brothers, a common practice that is referred to as **fictive kinship**. While the language of kinship varies across cultures and languages, horizontally the extended family can include in-laws, aunts, uncles and cousins. Societies in which families are strongly associated with conjugal relationships (marriage) favour having the marriage partners leave the family of orientation (the childhood household) and then set up a new household which in time may procreate.

?   Drawing upon your description of family roles, what affinal relationships can you identify? What are the differences in the way you and others relate to affines? Are some of their practices more or less tolerated than those of blood relatives? If you know any people who have entered civil partnerships are you aware of ways in which their families treated that relationship differently as a result of their change in legal status?

GLOBAL FAMILIES

One aim of this book is to locate information, explanations and debates about families in a global context and throughout the chapters we use examples from across the world to illustrate points and demonstrate diversity. Variation in families is evident in all societies and communities. Diversity in families is predicated on a range of factors which, as noted above, can include beliefs, personal aspirations and choices, health and illness, and income and resources. The explorations of global families remind us of differences nearby and further afield and highlight the fact that the definitions of families we draw upon tend to reflect the lived experiences of ourselves and of those with whom we come into contact (Leeder, 2004).

We begin to explore some of these differences and similarities in global families here through two topics:

- Topic 1: The impact of welfare polices on families and work in the countries of France, East and West Germany and the Russian Federation

- Topic 2: Religious and cultural beliefs, grandparents and family types in China, Japan, Singapore and South Korea

The choice of these countries and contrasting continents illustrates trends in ethnicity, cultures and economic opportunities. In the first Topic, drawn from a recent review of research from France, East and West Germany and the Russian Federation, we explore how rapid political changes have impacted on family decision making, including the choice to have children (fertility rates), employment of mothers (maternal employment rates) and the use of public policies and services (welfare regimes). Again, we offer an overview here of issues that receive closer attention in Chapter 4 on politics, policies and practices. In the second study we review information on family life in three Asian countries, namely Singapore, Japan and China to explore continuities and changes in the role of grandparents.

TOPIC 1: THE IMPACT OF WELFARE REGIMES ON FAMILIES: FRANCE, THE RUSSIAN FEDERATION, EAST AND WEST GERMANY

Kreyenfeld et al. (2009: 34) examined family diversity in France, the Russian Federation and East and West Germany. The aim of their review was to identify and assess the impact of political, demographic and economic changes on families. Of particular note in this comparative analysis are the changes that took place in political regimes between 1989 and 1991, marking the end of what was known as the Soviet Bloc. The effect of these changes was felt across the continent of Europe.

The term Soviet Bloc is used to refer to the states under communist government control in eastern and central Europe between 1945 and the 1980s. Communism is a philosophy in which classes are abolished and property is commonly owned and controlled. The Soviet Bloc emerged at the end of the Second World War as occupying Soviet troops ensured that communist governments and economic regimes could be imposed on a number of states. This resulted in the separation of families and friends as people found themselves unable to travel freely between states. For several decades tight controls by governments ensured little resistance, and what resistance that took place was put down by the use of force. Alongside strict controls on travel and freedom of expression was the evolution of common policies and services for families and workers as part of a 'contract' with citizens. The core of this was the provision of universal and largely free welfare services for all over the lifespan, linked to engagement in employment, or in effort for the good of the economy and state, including care for dependants. For many sectors of the population the introduction of these services heralded a sharp increase in their standard of living. These benefits though, were set against a loss of what had become accepted freedoms in much of Europe.

During the late 1980s, a weakened Soviet Union gradually stopped interfering in the internal affairs of other eastern European nations and a trend toward greater liberalization emerged. Mikhail Gorbachev launched a policy of *glasnost* (openness) in the Soviet Union, and emphasized the need for *perestroika* (economic restructuring). In 1989 during a period called the 'autumn of nations', a wave of revolutions swept across eastern Europe. On 9 November 1989, following mass protests in East Germany and the relaxing of border restrictions in Czechoslovakia, tens of thousands of East Berliners flooded checkpoints along the Berlin Wall, crossing into West Berlin. This date and related events heralded the end of the Soviet Bloc. In addition to major political changes it also led to revised and reduced levels of welfare benefits and services. Families could no longer depend on the availability of comprehensive childcare, health or education services, or pensions upon retirement. The Russian Federation emerged from this period with Russia at the core of this grouping of countries.

Across Europe as a whole there have been other major changes in the decades after the Second World War. Developments post-war, combined with economic growth in much of the minority world brought changes to families. Marriage and fertility rates have declined while rates of cohabitation, birth outside marriage and divorce have increased, and the average age at which first marriage and births take place have risen. Added to these trends is a growth in the number of adults choosing to remain childless, as well as an increase in those living alone for all or part of their adult life. What are the consequences of these trends in different countries?

- The Russian Federation has 83 parts which include regions, provinces and cities. It is the world's largest country and covers a ninth of the global land mass. Extending from northern Europe to Asia it covers 11 time zones and is also the ninth most populated country in the world with over 140 million inhabitants. Following changes in the political regime, the early 1990s saw major upheavals, not least of which was a rapid growth in unemployment. Core elements of the economy declined or collapsed, including manufacturing and steel production.

Levels of state employment also faltered and living standards declined for a majority of the population. Such a dramatic change in living standards took place that life expectancy declined; a trend in complete contrast to the rest of Europe and much of the world. Diverse family forms are a notable feature of the Russian Federation, as are relatively low rates of non-marital fertility when compared to the rates in France or the UK. Marriage remains a pathway to childbearing and parenting but high divorce rates ensure that families form, split and reconfigure, often involving multiple generations.

- Economic crisis and growing inequality have been defining features of the Russian Federation over the past 20 years. One of the most important changes has been the withdrawal of rights to low-cost, full-time daycare. Prior to 1989 it was unusual for mothers not to work full time and while work continues to be a crucial element of income for women, lower rates of pay and higher childcare costs have encouraged families to seek support for care responsibilities from among family, friends and neighbours. Current generations of adult women active in the labour market experience greater tensions between employment and care responsibilities than previous generations.

- East and West Germany. Soon after the changes in 1989, families in the former Soviet Bloc state of East Germany experienced some of the same dramatic changes that took place in the Russian Federation. Unification between East and West Germany softened a number of these changes but different standards of living continued. The Unification Treaty of 1990 ensured that West German legal and political systems replaced those in East Germany. Childcare, however, is organized on a federal basis, so each state determines the level of provision. Following unification, many daycare centres closed and the decline in the availability of childcare was described by many analysts as 'sharp'. The need for full-day, low-cost childcare was, however, recognized by employers, politicians and communities in the East German states and local governments went on to develop provision. While this did not reach the pre-1989 levels, by 2000 it was higher than the provision available in West Germany; for children aged below three years, there were 37 public places for every 100 children, while in West Germany the comparable number of places was eight per 100 children (Kreyenfeld et al., 2009: 37).

- It would seem that the expectations for families are reflected in contemporary histories. In West Germany the male breadwinner, female carer/homemaker dichotomy is evident in a taxation system which rewards this model of family life; only 20% of women with children under 16 work full time in West Germany, while in East Germany the comparable figure is 50%. Fertility rates in East Germany are lower than most of Europe, especially West Germany. A unified Germany illuminates how differing histories and expectations persist between the east and west parts of the country, despite their having the same policies and national government.

- France has a long history of support for mothers and children in the taxation system and in care services. A variety of measures support mothers, whether married, cohabiting or single, to maintain care commitments alongside employment. Any arrangement in which children live is considered a family; over the past 30 years France has been at the forefront of policies to treat all mothers as equal and, more recently, to enable unmarried couples to access the same rights as married couples. There remain however, incentives to get married, especially for higher-rate taxpayers. Thus the French welfare regime both supports any arrangement which includes children while engaging in social engineering through incentives for marriage among those with higher incomes.

In any overview of trends the patterns identified may be oversimplified. For example, in all countries, women with higher levels of education and social class status fare better regardless of policies, as their financial resources allow for a greater degree of choice. Nevertheless there are distinct differences promoted by histories, welfare regimes and cultural acceptability. The Russian Federation shows a continued trend towards divorced and widowed single mothers with high rates of full-time employment despite the decline in childcare services. Grandparents and friends are crucial in the provision of practical and economic support. The demise of welfare benefits and the growth of insecure and low-paid work has fuelled this trend. In complete contrast, West Germany is a country that promotes a more traditional notion of the family with low rates of unmarried motherhood and low levels of full-time work among all mothers. While East Germany works with similar policies it demonstrates a different pattern. Here the higher availability of childcare and a long history of women working full time have resulted in more diverse forms of families than is seen in West Germany. In France, too, less stigmatization of single motherhood is evident as are diverse family arrangements. Regardless of living arrangements, in all these countries being in employment is now important to personal and familial wellbeing as welfare benefits and services are more keenly linked to labour market participation.

> **?** Topic 1 draws attention to the impact of sudden economic changes on families. From 2008 much of the minority world has experienced economic recession. What has been the general impact of that on your immediate and extended family? Are you aware of impacts on other families and of the variables that have determined those impacts?

TOPIC 2: IDEAL AND ACTUAL FAMILIES IN ASIA

There is no such thing as a typical family but there are stereotyped views of what families should or could look like. These views are drawn from perceptions of sex, age, country, culture and the composition of a household. The notion of an ideal family type is, perhaps, more strongly identified in Asian countries such as China, Japan, Singapore and South Korea than in non-Asian countries. For example, common presumptions about families in Asia include multiple-generation Chinese families sustained by a deep respect for their elders. Strongly delineated gender roles with a focus on long-term secure employment might come to mind when reflecting on Japanese families. Young adults in South Korea appear highly versed in technologies and global networks, seeking marriage based upon *yeonae* (romantic love) while continuing to negotiate traditional patterns of arranged dating. How do these perceptions stand up to scrutiny, given the breadth and depth of economic, political and social changes in the region of Asia?

?   There is no such thing as a typical family. Yet we hold strong images of 'the typical family'. Why do you think this is?

First, most Asian countries have been experiencing demographic changes and trends in living arrangements similar to those in Europe and other post-industrial countries. People are living longer, fewer children are being born, people are postponing marriage and the arrival of the first child, and women are much more likely to be economically active. As in Europe, these broad trends differ in impact when you take into account inequalities in income and resources between social classes. Further, these trends are taking place against a backdrop of strong notions of family life. There is also a subtle difference in emphasis between Europe and Asia; in Asia the notion of the ideal family based upon traditional, if changing, beliefs continues to receive prominence in everyday conversations, in the media and in many policies and services. As Quah comments, regardless of the notion of an ideal type, the family in practice is what 'people can "afford" to have according to the specific circumstances of their lives' (2009: 2). Families which diverge from the 'ideal', she calls the 'actual' family (2009: 2), and while people and governments know the ideal is unobtainable or unacceptable for many, divergent family arrangements sometimes come under fierce criticism. It is not unusual for some families to be denied social recognition and participation in familial networks for diverging from idealized notions.

An examination of the changing role of grandparents in the Asian countries of Singapore, Japan and China illustrates the tensions between ideal and actual families. Grandparents are a key source of familial memories and cultural traditions and are purveyors of values, and these are shaped by interactions across generations:

> For each generation, its scope of personal and collective horizons contains both a stock of cultural traditions (partly transformed in its journey across time), and new elements that are created by their members or that they borrowed and adapted from other cultures. (Quah, 2009: 78)

An intergenerational contract has always existed but has varied in content. In previous centuries there was a focus on the role of grandparents offering knowledge, practical advice, physical labour and care for others in the three-generation household. As economic structures changed so too did this unwritten but understood 'contract'. Industrialization, global networks and integrated economic systems have had an impact. For many governments this is centred on the delivery of welfare benefits, particularly pensions, while for families, grandparents offer resources not only in terms of childcare and income, but may also become the recipients of care and resources from other family members.

In economic approaches an assumption has evolved that the number in retirement should be smaller than those in employment. Taxes from those in employment are to help fund services and pensions for the retired. This equation promotes the notion that declining numbers of working-age people, as the number in retirement rises, places intolerable pressures upon services and governments. In this equation the contribution of older people is often ignored in spite of the fact that their contributions to their families and communities may go well beyond childcare. Elders may also care for family members, neighbours and friends, engage in economic activity in family and other businesses at low or no pay, and volunteer to support community or other activities. All too often 'retired' is presumed to mean disengaged and less valued. A compulsory retirement age limits the economic opportunities for those over 60, as well as stigmatizing those who are retired as being drains on welfare, health and social care. Nevertheless, the younger and the older achieve a partnership of past, present and future as individuals grapple with change and traditions in ways that transcend age. Global networks have created broader horizons for younger people in Asia; technologies, media and travel have ensured a dramatic change in experiences and aspirations. Yet these are tempered through ongoing engagement in the continuities of family life. Grandparents are visible pinnacles of family life and interactions. In addition to values transmission they also play a practical role through their potential to care for others especially children and offer advice and resources for support.

One of the continuities that can be perceived in many parts of the world is adherence to religious or philosophical belief systems. The role of Confucian ideas about intergenerational support and respect is pertinent in many parts of the world. Writing around 470BC Confucius promoted the virtue of filial piety. In broad terms this means to be good to one's parents and take care of them and the family name. Filial piety is considered to this day in China a strong virtue in family life and is often the central content in paintings, plays, novels and films. Further, the Chinese idea of dynasty and the worship of late ancestors were adopted and adapted in belief systems that straddle much of Asia. Similar views were expounded by the Greek philosopher Socrates a decade after the death of Confucius. His call to respect senior generations has not stood the test of time in many European countries, nor has the Judeo-Christian commandment to 'honour your father and mother'. In parts of Asia, however, traditional values have merged with economic changes to see the continued existence of many three-generation households.

> **?** Explain the social standing of elders in your country or community. Can you identify the values of Confucius or Judeo–Christianity in attitudes to older people?

The education of the young and lifelong learning for adults has been a key component of many Asian religions and belief systems. The economic and social benefits of education have evolved over centuries, and in Japan, for example, it is not uncommon for people to describe society as largely orientated towards educational qualifications, *gakureki shakai*. That said, there is a cultural tradition of 'kin-come-first' which, while not a central tenet of many belief systems, has posed a barrier to progress for those qualified individuals who find opportunities blocked by intergenerational support among family members. Political change has impacted on traditional values. One prime example is of the challenge posed by the Cultural Revolution in China in the 1950s in which the young were encouraged to reject common belief systems and to spy on elders. Forty years on and the introduction of a quasi-market economy has led to a transformation in China, promoting disjuncture in intergenerational co-residence as many adults migrate for education and employment. However, the transmission of beliefs and ideas is strong and many thoughts originating in Confucianism continue to impact on the way families are talked about, if not experienced.

In the case of senior citizens and grandparents what really happens in practice? Drawing upon data from Singapore, Japan and China, we illustrate actual experiences:

- **Singapore**: In 2000, nearly 74% of Singaporeans aged 65 or over lived with their children and by 2005 this percentage had risen to 87%. This is a staggering contrast to the case in many countries in the minority world where an extremely small number of older people live with their families (Singapore Department of Statistics, 2006). This Singaporean trend is based upon beliefs, limited accommodation in a densely populated state and the limited provision of childcare. The three-generation household is a reality and a cherished one. And by 2040, those aged over 80 in Singapore will be among the most educated in the world with over half having high school or university educations, the majority of whom will speak two or more languages, and 75% of whom will have personal pension benefits. Thus older Singaporeans are a potentially strong resource for value transmission, continuity of care and resources.

- **Japan**: In contrast to Singapore, three-generation households are decreasing in number in Japan. Between 1975 and 2001 these declined from 78% to 53%, although the economic downturn starting in 1990 has led to a steadying off of this figure at less than 50%. The reasons for the decline are often pragmatic as those in younger age groups, in a society dominated by education, put their qualifications to use in professional jobs that require a high degree of mobility. Further, the power of older generations has been the source of some tension and not viewed as benevolent, especially with the changes in gender roles as Japanese women seek increased freedom in their personal life and wish to avoid the sanction of parents (Sugimoto, 2003).

- **China**: Across this vast country inhabited by many diverse groups, filial piety remains highly evident. While there are urban and rural differences in the formation of households, with three-generation households more prevalent in rural localities, the idea of grandparents constituting the 'family home' remains very strong. Some 20% of households are three-generation, and although this seems a low figure in comparison to those for Singapore and Japan, the adherence to filial piety is strong and often fulfilled by two-generation households as the economically active migrate to find paid work (Cheung et al., 2006). Rapid economic growth has resulted in generations moving away, but the impact of the policy to penalize those with more than one child has witnessed a rise in three-generation households again (Yi, 2002). Due to gendercide, sex disparities are marked, and in some provinces there are now 124 boys born for every 100 girls. When this generation grows up, one in five men are unlikely to find a partner. This may cause social unrest, sexual violence, crime and the questioning of masculinities and pro-creation practices. For the moment the trend is tolerated and in times of economic stress, the number of three-generation households will also increase further.

The ideal of the multigenerational family works well for many when family members have a reasonable quality of health. The onset of chronic conditions, impairments or decline in income presents families with a new set of challenges. With welfare regimes that assume a high degree of familial care, there are limited sources of provision to draw upon when versions of the ideal type become stressed or fractured. Nevertheless, it would appear that key aspects of the ideal, three-generation family remain prevalent. Further, where economic change and governmental policies make this difficult, a modified version has developed of two-generation households combined with communication technologies and transport systems to keep generations connected. Sex selection of children, and personal choices among adult women however, will make care more complex and family formation problematic in decades to come.

SUMMARY

In this chapter the broad structures and processes of families have been presented. We have introduced common ways in which families may be defined and described including blood ties, kinship, relationships and legal arrangements, as well as emphasizing the diversity and complexity of families from a global perspective.

Drawing on data on trends in families and relationships across the world between years 1900 and 2000, and speculating about the future of the family, Therborn comments that 'complexity is likely to remain'. Even with the diverse living and family arrangements evident across the world, there abides 'the longing for deep, lasting and exclusive emotional bonding' (Therborn, 2004: 314). Families and relationships continue to be imperative to human flourishing. They do, however, evolve and transform at various speeds and in differing ways; for example, in certain areas of sub-Saharan Africa families have experienced rapid changes and as a consequence have had to adapt through migration, mobility, and revised kin and intergenerational arrangements.

Natural disasters such as droughts have caused farming land to diminish while changes in patterns of diseases, too, have promoted the movement of adults of working age and encouraged intergenerational care arrangements between young and old, grandparents and grandchildren. Further, some people have been affected by ethnic tensions, war and fluctuations in food aid. Responses to clusters of these factors have required people to change their living and care relationships, sometimes losing homes and income as some family members become refugees while others move to find paid work.

The nature and pace of these shifts contrast with the experiences of families in western Europe, where many of working age strive to combine ongoing gender changes, and increased participation of women in paid work, along with the demands of domestic and care tasks. Many families in eastern Europe are grappling with the consequences of a rapid change in political systems from communism to capitalism. This has led to a growth in unemployment, to reductions in income levels as well as to a reduction in access to welfare provision and benefits. Historians continue to document the many ways in which family life has evolved over the centuries to ensure stability, nurturing and cohesion. Families adapt, survive, flourish and move on.

> **?** After reading this chapter you may be able to identify some 'taken for granted' assumptions you held about the 'naturalness' of the ways your own family functions. To what extent were these the result of economic, cultural or emotional factors that are somewhat specific to your circumstances and therefore unlikely to lead to the same practices in other families or societies?

EXPLORE FURTHER

Baker, M. (2011) *Choices and Constraints in Family Life* Don Mills: Oxford University Press Canada. 2nd edn.
Ribbens McCarthy, J. and Edwards, R. (2010) *Key Concepts in Family Studies*. London: Sage.
Scott, J., Treas, J. and Richards, M. (eds) (2007) *The Blackwell Companion to the Sociology of Families*. Oxford: Blackwell.

USEFUL WEBSITES

The Centre for Family Research at Cambridge University is a multidisciplinary centre that carries out research on children, parenting and families. See www.ppsis.cam.ac.uk/CFR/

The Centre for Social Justice is a Westminster-based 'thinktank' or policy research centre that emphasizes the role strong families can play in comprehensive solutions for addressing poverty. See www.centre-forsocialjustice.org.uk

The Centre for Research on Families and Relationships (CRFR) is a research centre founded in 2001, based at the University of Edinburgh, UK and is a consortium involving the universities of Aberdeen, Edinburgh, Glasgow, Glasgow Caledonian, Highlands and Islands and Stirling. See www.crfr.ac.uk/index.html

Eurostat is the EU statistical website providing a range of data on work, families and life in the EU. See http://epp.eurostat.ec.europa.eu/portal/page/portal/eurostat/home/

The Morgan Centre for the Study of Relationships and Personal Life is a research centre founded in 2005 at the University of Manchester, UK. See www.socialsciences.manchester.ac.uk/morgancentre/

United Nations. With 192 countries as members, the databases of the UN consist of global and country-specific information on policy and statistics for a large number of countries. The webpages of the UN Economic and Social Council are of particular relevance to those studying global families. See www.un.org/en/ecosoc/

2

Explaining Families

Keywords: ideology, theory, structures, interaction, conflict, 'doing family', feminism, queer theory, intimacy, individualization

INTRODUCTION

In this chapter we explore the ways in which sociologists have explained family life through the use of *theories*. Theory is about describing and explaining what happens around us. In the case of families, theory aids our understanding and assessment of past, present and future: for example, how do family members describe and explain their histories, activities and plans? In Box 2.1 we define theory in greater detail, and in the subsequent sections and boxes we identify and examine how sociology can offer insights into the structures and processes of family life.

> ➔ This chapter draws heavily on the content of Chapter 1; we presume you will have read this and are familiar with the characteristics of families, the principles underpinning families and relationships and statistical information on contemporary trends.

The words 'theory' and 'theorizing' conjure up images of academics and policy makers debating seemingly complex ideas and information on family life. For many people the mention of the term can be somewhat intimidating: theory is too complex, not easy to read or to understand. People can struggle to see the relevance of theoretical work. For example, what relevance does the study of theory have to an analysis of the use and outcomes of health services for families? But theories can help us to describe and explain the uses of health services and the longer-term impact on families.

Theory is not an exact science and we all have our own theories of why families form, dissolve and reconstitute. What makes the academic study of theories different is that these are substantiated by carefully collected information, including statistical data, and the analysis of policies and services. No one theory can explain the many changes and possibilities in family life. Further, theories, regardless of the information available, reflect the ideas and subjective interpretation of the authors. Thus the interpretation of the one set of statistics can differ between two or more sociologists; for example, data on changes in number of divorces each year in the UK may be explained by one theorist as indicating a breakdown in family life while another may point to the continued stability in the institution of marriage given a levelling off in the number of divorces. So if interpretations can vary, why study theory? Examining theoretical perspectives encourages us to scrutinize data sources and question the interpretation of these. This also aids our analysis of family life and families through the development of critical skills and the need to offer our own understandings of both theories and data. In short, through working with theoretical perspectives we can develop our own critical insights and thus inform debates, research, policy and practice work.

Box 2.1   Defining theory

The word *theory* originates in classical Greek politics and philosophy. The Greek word *'theoria'* means looking at, viewing or beholding. It was adopted by Greek thinkers (or philosophers) who were examining issues such as how nature and human reality interweave (metaphysics), the relationship between language and reality (semantics), the principles of moral judgement (ethics), and the nature and limits of knowledge (epistemology). Theory, as a term and process, evolved to include contemplation and speculation as opposed to action. Consider the following: theories on families involve trying to understand the formation and workings of family groups, while the practical dimension is associated with teachers, social workers, doctors, community workers, neighbours and friends, all of whom are engaged in supporting, monitoring or evaluating families. Theories contain ideas that aid explanation and those ideas can be called concepts.

A theory in social sciences is drawn from predictions based on the findings of previous observations and information collected through a range of research methods. In theory building, an interpretation of findings informs explanations of variables and thus, in this case, families and relationships. In social sciences two or more variables drawn from statements constitute a *hypothesis*. A hypothesis is tested through the use of statistics to assess the relationship, if any, between variables. Theories offer explanations and ideas on new, existing and differing combinations of events and activities. A hypothesis may be proven or dismissed as the outcome of an assessment of new information or conditions, often through statistical testing or modelling. Social scientists collect data that can be analysed in a range of ways, not just through the testing of hypotheses. Interviews, observation and surveys are among the many research methods available to gain depth of understanding on families and family life. These issues are explored further in the following chapter, 'Researching Families'.

Further discussion of theory can be found in:

Elliott, A. (2009) *Contemporary Social Theory. An Introduction,* and Fulcher, S. and Scott, S. (2011) *Sociology,* 4th edn.

? In Chapter 1 we noted that in much of the minority world families can break down, divorce has become more acceptable, and second marriages are on the increase. How would you explain these changes? Write down your ideas and at the end of this chapter we will return to these.

SOCIOLOGICAL EXPLANATIONS: PREMISE AND ORIGINS

At this point it may be useful to reprise that at its most basic level sociology is concerned with the study of groups in society and how these interact. Sociologists help to explore and explain the world we live in through challenging the existing assumptions about the ways in which people view families and relationships. Social pressures to conform, or opportunities for choice, will have a bearing on the age at which we form long-term relationships. This can vary from the late twenties in northern Europe to the early teens in parts of Africa. Religious beliefs, economic necessity and what is considered to be normal, or *norms*, will all have an impact on decisions about families and relationships. Norms can be defined as rules of behaviour which reflect a culture's values and expectations, either prescribing a given type of behaviour, or forbidding it.

Throughout this book we refer to family structure, the way relationships are patterned within a more or less recognizable family unit. Similarly, sociologists use the term *social structure* to refer to the relatively stable pattern of relationships between people in families, organizations, neighbourhoods, regions and countries. People do not always follow the path proffered by social structures as promoted by older relatives, government policies or wider ideas in the media about lifestyle and living. However, challenging the pathways commonly promoted by key groups, social structures and cultures can bring isolation, exclusion and even violence. Examples include women excluded from families and communities if they say no to an arranged marriage; single parents who are criticized for early parenthood; and fathers who have custody of their children and find it hard to negotiate with their employers for flexible working arrangements. In these examples a combination of social norms, including gender and age expectations, come into play. Transgressing these culturally specific norms can bring about judgemental comments, stigma and potential violence. 'Transgressions' can also herald change and adaptation on the part of families.

Sociological theories develop through observing and analysing trends and events, documented through the collection and analysis of information, whether these are contemporary, historical or anticipated:

> Sociological theories are attempts to highlight interesting aspects of social situations by drawing out their general features. They abstract from the particular and unique features of events and situations in order to isolate what they have in common and what can, therefore, guide us in understanding events and situations that we have not yet encountered. (Fulcher and Scott, 2011: 21)

As Hill comments, 'the family is a central systematic concept in theory ... serving as the central target concept for public policy and ... service' (1984: 10). This dual aspect – abstract concept and yet a practical target – makes families, and ways of understanding families, a powerful tool for informing policy and services. In some services the underlying ideas about families, roles and responsibilities inform the work that is done, as in the case with family therapies or family counselling. These approaches to policies and service provision, in the case of alcoholism, for example, could be understood as reflecting family processes as well as individual actions. Such approaches are, however, criticized for suggesting that too much can be achieved if families just worked in certain ways. Families evoke strong views and ideas. To explore how strong views and ideas on families are forged and promoted we now examine ideology and the family.

IDEOLOGY AND THEORY: WHAT IS THIS THING 'THE FAMILY'?

Throughout this book we have chosen to use the term 'families' as the best way to reflect the diverse forms that this human social grouping can take. We have avoided references to 'the family' as the use of this term encourages thoughts of a fixed and reified family type. (A term becomes 'reified' when it has been conceptualized in a way that distances it from everyday reality for most people who might use it.) Talking of the family encourages us to lose sight of diversities. Many politicians refer to the family when trying to evoke a sense of cohesion with a range of services named as family-specific, such as family policy, family welfare and family health services. That said, the idea of the family can all too often become one that promotes a family type, and this draws attention to the role of ideology in any discussion of families.

It is important to differentiate between ideology and theory; the former is about dominant ideas that form beliefs and the latter is concerned with explanations based on interpretations of information. That said, ideology and theory can and do intermingle, and so we would encourage any student of family studies to look long and hard at the origins of information, interpretations and explanations.

More persistent and persuasive than any television talent show, the idol of the family pervades all our lives. Ideology can be defined as a dominant set of ideas, comprising thoughts, notions, opinions and meanings that people come to attach to a phenomenon. As these ideas are talked about and become incorporated into debates, policies and activities, over time they become accepted as a dominant view. Many argue that ideologies are used as a screen for inequalities and for structures that create and justify unequal relationships. Ideologies present differences and inequalities as inevitable and universal.

The ideology of the family has been especially powerful in promoting the nuclear family in many industrial and post-industrial societies. In complete contrast, in parts of Africa, extended families based around polygamous marriage are not uncommon. Ideologies of family life form patterns that structure much of our thinking about, responses to and activities in relationships and families. Despite all the evidence of inequalities, abuses and tensions, family life is generally viewed as a positive goal, as something we all want to be part of. This mystification plays a key role in how societies and people talk about and engage with families. Talking about and being in families seems to offer 'natural' and straightforward ways to organize our lives.

Bernardes called for the recognition of family ideology, asserting that this promotes 'sets of partisan beliefs supporting a particular family form' (1985: 275). He expressed his concerns that an 'idol family' becomes standardized against which the 'virtues or deficiencies' of other families are assessed. Noting that we live with multiple social realities (for example, woman, worker, mother, daughter, sister, car owner, music lover, political activist, and so on) Bernardes examined the multilayered ideas and practices which appear to render the family as a natural and enduring universal form that can adapt to address changing contexts (Bernardes, 1985: 275):

> The family is awesomely powerful and clearly one of the key components in erecting and sustaining meaning in contemporary social life.

In his analysis Bernardes identified layers through which family ideology operates, namely:

- Individuals and groups – paradoxically, argues Bernardes, families are group formations and yet they require 'extreme individualism' in so far as roles are distinct (1985: 281). Being a father or daughter offers a strong idea about roles and responsibilities in the group context. Further, the individual operates within the family context as someone who can have their own space or time, a room of their own, desk space in a living room, or time to watch television and relax. The notions of the private world and the family world are keenly felt by many as the family and ideologies of families offer incentives and material rewards to take people away from the mundane and difficult public worlds of work and social spaces. Of course there are differences within families, and gender and age determine who has the power to access resources and spaces. Yet the notion of families as havens and domains in which emotions (love) can be created and sustained is dominant in all societies.

- It can seem so natural to be part of a family! Biology and reproduction seem to underpin the family, with childrearing presumed to be the key role of families. A range of ideas have informed services about families and the appropriate roles for families to play in childrearing, socialization and community life more generally. It would seem that 'family problems' require 'family services', as it is the failure of families to function that is at the heart of many social issues. Individuals may choose to challenge societal norms. That said, ideas about what makes up a functioning family are considered core to social cohesion and thus familial beliefs are hard to challenge.

- It structures views of others and legitimates differentiation into roles by age, sex, gender and ethnicity. Women's role as mothers and carers are emphasized through family ideologies and these ideas are further complicated when ethnicity is considered. For example, the role of mother for a woman originating from the subcontinent of India and living in a UK inner city might be further defined as that of carer for multiple generations.

- Mystification obscures the challenges and issues in the human condition. The family is represented as distinct from the realities of the roles and ideas it represents. Age, gender and resource inequalities, neglect, abuse and violence can all be found in family contexts, but the power of family ideologies clouds and even renders these invisible.

Bernardes (1985) and Morgan (1996) have argued that these are powerful forces and that family ideologies play a key role in social structures, formations and socialization, and are not always for the good of those involved. In complete contrast, others argue strongly that family ideology is necessary to ensure that social cohesion is created and reinforced. To dilute the ideology of the family leads to breakdown in family life and resultant social fractures. This can, some assert, be directly linked to anti-social behaviour and criminal acts such as indiscriminate violence or violence within families, friendships and neighbourhoods (Almond, 2006).

SOCIOLOGICAL THEORY

The body of theoretical work available is vast and so we have chosen to organize these ideas under four key themes:

- theories which focus upon families as creating and being created by social structures
- those which reflect on the ways in which people and groups interact to develop intimate and kinship relationships
- theories which examine the role of families as part of the ongoing conflicts and tensions in societies focused on the demands of economic systems
- gender and sexualities and the growth in feminist and queer theory.

There are a number of explanations for the emergence of, and changes in, families. These draw on shifts in economic and political systems, and on related trends in demography, as well as ideas on human relationships and on individual thoughts and actions. Sociological explanations of families began in the eighteenth century with attempts to examine the social world in ways similar to the natural world. Frenchman Auguste Comte (1798–1857) is said to have invented the word 'sociology' and it is drawn from the Latin '*socius*', companion, and '*ology*', the study of. The word sociology evolved from early attempts to develop a social physics.

Comte advocated a 'science of man' [*sic*] that would emulate the ideas and methods of natural sciences. He developed the notion of positivism as an approach to exploring societies. Positivism places an emphasis on the documentation and study of observable phenomena and events; for example, the number of people in a dwelling, the type of relationships in the household, the age of residents, and so on. In the end, the evidence collected can be examined to identify trends, similarities and differences within and between phenomena and events. Explanations can then be sought that are based on the trends identified. For Comte, the role of the social scientist is to produce explanations – or theories – that can be used to underpin laws, regulations and services and thus ensure the smooth running of societies.

> **?** Drawing upon Comte's ideas one example might be the number of people living in a particular type of dwelling. If, for example, previous studies indicate that an increase in number of people living in a family dwelling results in higher rates of partner separation, family breakdown, and other tensions in families, governments might take action. This could include legislation to restrict the number of people in a dwelling, a programme to build new homes and financial incentives for adult members of households to form their own home. Returning to the previous example of family breakdown and divorce, what evidence might a sociologist seek? And what laws, regulations or services might they initiate as a result of changes in family formation?

Lest you consider these ideas simplistic or old fashioned, Comte did recognize the complex nature of societies and the need to study social systems in terms of their structures and dynamics. Securing coherence in societies was his overarching aim and for most people and governments the establishment of conflict-free societies remains a critical objective. Key elements in achieving coherence are the organization of production (division of labour), language to communicate and pass on knowledge and ideas among people and across generations, and shared views or beliefs, including religion. In Comte's work we also see the origins of the study of both industrial societies and technologies, as well as differences and inequalities in societies. Comte called for the moral regulation of societies to lessen resentment between rich and poor, arguing for what he considered to be the pivotal role of systems of education and religion in the promotion of stability.

Several decades after Comte began his work, Herbert Spencer (1820–1903) developed the idea of a 'synthetic philosophy'. He too was interested in economic production and paid work, but Spencer's distinct contribution drew together the three dimensions of evolution, individuals and their actions, which enable social evolution. Working at the time of the publication of Darwin's *On the Origin of Species*, Spencer was drawn by the idea that species adapt to their conditions in the ongoing struggle for survival. Structures evolved in societies to support survival, for example, healthcare, education and housing. Just as important was functional adaptation, namely how societies organize to produce future generations and support individuals to adulthood and through later years. Spencer examined families and kinship relationships, noting their importance in achieving stability. He also noted that as economic production changed and structures and services grew, families lost some of their specialized roles such as the transmission of knowledge, large parts of which were supplanted by formal schooling.

TIES THAT BIND: MAKING SENSE OF STRUCTURES

As we noted in Chapter 1, family life evolves as members arrive, grow older and sometimes leave. Families also experience tensions and stresses for a wide variety of reasons which can include managing limited income and resources, the arrival of a baby, or the death of a partner. Most families emerge from these tensions and stresses changed but fundamentally intact. The ability of families to adapt to change and the resilience of members to ensure familial survival has been considered by a number of sociologists. Emile Durkheim (1858–1917) contributed the notion of solidarity in relationships. Feelings of solidarity are, Durkheim argued, essential to the integration of people, groups and societies. Solidarity includes the integration of people into social groups and the regulation of them by shared norms. A system of law provides a base from which solidarity can grow. For Durkheim, as societies become more complex the law is less about repression and more about establishing, retaining or restoring secure ways for people to live. People tied together through economic interdependence and through beliefs in societal cooperation and give and take (reciprocity) achieve organic solidarity.

In contrast, mechanical solidarity is identified with strong systems of beliefs and repressive force, such as seen in ancient and feudal societies. While organic solidarity is integral to modern societies, encouraging individual freedoms and integration, Durkheim identifies two potential tensions, anomie and egoism.

> **?** In his study of suicide, Durkheim (1897) deployed the term *anomie* to describe situations where individual actions digressed from organic solidarity. This can result from *egoism*, which occurs when individuals are not properly integrated into social groups. Can you think of examples of anomie or egoism drawn from your experiences of family life?

Through the study of actual figures on suicide, Durkheim identified patterns or what he termed, social facts. He demonstrated that suicide rates were influenced by certain factors, including:

- religious beliefs – Catholic teachings ban suicide, and among Catholics the suicide rates were lower
- family relationships and specifically family structure; those who are married are less likely to commit suicide than those who are single, widowed or divorced
- during the time of war when the suicide rates drop
- economic crises when suicide rates increase.

Explaining why these patterns occur requires the analysis of social context, personal relationships and beliefs, economic and political activities, and governmental responses. The identification and examination of wider contexts and systems can offer insights into the seemingly individual act of suicide.

FAMILIES AS A FRAMEWORK: PARSONS

Talcott Parsons (1953) is closely associated with the study of families, in particular his idea of an action frame of reference. The action frame of reference incorporates:

- actors: the people who carry out actions
- ends: the goals that actors pursue
- means: the resources available to achieve these ends
- conditions: the particular circumstances in which actions are carried out
- norms: unspoken or unwritten rules or standards which people choose to adopt in their choice of ends and means.

These five elements bring together ideas on structures and actions. That said Parsons' work fuelled much debate on the topics of structure and function. Structural features of society provide the framework for society. At the core of this framework are the expectations and obligations which seem to govern people's actions. Social position and the division of labour drive these. So a wife, grandfather and child might all be presumed to have certain roles, responsibilities and requirements. The wife might also be a lawyer or teacher, and the grandfather of the child might undertake voluntary work for a local social club while the child attends a primary school nearby. Positions define roles and to varying degrees these are bound by age, gender and social class. People are surrounded by structures which create, reinforce or challenge social roles – families, education, labour markets, political systems. Thus what may be an appropriate role for a worker and wife in France where she is a lawyer working part-time, may be inconceivable or impossible in another context; for example, a mother and worker in rural Egypt or in a poor area in Shanghai. The key to creating and sustaining structures and roles is socialization. Here families are critical, for in early years people learn how to behave and what is expected of them. Fundamental to this analysis are stable societies in which a high level of agreement is possible on everyday life, institutions and structures. This suggests, however, a highly idealized state of affairs.

SOCIALIZATION: MERTON

Following the work of Parsons, Robert Merton developed ideas on structure and function which had a specific impact on the study of families through his concept of socialization. Arguing that families are central to stability and the cohesion of societies, Merton asserted that families undertook core work in socialization throughout the lives of individuals, teaching members from infancy onwards about what is acceptable. Ideas about culture – values and norms – are first shared in families. Subsequently other influences begin to have an impact, including relatives, friends, and various forms of the media, schooling and other services. Merton, however, argued that there is not a blanket acceptance of values. Individuals may commit to some but not all the values of their culture. For example, a parent may challenge identity stereotyping at the earliest stages by not dressing the baby in clothes that signify one sex or the other; in many cultures blue is assigned to boys and pink to girls.

Merton developed his own notion of anomie, drawing upon the ideas of the goal or ends and the means one is expected to follow to achieve it. When people are fully committed to the norms of a society or community, they will follow both the ascribed goals and means; they will dress babies in the gender-coded colours and thus achieve conformity. If, however, they seek to challenge these through beliefs or awareness of the lack of opportunities that might follow for their child, then they experience a degree of anomie (see the think box on page 51 on Durkheim for an explanation of anomie). In societies where financial success is important and inequalities are evident, those without the means to achieve this particular goal can seek various paths. These may include crime or other acts that Merton identifies under the broad heading of innovation in societies, i.e. bending the rules. Some may retreat and not engage in aspects of society as they feel the goal is impossible to achieve. Others may demonstrate 'ritualism', in which people remain loosely committed to the goal, and go through the motions but in a half-hearted way. For example, one teenager may hear their teachers talk of university courses and wonder what all this is about as no one in their family has been to university. For another young person, university seems completely irrelevant as they plan to train for a skilled occupation that does not require a university course, for example, to become a qualified electrician. Both agree to attend an open day at a nearby university to keep the teachers happy but do not reveal their true feelings. A third student in the same class attends the open day keen to find out more as they plan to take a degree course.

Explanations that focus on structures are more complex and nuanced than many commentators suggest. While the core idea of structures around and through which societies organize seems straightforward, many theorists have addressed issues of needs and relationships to offer insights on how families integrate, adapt to changes, fracture and offer spaces in which people may be both frustrated and flourish. For example, images of happy families sitting together at mealtimes and talking pleasantly to each other, regardless of their limited social choices and economic resources, may seem implausible. However, it can and does happen and family processes may reflect mutual support, group tasks to prepare and serve the meal, and conversations imbued with care and concern. That said, as we have noted on several occasions in this book and considered in some depth in Chapter 5, family tensions and abuses can be found in households regardless of social class or income levels. Families work together, gain support and solace through everyday practices, and these matter more in times of tension, stress and resource constraints. When tensions and abuses are evident, family processes may reflect division, disharmony, and may also create a screen to limit the visibility of these actions.

ACTORS AND ACTIONS: THEORIES OF INTERACTION

A focus on social and economic structures dominated key dimensions of early sociological thinking. The work of Max Weber (1864–1920), however, is notable for its emphasis on people's actions. Weber argued that it is impossible to start the collection of information and research on social issues without recourse to existing knowledge. Further, we all bring to each and every topic our personal perspectives and these are tempered by a host of things, including what we have read and know about an issue, and which information we choose to collect and examine; in short, our values inform any critical analytical work we undertake. For example, those who assert that religious beliefs have a bearing on decisions about whether to marry or cohabit are likely to collect information on religious and social beliefs. Others may have an interest in economics and focus on people's perceptions of the effect that different types of living arrangements have on financial interdependence and independence.

Although these examples suggest sociological analysis is driven by personal viewpoints, knowledge can be objective. Sociologists, Weber argued, should be open and critical about the ideas that underpin their research and their choices about the data they collect. So while the researcher concerned with religious beliefs and the one interested in economics start from differing perspectives, they can assess how honest and self-critical the other is and decide whether or not the research can be replicated. The possibility of replication is critical to Weber. If replication is possible then a factual judgement, as opposed to a value judgement, can be made. Thus a sociologist may start with the assertion that marriage is unnecessary (a value judgement) and through research find that many consider marriage an important commitment prior to having children (a factual judgement).

Understanding social actions was the focus of much of Weber's work and he also developed the notion of the *ideal type* to help understandings of the social world. Ideal types do not necessarily exist. They offer categories or compartments which are labelled to offer identification of key characteristics. Examples include capitalism, feminism and bureaucracy. It would be hard to identify the pillars and structures of, for example, capitalist systems or bureaucracies across the world. They do, however, demonstrate many similarities and thus the description offers strong identification of most characteristics. Social actions are ideal types in so far as we can consider actions to be external to, or independent of, individuals and can attribute meanings to actions.

For Weber actions may be:

- instrumental: actions are undertaken to secure a predetermined goal, for example, moving into the locality of a preferred school or family doctor

- value-rational: these are actions based on chosen values such as 'marriage is a prerequisite to cohabitation'

- traditional: these are unreflective and habitual actions such as always talking about the weather at the bus stop or in a conversation making the presumption that in a married couple the man will earn more than the woman

- affectual: these are actions based upon emotions; for example, anger, frustration and love combined promote the actions to speed the recovery of an older relative who needs to be mobile despite all their protests about discomfort.

Ideal types are meant to aid understandings of actions, and Weber used the German word *verstehen* to describe the analytical processes associated with using ideal types. Actions and ideal types can often intertwine; in the last example in the list above the affectual action is also instrumental as it is likely to help an older relative achieve the goal of greater independence. Clustering the characteristics of a phenomenon together, not all of which necessarily coexist at any given time, produces a sharply defined picture that people may relate to.

INTERACTIONS: GOFFMAN

Other sociologists have considered issues of social interaction in some depth. Goffman's work considered face-to-face interactions in everyday small-scale contexts, and so has particular relevance to the study of families. His ideas on the presentation of self draw much from notions of drama; these are the play, the set, the roles and the actors, and it is here we see the interweaving of structures and interactions. These ideas were termed 'dramaturgical' and Goffman emphasized the ability of people to manipulate identities. Thus the teenage son will behave very differently in front of his grandparents than with his male friends, or differently again when talking to a teacher about the future. People can choose to present images to others that they feel are appropriate to that context (polite manners with a teacher) or that offer a direct challenge (anger and swearing in a meeting with a teacher). Thus interaction involves continuous negotiation and refinement. Pahl (2000) argues that a refashioning of relationships takes place and this is characterized by both dependence on another person and obligations towards others, a process he terms confluent associations. In these associations, for example, men and women might be relearning how to talk about roles and actively engaging in what they consider to be fair and more equal relationships.

Despite the ongoing nature of negotiation, the notion of roles leads to labels and these may be construed in numerous ways, both positive and negative. For example, the terms teacher, parent and doctor might all suggest roles and responsibilities that promote social cohesion while the terms junkie, thief or teenage mother can create identities that are hard to loosen from associated negative connotations.

STRUCTURES AND PRACTICES: GIDDENS AND WALLACE

One way of examining interaction that has gained ground in recent years is structuration (Giddens, 1986). A broad explanation is that individuals and groups work within existing social structures. Both the structures and actions take place within the context of social norms and these norms may be followed or transgressed. Nevertheless, structures and norms predetermine actions to an extent. But structures and norms are not permanent parameters. They do change as is seen in, for example, the growing availability and acceptance of assisted reproductive technologies (ART). ART provision is evident in the structures and provision of health services and many people talk openly about using technologies to enhance fertility.

> → In Chapter 1 we noted the distinction between the terms 'household' and 'family'. Household, however, remains a popular and useful term in the explanation of living arrangements and relationships. In her article *Household strategies: their conceptual relevance and analytical scope in social research*, Claire Wallace (2002) provides an overview of debates and offers suggestions on future use of the concept. As a unit of analysis, the household allows researchers to focus on groups rather than individuals. It provides potential to explore the motivations and actions of people living in a group in the same dwelling.

In most societies people live in households of one type or another, be it a shanty dwelling on the outskirts of São Paulo or a large detached house in a suburb of Los Angeles, organizing their lives and managing resources. The organization of everyday living goes on in the midst of plans for the next day, next week, next year. Households provide a key context in which reproduction of people and domestic services take place, 'from day to day and from generation to generation' (Wallace, 2002: 281). Thus households may contain families or members of other friendship or intergenerational groups, but at root they comprise groups that have a common understanding.

Households adapt to social change, for example, a decline or increase in the resources coming into the group. Adaptation may be conscious (for example, household members may suggest sitting down to discuss a decline in income due to the unemployment of a member) or it may be less conscious and more role specific as in the case of a household where an adult woman is viewed as the main manager of resources. Thus there may be strong or weak strategies (Warde, 1990), referring respectively to members of a household sitting down and planning a strategy, or to a household inferring strategies through the actions of some. So the idea of the household can enhance the potential for researchers and theorists to explore how people interact and organize their lives.

The notion of household strategies has been used by a number of sociologists and it has also come under some scrutiny. Key work by Gershuny (1978) and by Pahl and Wallace (1985) drew on the concept to propose that households could shape the environment in which they lived rather than be shaped by it. One example would be the pooling and closer management of resources in times of recession to ensure day-to-day survival. It was also proposed by Morris (1997) that the notion of strategy allowed for closer examination of household tasks and relationships, and in particular allowed for keen analysis of physical and emotional domestic work. In many of these studies sociologists emphasized the on-the-ground or micro-level decisions and the choices household members could make. In a notable study and resultant assertion, Pahl (1988) used the notion of household strategies to identify what he termed 'work-rich' and 'work-poor' households. In the work-rich households, resources allow for greater choice about how the family manages day-to-day living and longer-term decision making. By contrast, in work-poor households choices are restricted resulting in a focus on the daily maintenance of the family and household. Day-to-day survival for a work-poor household can make any notion of a longer-term family strategy seem fanciful. How people view their life possibilities is based upon a moulding of time, space, resources and relationships.

Household strategies have received the most attention in economic analysis (see for example, Harding and Jenkins, 1989). But for many sociologists it does offer ways of exploring how the structures of societies are perceived by, and interact with, the agency of household members. Wallace (2002) asserts that household strategies may be more important at certain times in people's lives and in periods of notable socioeconomic change. She offers three examples: when women enter the labour market and need to reschedule or organize unpaid work; times of rapid change such as economic downturn or technological advancements; and where informal work dominates, for example, in developing countries. The latter two examples overlap in so far as the informal economy becomes prevalent in times of recession or with dramatic political change, as seen with increasing informalization of large parts of the economies of eastern Europe.

THEORIES OF CONFLICT

Tensions and conflict wax and wane across families and relationships. Tensions and conflict also infuse the work of Karl Marx (1818–83). Starting from the analysis of economic relationships, Marx developed the idea of alienation to explore how the labour of people had become disassociated from personal creativity. The necessity to work for payment and on behalf of others results in the creation of products that are removed from – or 'alien' to – workers. Thus the people who produce products find their labour is restricted to tasks that largely fulfil the needs of others. Wage labour reinforces differences in income as well as inequalities in opportunities. Observation of these processes led Marx to his second core idea of social classes, namely categories of people divided according to their type of labour and level of ownership. A fundamental divide, Marx asserted, is between those who own property and those who do not.

In the first volume of *Das Kapital* published in 1867, Marx developed a number of assertions about conflict and tensions between workers and those who own the methods of production (see Marx and McLellan, 2008). Marx also offered the notion of 'ideologies', a term used to describe how the ideas of people are constrained and shaped by the material conditions in which they find themselves. The dominant ideology for Marx was that of capitalism in which, to briefly summarize, workers accept payment for their labour and this fuels consumerism as a system of beliefs and actions. In order to consume and to be part of a capitalist society people adapt their lives to the necessity of paid work and to the need for the income generated by this. In all of this analysis, families are exploited by capitalism to undertake the reproduction of future workers, together with current and former workers, while offering a haven from the pressures of production and work.

➡ Refer back to the section earlier in this chapter 'Ideology and Theory: What Is This Thing "The Family"?' (page 47), where there is a full explanation of what is ideology and the relevance of this to the study of families.

Marx considered historical changes in family forms in response to economic systems. Modes of production have changed over the centuries from the ancient slave-owning systems through feudalism to capitalism. There remain, however, examples of slave ownership and feudalism, and the inequalities and exploitations associated with these systems are stark. Many would argue the same could be said of capitalism in its creation of a range of inequalities. Why do systems of inequity continue? Marx maintained that the social world could not be considered objectively. Personal experiences and judgements are influenced by available information, social norms and emotions. As we noted earlier, when people come into contact with information and explore possible interpretations, their own views and bias will become evident.

> **?**   People have 'standpoints', and these illuminate their experiences and back grounds but they are also structured by the powerful; the dominant class. Rather than question differences and inequalities, individuals draw upon different ideas to create varied standpoints. On the one hand, individuals may believe that capitalism creates inequalities, but on the other hand, they could feel that while living within a particular economic system they need to play by key norms, such as being active in labour markets and participating in family life. What 'stand-points' do you hold?

THE 'LIFEWORLD' OF FAMILIES: HABERMAS

Many sociological thinkers have been concerned about documenting and analysing con-flict in societies. A contemporary group of theorists have kept conflict as a core element in the analysis of societies. From this group, known as critical theorists, the work of Habermas has particular relevance to explaining families. People, Habermas argued, need to understand the everyday: settings, structures and interactions. Knowledge of these dimensions provides meaning to people's lives. Habermas draws upon the work of the positivists with a focus on structures, on the work of the interactionists and their concern with relationships and roles, as well as ideas about divisions and conflicts. Sources of social division (for example, gender, occupation, income) have changed from the time of Marx's writings and these are now more complex and subtle. That said social divisions do not result in conflict generally, given the needs people have to sustain income, resources and the livelihood of themselves and their families. Habermas drew upon a range of theoretical approaches and offered multilayered ways in which families might be analysed and explained.

Habermas notes the relevance of structures and systems to the context in which people communicate and attribute meanings. The resultant face-to-face encounters determine what Habermas calls the 'lifeworld', and through this we form communities and families. While the lifeworld is concerned with the forging and understanding of human relations, it also promotes cohesion. Habermas noted how this taken-for-granted framework of the lifeworld cloaks tensions, misunderstandings and conflicts, many of which are created by the economic system of capitalism. The lifeworld of families is also informed by global trends in economic production and linkages. For example, migration creates physical distance between family members and yet deepens mutual support with dependence upon income sent home.

Following the work of Habermas, in Box 2.2 we introduce David Morgan (1996) and his development of the theory of family practices. Morgan asserts that the doing of everyday family activities offers critical insights to what it means to be part of, or excluded from, family life.

Box 2.2   Family processes explained as 'doing family'

'Doing family' is a term used to describe the various relationships and activities that take place in families. This includes the processes that go on inside and outside a household. These involve a range of people who consider themselves to be family members or linked in some way. Doing family offers a more active appreciation of families' processes and family life and encourages us to consider variation in the types of arrangements and array of activities which come within the orbit of families. Sometimes people 'do family' in more obvious ways than others. Examples of this can include travelling some distance to attend a family festival or wedding, making particular efforts as a step-parent to develop a parental role or visiting a family member whom you rarely see but who has just experienced bereavement. In all of these examples, and the many activities of daily life, the notion of doing families points to the myriad ways we engage in an emotional and physical sense with those who are linked to us in a significant way. Doing family is also predicated on engagement with various agencies and professionals and can include schools and teachers, hospitals and health workers, banks, employment agencies, housing departments and, for some, aid organizations.

The development of *doing families* as a theoretical framework owes much to the work of David Morgan (1996) and his major contribution to debates on defining and researching families. Key to his ideas is the recognition that contemporary families are defined more by doing family things than by presumptions or assertions of being part of a family. Morgan draws upon the concepts of fluidity and diversity. Further, he considers the many ways in which family life draws upon memories, experiences, anticipations and potential arrangements and plans. Doing family can include, for example, the annual trip to households of other family members at a given weekend in the year, 'as we always do this'. This may be described as a family ritual, and these as well as many other activities and thoughts make up doing family; 'family represents a quality rather than a thing' (1996: 186).

If the overarching notion of doing family asks us to reflect on the range of activities, locations and people, then Morgan's concept of family practices is more firmly rooted in daily life: 'Practices are often little fragments of daily life which are part of the normal taken-for-granted existence of practitioners. Their significance derives from their location in wider systems of meaning' (1996: 190).

Actors and agency are emphasized. Individual biographies are central to this explanation. People's experiences, rooted in personal biographies, change over time and in various locations and social settings. At a meal with family members in a restaurant it may seem appropriate for adults to continue to use the name 'Granma' [sic] rather than the first name, Ann, as the family term expresses endearment. In this example we find doing family reflects a family practice through the use of the term Granma.

WOMEN, MEN, GENDER: FEMINIST PERSPECTIVES

It is notable that all of the social theorists discussed in earlier sections are men and their analyses have generally offered gender-neutral or gender-ascribed analysis of families. For example, in Parsons' analysis the functions of the family are gender coded such that the main provider of resources is assumed to be a male worker, partnered by a female home-maker who undertakes most of the care for children and other dependants. Through these ascribed roles the family unit ensures that the main worker is freed up to participate in the labour market while the next generation is socialized and older or sick relatives can be cared for with limited recourse to welfare services.

One of the most significant aspects of contemporary sociology is that of feminist and pro-feminist perspectives on families (Oakley, 1974; Luxton, 1980; Hochschild, 1983; hooks, 1984; Smart, 1984; Connell, 1987; Morgan, 1996, Tong, 2009). While there are a number of feminist theories, the common premise is that men and women have different experiences and thus different standpoints from which they generate knowledge. For feminist and pro-feminist theorists, gender is the main organizer of one's experience of the social world, and gender, they argue, is socially constructed.

In sum, most feminists argue that woman's experiences, and those of men and women as they interact, have been marginalized. The only way to redress this and to provide a clearer analytical dimension to the study of families is to develop knowledge from the standpoint of women and feminists. Here we differentiate between women and feminists, as a feminist perspective constructs knowledge upon the presumption of patriarchy or the domination of women by men. Patriarchy takes many forms rang-ing from explicit gender discrimination through to implicit vehicles for the workings of power such as gender coding. Examples include the gender segregation of employ-ment with a disproportionate number of women in caring professions such as teaching and nursing, fewer of whom achieve senior posts in comparison to their male counter-parts. Men who enter caring professions achieve career advancement at a swifter pace than females and as a result males in these professions are over-represented in senior and better paid posts.

FEMINIST AND GENDER PERSPECTIVES ON FAMILIES

Feminist explanations of families and family life are generally based on the notion of patriarchy, namely, that women are undervalued, denied aspects of their rights and thus oppressed. Further, it is argued that the power resources of societies favour men, and women are exploited in numerous ways, including, the division of domestic labour, access to higher paid jobs and ensuring equal pay for work of equal value. Women are persecuted for being women through various forms of violence and violation, including rape, domestic abuse, sexualized stereotypes in advertising and media, so-called 'honour' killings, female circumcision and female infanticide. Within the family, gendered and oppressive power dynamics are sustained, learnt and evolved. Combining economics with this oppressive working of gendered power generates, for example, capitalist patri-archy or communist patriarchy. If you consider race, ethnicity, sexualities, age and so forth, there are myriad ways in which differences and oppression can manifest. Power is not merely that of men over women but of dominant groups of men who achieve domination over less powerful groups of men and women (Connell, 2009).

Women's experiences of patriarchy and gender differ (Butler, 1990). Delamont (2001) has argued that differences in social class between women are more powerful in determining life chances than gender-based similarities or differences between women and men in the same social class. However, differences do exist and it is in the family that all of us have our first experiences of gender identities and the consequences of these (Delphy, 1977). Yet identities are malleable and flexible, and as Goffman noted, open to renegotiation and change. Thus there are possibilities for change. That said, feminist theorists argue that society and culture create gender, not biology. Under this umbrella are a number of perspectives, which we explore in subsequent paragraphs including:

- liberal feminisms
- socialist and Marxist feminist perspectives
- radical feminisms
- queer theory.

Liberal feminists focus on the potential for policies and legislation to promote equality and combat sexism (Tong, 2009). The main assertion among such theorists is that elimination of prejudice and discrimination can be achieved through laws and changing practices. Most governments have chosen this route with a range of laws, policies and codes of practice. These views may be termed a neo-liberal approach to gender equality. Many argue, however, that we remain far from achieving equality, certainly in family roles and tasks. While younger generations may contend that they treat men and women as equals, the arrival of a child is often a trigger to moving into gendered roles. Women and girls continue to undertake more than a fair share of caring and domestic labour in family processes. Kin-keeping and extended family relationships are likewise considered a female domain. One symbol of this is in birthday or Christmas cards, which are over-whelmingly organized and bought by women.

Gender coding of roles also places men in specific domains whether they like it or not; for example, home improvements, general car maintenance or playing ball games with children. These roles are evident across the private and the public spheres of life with women and men segregated in the subjects they study in education and training, and the jobs they undertake in the labour market. The implications of these processes of segregation are evident over the lifecourse. For example, in the EU in 2008, the gap in average pay was estimated at 17.8% between men and women (Eurostat, 2008). This leads to reduced access to lifetime earnings, welfare benefits and pensions, with women making up the majority of the global population identified as living in poverty.

Socialist and Marxist feminists range widely in their perspectives, but at the core of this body of work is the way in which capitalism creates and is sustained by gender inequalities (Gittins, 1993). The challenge, however, is to address the class inequalities created by capitalism as it is through these that gender inequities flow. The family is central to the capitalist economic system, and gender relations in families reflect the economic system they serve. Women serve capitalism in many ways, including as providers of unpaid care and domestic work, as consumers of goods and services, as employees who are often paid less than male counterparts, and as untapped labour in the form of those not in full-time employment. Capitalism relies on families to sustain workers and produce future generations. It also creates differences among socioeconomic groups. The experience of families in low-income groups, who may be migrants, unskilled or casual workers, is very different from those of the family of the multinational chief executive. Marxist feminists argue that without changing the economic system little will shift in these multifaceted and exploitative relations.

Radical feminists argue that patriarchy is not specific to capitalism but forms the basis of all societies. Love, sex and relationships are viewed as closely linked to male domination, and potential violence and abuse. They reject the liberal focus on reform through legislation and the potential for change in social and political order. For some in this school of thought, women are considered both different from, and superior to, men.

?   In most families women undertake more unpaid domestic work than men. How would liberal, socialist, Marxist and radical feminists explain this?

In recent decades masculinities and men's studies (Kimmel et al., 2004) have evolved offering distinct perspectives on families. The experience of men as lovers, partners and parents has undergone a series of changes. Policy makers, social movements, men and women, critically reflect on the role of fathers as providers and offer new dimensions to the sociology of families, not least of which is the analysis of power in parenting, heterosexual, same-sex partnerships and families (Whitehead, 2002). The expectations and anticipations which imbue men's experiences in families also draw attention to the interweaving of social class and masculinities. For women, and men, social class matters. Middle-class men and women often have more in common than with those in other social classes. That said, the workings of masculinities and femininities in families offer insights into 'doing family' and the potential for development alongside exploitation.

Queer theory offers a further dimension and additional possibilities for the analysis of families (Eng, 2010). This body of work rejects the binary divides of sexes and sexuality arguing that the categories of heterosexual and homosexual are the products of the discourse in which heterosexuality dominates. Queer theory asserts that sexual categories are socially produced and not biological in origin. These bodies of work have challenged common conceptions of families, intimacy and sexualities with the focus on women as the key providers of parenting and emotional work. The implications of feminist standpoints, masculinity studies and queer theory are manifold and encourage us to recognize and reflect upon the dominance of ideologies about family roles and life. These include the issues of parenting, fostering and adoption, and assisted reproductive technology (ART).

➜ In Chapter 7 we consider the future of families and the potential impact of ART. The development of ART has resulted in the proliferation of fertility services across the world. Further, same-sex couples can be helped to give birth to children. Technology and changes in roles illustrate the acceptability of diversity in parenting, parental origins and familial composition.

GLOBAL DIMENSIONS

Global trends in poverty and income have received attention from numerous commentators and theorists. These trends are marked. The Global Policy Forum offers a portrait of increasing disparities between rich and poor countries from 1970 to 2000. Economic growth has steadily risen in the 20 richest countries while the poorest 20 countries have experienced modest or declining gross domestic product (GDP) (Global Policy Forum, 2008). An analysis of trends from 1820 to 2004 comparing data from the wealthiest and most powerful countries, commonly referred to as the G8 (Canada, France, Germany, Italy, Japan, Russia, the UK and the USA), with data from China, India, Latin America and Africa illuminates such inequalities (see Table 2.1).

Within the world's wealthiest nation inequalities are also stark. In the USA at the end of 2001, 10% of the population owned 71% of the wealth and the top 1% owned 38%. On the other hand, the bottom 40% owned less than 1% of the nation's wealth (Phillips, 2006). Women, in all countries, are over-represented in poverty statistics and this has been the focus of numerous global and national campaigns led by supra-national organizations such as the UN, the World Bank and the EU.

TABLE 2.1   Share of the gross domestic product (%) from selected countries and groupings 1820–2004 (Global Policy Forum, 2008)

	1820	1975	2004
G8	29	55	44
(US only)	2	22	21
China	33	5	13
India	16	3	6
Latin America	2	7	6
Africa	5	3	3

> → In Chapter 4 we consider how women and men may choose to use their resources (money, time, emotion) in differing ways. A body of research suggests that women are more likely to spend on children and on household members than are men. Of course, how these practices are worked out in families and relationships must be set in the context of household decisions and opportunities. Also refer to the section 'Structures and Practices' in this chapter (page 55) where we discuss family strategies (Wallace, 2002).

Researchers and commentators have become concerned at the centrality of theories from developed economies and how these contexts have channelled explanations of families towards an Anglo-centric debate. Fevre and Bancroft (2010) draw attention to the dominance of *Dead White Men* in the evolution of sociology. 'Live' women of many cultures and backgrounds have moved debates with their feminist perspectives (Leeder, 2004: 60). However, as discussed in Chapter 1, there is a multiplicity of families. Ideas about families are shaped across the globe through a range of factors, including race and ethnicity, politics and international relations, economics, and cultural and belief systems. Most notably, world politics is in a post-colonial era and feminist theorists are identifying and drawing attention to the fact that 'vectors of subordination and privilege – gender, race, class, age, ethnicity, global location and affectional preferences – both interact structurally and intersect dynamically in people's lives to create oppression and inequality' (Lengermann and Niebrugge-Brantley, 2000: 468).

Women's life experiences differ and so do their experiences of subordination and/or privilege. Contrast a young middle-class woman in New York worried about getting better marks than her boyfriend in her university course with the experiences of a woman in her sixties, recently widowed and living in a rural area of Egypt. The Egyptian widow is worried about how to sustain herself and where her next meal will come from. There is no one set of experiences for women, except that they are oppressed. Further, as capitalism becomes the dominant economic system, so too are the associated family forms and the gendered oppression of both men and women (Mies, 1999).

In Box 2.3 we draw attention to the social theory of post-modernism in which trends in capitalism and families are explained through documenting diversity, fragmentation and changes.

Box 2.3   Social theory and post-modernism

Post-modernism can be defined as a school of social theory which recognizes and places centre stage diversity, fragmentation and major changes in economic systems.

Theories of the post-modern have tended to focus on the minority world. These originate from explanations of industrial societies which have moved to higher level technologies and no longer depend on traditional industries of, for example, ship building, steel production and large-scale manufacturing. Further, demographic trends, changing gender roles, ethnicity, migration and care issues are among the issues which post-modernists argue benefit from recognizing the complex interweaving of change and how this is manifest in families. See Foucault's *The Archaeology of Knowledge* (1971).

CONTEMPORARY VOICES ON INTIMACY

Feminist theories draw attention to the emotions and relationships of family life – of partners, parents, children, grandchildren. The study of emotions in families and relationships is the focus of a number of sociologists concerned with individualization, namely, discriminating the individual from groups such as families. Much of this work has been driven by Beck and Beck-Gernsheim (1995). They contend that a shift to greater individualization, a notable trend in the minority world, brings with it the possibility of societies without families and children. People seeking a life unhindered by commitments and seeking to achieve personal fulfilment may choose to remain single and pursue their individual agendas. While the push to individualization is seemingly documented through statistics of an increase in solo living at all adult life stages, a deeper analysis of living arrangements, relationships and friendship groups illuminates a world of intimacy. Individuals are creating and inhabiting networks of friends, families and partners alongside pursuit of personal fulfilment. Beck and Beck-Gernsheim (1995) have proposed the notion of post-familial families; people create families, leave them for moments of time or longer periods and yet return to familial relationships.

Key elements of this thesis are based on notions of 'risk' and the idea of risk societies. What is a risk society? One common definition is of a collective sense that individuals have the potential to engage with or avoid events or activities considered to be hazards. For example, risks might be related to concerns about job security and for others risks may be viewed positively with insecurity and mobility in employment perceived as exciting and exhilarating. For a minority of the world's population, risks from famine, war and infectious diseases may have reduced, and yet anxieties about new problems and dangers have come to the forefront. These risks can include food and diet, employment and income, environment and ecology. Thus while not immediate, nor likely to lead to imminent danger, these risks form the basis of calculations engaged in by many of the worried better off. The implications for families include standards of living, access to education and employment, climate change and future survival. In the majority world, the struggle to ensure survival and sustenance remains for many.

Reflexive practices are determined by a range of structural and cultural factors; for example, a middle-class woman in France decides to return to work within six months of giving birth regardless of prevalent attitudes to being at home in the first year of a child's life. The household income has the resources to pay for childcare and her partner is supportive. Contrast this with a young mother in a rural location in Malawi for whom there is no choice in her society, although she can see different routes for women in Europe as she watches the television and digests images of other ways of living. Her life may seem constrained in the eyes of the French mother, while for her this is a path that ensures familial and community support.

With the availability of low-cost or free contraceptive methods, sexual activity need not necessarily lead to reproduction. In the minority world, sex free from concerns about pregnancy is a possibility for many couples. Pleasure in sex and intimate relationships can also be discussed and is the focus of many aspects of the media and culture. The work of Giddens (1992) on the transformation of intimacy sought to connect gender, sexuality and intimate relationships with reflexivity (Box 2.4). This theory has been criticized for emphasizing autonomy along with an inadequate consideration of gender and social class. Giddens asserts that individuals are creating personal portraits in their intimate lives and in doing so draw upon the past, present and anticipations; what has worked or not, what can I do now and what might I want to do in the future? Divorce and separation are cited by Giddens as examples of this notion of a personal project. Self, society and reflexivity are interwoven in dynamic ways. Relationships and families change although continuities remain evident in, for example, childrearing and gender codes in which mothers undertake much, if not all, of this work, and images and discourses generally represent children with women. This is too stark a picture to offer, for as Jamieson (1998) points out, negotiation of roles does take place, especially in dual-earner and middle class households. Jamieson and Tonybee (1990) chart the changes in family relationships and intimacy noting how 'good mothering' was conceived as largely functional in the early twentieth century and best suited to what are considered feminine skills. In many contemporary societies parenting – mothering and fathering – is now concerned with the emotional well-being of the child too as this is a notable change in the intimacy among parent and child to have taken place over the last century.

Box 2.4   Reflexivity

Here we draw attention to the notion of reflexivity. Simply put reflexivity is about cause and effect. In sociology to be reflexive is to undertake an act of self-reference. This requires the sociologist to refer back to the idea with reference to, and awareness of, their own place in the social structure. People are reflexive in their everyday lives as they look around, identify events and trends and decide on their personal interpretation and potential response. Elliott refers to the ways in which 'observation of, and reflection upon, the social world of human agents comes to reshape the very forms of life instituted by society' (2009: 287).

Debates on intimacy and individualization can be criticized for a Eurocentric approach, which does not give due attention to the experiences of many in the majority world still striving for survival and the basic necessities of life. As Jamieson points out we also need to be aware of 'the global in the local, and having a sense of connected histories' both over time and space (2010b: 9).

Box 2.5   Family displays

If families are based on 'chains of relationships' (see Smart and Neale, 1999: 72) with different people across various households, then connecting through phone calls, emails or letters, and talking about doing this, becomes a display. Displays allow for demonstrations of the quality of relationships as individuals may choose to 'display' some relationships more than others in practical ways (meeting up) or through talk. Choices to display can be developed as a proxy for the strength of a relationship, which (Finch, 2007: 72) refers to as 'degrees of intensity'. Talk about displays, or choosing not to display, can illuminate the strains and tensions in families. Displays also change over time with shifting roles and identities. Children grow up and move away and watching them become parents or end a relationship requires new and different ways of displaying families.

In addition to seeing or hearing about displays, it is important to consider who recognizes these, how and why this matters. Recognition may come from other family members, friends, colleagues, employers or agencies such as the police, social services or health services. It can take many forms and can draw upon very different types of relationships and displays. What is the significance of the 'family meal' or the mother accompanying her daughter to an antenatal clinic? Talking about these displays and interpreting them can be hazardous for they are open to inflation and incorrect interpretation. That said, it is the combination of practices and displays, and the quality as well as quantity of what we hear or see, which demonstrate the breadth and depth of relationships.

The concepts of practices and displays, of doing families, offer us a range of adjectives to bring the noun 'family' into vivid colour and meaning (Morgan, 1996: 193–4). Dermott and Seymour (2011) develop these ideas further in the book *Displaying Families: A New Concept for the Sociology of Family Life*.

?   In Box 2.5 Finch (2007) encourages us to consider how families display (show) what they have done as a way of asserting membership and uniqueness. Reflecting on the theoretical perspectives presented throughout this chapter, which do you think can help to explain what, how and why families offer displays to those outside their group?

SUMMARY

There are a number of ways in which sociologists seek to explain family formation, structures and processes. Sociological theories offer possibilities to identify and interpret how family structures are moulded by and respond to the wider context of the economy, politics and policy. Social norms and ideas about the processes in which families and family members should engage are also the focus of sociological explanations.

In the political and policy arenas, theories are drawn upon to inform debates and declarations on the family. A notable example of this is the Doha Declaration of 2004, adopted through a consensus resolution by all members of the UN (2004). The resolution before the General Assembly of the UN proposed protection of the family as the 'natural and fundamental group unit of society'(United Nations, 2004: 1) noting widely shared international values related to marriage, parents, children and human life. Much of the debate surrounding this declaration focuses on families as a basis to social cohesion and support for women and children.

> ➜ In Chapter 4 we discuss family policy in depth. It is important to note that sociological explanations and ideas about families have an impact upon policy development and implementation too.

The plurality of possible explanations and ways of exploring families may seem daunting, but families remain a major topic in any discussion of societies and social cohesion. Politicians, faith groups, employers' organizations, environmental groups, aid agencies and many others, have much say on, and about, families. Debates can be polarized, ranging from those who argue that families are core elements of integration and without strong models of the family adhering to certain functions, then cultural disintegration and moral decline will ensue. Others challenge this, noting the diverse forms of families that have always existed.

In this chapter we have outlined the major approaches to explaining families, namely:

- structural approaches – in which theorists argue that families provide ties that keep people in cohesive groupings

- social interactions and sociological ideas – on how individuals are actors and engage with each other in varied ways which create interdependencies

- conflict theories – with the focus upon economic systems and the role of families in supporting and sustaining dominant means of production

- feminist and gender approaches – in which the issues of gender, sexualities and power were brought to the fore for both the majority and minority worlds.

To end the chapter let us draw attention to the blurring of boundaries between the various approaches in the hope that this may encourage you to develop your own perspectives on explaining families.

The work of the structural functionalists, so popular in the 1950s and 1960s, could not adequately address dysfunctions of families. What of psychological and physical abuses? Of intimate partner relationships which break down? And what of major changes in roles? Morgan (1975) drew attention to the successful adaptation of individuals achieved at the expense of the main carer in families, often adult women. Many women sacrificed work, education and personal opportunities so others could, for example, develop a career. Further, many analysts did not address the love-hate ideas we have towards families. We might feel comfortable with our immediate family but dislike large family get-togethers such as Christmas celebrations. We may not wish to spend time with certain family members, but in times of personal crisis we seek support from them presuming this will be forthcoming; if it is denied, we feel more aggrieved than we might with friends.

David Cheal (1991) has written extensively on sociological theory and families. In a historical perspective on this topic he suggested that the 1970s witnessed an explosion in the sociological study of the family that coincided with the development of the topic in American and European universities. This was also, he contends, the 'high point' of positivism and the height of the struggle to privilege one perspective; one particular kind of 'socially constructed world', be that based on structures, interactions or conflicts. Such struggles for theoretical dominance led to a decline in the status of the sociology of families. Others recognized how families are critical to all aspects of societies from health to politics, from work to social life, and the exploration of families became critical to the study of health, social care, social work and psychology.

Debates about families as models of developmental change and of rupture and liberation encourage us to examine again the fuzzy boundaries between the private world of families, and the public gaze on people, relationships and identities. Regardless of how we try to explain families we may draw towards or pull away from families, and at times have these feelings and actions working in parallel. Families form social groupings which are seemingly so obvious to everyone that there is temptation to see the family as simple and monolithic. Yet both broader and closer study reveals that families are rather more complex.

> **?** To end, return to the notes you made at the outset of this chapter on your explanations of family breakdown and the increasing acceptance of divorce. After reading this chapter how would you explain these changes?

EXPLORE FURTHER

Allan, G. and Crow, G. (2001) *Families, Households and Society*. Basingstoke: Palgrave Macmillan.
Cheal, D. (2002) *Sociology of Family Life*. Basingstoke: Palgrave Macmillan.
Gerhardt, U. (2002) *Talcott Parsons: An Intellectual Biography*. Cambridge: Cambridge University Press.
Leeder, E. (2004) *The Family in Global Perspective: A Gendered Journey*. New York: Sage.

USEFUL WEBSITE

Social Science Information System based at the University of Amsterdam offers a range of definitions of theories and concepts: www.sociosite.net/topics/theory.php

PART II

RESEARCH AND POLICY

3

Researching Families

Keywords: research, methods, historical research, secondary research, policy, sociological imagination, change, continuity

INTRODUCTION

In regard to families, social research has addressed many issues and themes, including the history of families across the centuries, the experiences of families in different countries and cultures, roles and relationships, and how families engage with institutions and services such as education, housing and health. The topic of families has generated a vast amount of research ranging from school projects through to global studies led by supra-national organizations (Bibi et al., 2010). National governments often fund research on families, investing time and resources to gain evidence on family structures and processes. Policy makers and politicians consider families to have a critical role in most aspects of society, not just in the upbringing of children. Policies, and resultant services, are generated and refined so as to support, cajole and manoeuvre families to behave in ways that reflect certain norms (Lewis et al., 2009).

> → In Chapter 4 we consider family policy and the relationship between research and policy in greater depth. In particular, you might want to look at the section 'Families and the Welfare State', which considers the relationship between research and family policy in greater depth.

Through the many studies on families we can see that there are clear and fundamental changes in family life and thus in our appreciation of 'families'. Diversity in family composition and in lifestyles is generally recognized and these trends necessitate research to map, understand and develop ideas. The increased prominence of research on families offers:

- myriad descriptions of how people live their lives and engage with others
- identification and exploration of relationships, including how paid and unpaid work combine and collide
- explanations as to why individuals and families across the world live as they do and how, for example, they view their futures.

In the majority world, sociological research on families has proved to be imperative to the documentation of maternal and childhood deaths, poverty, paid and unpaid work, migration, disease, food production and consumption, natural disasters and climate change, war and conflict. Supranational organizations, for example, the UN and the WHO, devote a large proportion of staff time and resources to collecting, collating and analysing data on families. Research underpins programmes such as those focused on delivering the UN Millennium Development Goals to address poverty, offering insights into the depth and range of problems and solutions as well as an assessment of what countries need to do to reach targets (see http://www.un.org/en/mdg/summit2010/). In the minority world sociological research on families has evolved from the 1950s, reflecting trends in:

- family structures and processes. Sociological work on families witnessed notable growth around the time of Parsons (1953), evolved through the 1960s to the rise of what has become known as second-wave feminism (Tong, 2009) and contemporary work on diverse families (Gabb, 2008)

- welfare regimes and the range of policies concerned with families, including the growing participation of women in employment as well as changing consumer demands and the impact of science and technologies on labour markets

- professional education for social and health services and policy analysis for government. The development of evidence-informed practice and policy work has also generated a demand for the monitoring and evaluation of services and policies for families

- the growth in communication and technologies that enhance the potential for family practices to take place over time and space. These technologies also offer the potential to document and explore families and their processes and practices in new and innovative ways.

This chapter is not an exhaustive review of sociological research methods or studies. The overall aim of the chapter is to highlight how families have been examined across the centuries, continue to be the focus of much social research, and the relationship between sociological theory, the design of research projects and potential impact of findings on policy and practice.

> ➜ In Chapter 2 we considered the development of sociology and in particular the evolution of sociological theories. To reprise, theories offer possible explanations to aid an analysis of how societies operate. They comprise a set of ideas connected by the authors (theorists) in ways they consider have explanatory power or explanatory potential.

RESEARCH METHODS

In this section we offer a brief résumé of the potential research methods available to design studies. We consider this relevant to the reader as appreciating how research is designed and undertaken offers critical insights to the process and findings of projects. Williams and May comment that neither social nor natural sciences are 'a value-free endeavour' but 'we should be vigilant about the ways in which some values inform our activities in the conduct of research' (1996: 192). At the heart of the research process is the individual researcher who takes a lead in the creation of knowledge. Decisions about the design and methods determine what is available in the process of knowledge creation. Researchers design projects that draw upon assumptions about the topic. There are also tactical and practical issues of what might elicit a better response, provide more data which offer explanations and ideas drawn from individuals and families, for example, how far resources will stretch and what skills and money are available.

As noted this is neither an exhaustive list nor does it provide an in-depth treatment of these. Our goal is to equip the reader with skills to assess the content of subsequent sections and chapters. Methods introduced are:

- survey research

- ethnographic research – this includes methods relevant to 'writing about people'

- secondary analysis of research studies.

SURVEY RESEARCH (BOX 3.1)

Box 3.1   Defining a survey
A survey allows for a 'mapping', meaning the collection of information on the extent of a topic or problem; for example, the number of people in a household, the hours adults work, the schools children attend or the location of the nearest hospital. Surveys can also offer information on people's attitudes to, for example, marriage, parenting, elder care or work–home issues. Theories inform survey development in so far as the relevance of one or more explanations of families, family structures and processes, can be explored through questions with preset categories or attitudinal scales for responses or open-ended questions. A questionnaire is the printed list of questions used in a survey.

The UK Government's Office for National Statistics undertakes over 100 surveys per annum/every year. Some take place every 10 years, as does the census, with preparation and analysis work taking place throughout those years, while others take place every three months, for example the quarterly survey into job vacancies. The array of data this process produces are considered a 'building block for open and transparent government, effective public administration, and efficient operation of the economy and society' (http://www.ons.gov.uk/about/our-statistics/the-value-of-statistics-to-society/index.html). Most of these data are of relevance to families as they create and monitor pictures of society and how groups and individuals interact. Statistics provide a range of audiences with information and insights.

The Office for National Statistics is an example of the kind of service most governments use to collect invaluable information on families and relationships. This organization is a member of Eurostat, the body which collates and collects statistical and other research data across the 27 Member States of the EU. The role and benefits of statistics are summarized thus:

> Democratic societies do not function properly without a solid basis of reliable and objective statistics. On one hand, decision makers at EU level, in Member States, in local government and in business need

statistics to make those decisions. On the other hand, the public and media need statistics for an accurate picture of contemporary society and to evaluate the performance of politicians and others. Of course, national statistics are still important for national purposes in Member States whereas EU statistics are essential for decisions and evaluation at European level. (http://epp.eurostat.ec.europa.eu/portal/page/portal/about_eurostat/corporate/introduction)

Surveys are also undertaken by other organizations and networks. One example is Growing up in Scotland (GUS). This ongoing survey is in its sixth year and is an example of a longitudinal study, following 8,000 children from infancy through to teenage years. Commissioned by the Scottish Government, it is run by the Scottish Centre for Social Research in collaboration with the Centre for Research on Families and Relationships and the Medical Research Council, Social and Public Health Sciences Unit. A recent topic that the survey data illuminated is child poverty in Scotland. One headline-grabbing result was the finding that almost one in four (24%) of all three to four year olds and one in five (21%) five to six year olds were persistently poor; the context to this experience varied according to the children's background circumstances. This result received a lot of media attention illustrating the degree to which poverty among children impacts on about a fifth of the under-six year olds. For further information on GUS see http://www.crfr.ac.uk/gus/publications.html and http://www.scotland.gov.uk/Publications/2010/04/21131609/1. Given the relative wealth of the UK, these findings surprised many commentators, policy and service providers and provoked a debate on the relationship between research and policy (Box 3.2).

Box 3.2 Contested terms used in surveys: determining poverty and income

In the GUS survey the definition of poverty used in the research came under scrutiny. The project as a whole defined poverty according to the Scottish government's most often used poverty indicator, that is, relative low income, or more precisely below 60% of median equalized household income before housing costs (Barnes et al., 2010). Adoption of government measures does not mean universal acceptance by the public, charities, local government and supranational organizations. Two major issues in survey work are how indicators are defined and how the relevant data are collected. Central to the assessment of poverty is determining household income. In the case of the GUS survey the main carer is asked to select a monthly or annual band of income which should

(Continued)

(Continued)

reflect their total income in their household from all sources before tax, and should include benefits, interest from savings and any other types of income. Again, how the bands are set, the wording of the question and the approach taken to collect an answer will all have an impact. Thus, although survey data may appear to offer a clear picture of family life, the ways in which indicators are defined, measurements are determined, questions are worded and answers are sought will have a bearing on the result.

? Drawing upon the contents of Box 3.2 and thinking about the majority and minority worlds, if you were designing a survey what would you consider when writing questions on poverty for a survey in (a) Kenya and (b) Sweden?

WRITING ABOUT PEOPLE AND FAMILIES: ETHNOGRAPHIC RESEARCH METHODS

Ethnographic research is a term which may loosely be defined as 'writing about people' (Fulcher and Scott, 2011: 80). Under this umbrella we can group a number of the methods often used in research on families and considered in the paragraphs below. These are:

- interviews

- focus groups

- observation

- diaries

- biographical approaches

- participatory and creative methods

- documentary research.

There are several types of *interviews* – from an unstructured conversation, through to the highly structured format with predetermined questions. In the arena of researching families there are a number of examples of projects based on interviews. The study by Young and Wilmott (1957) on family and kinship in East London is based on data obtained via a combination of survey questions and structured interviews. Almost a thousand residents who had at that time been residing or had previously resided in Bethnal Green were interviewed between 1953 and 1955. The depth and breadth of this study, coupled with the level of detail on the research process, makes this a classic project and one worthy of examination by any prospective researcher. More recently, Fiona Williams (2004) reported on the research programme on care, values and the future of welfare, referred to using the acronym CAVA. Using in-depth interviews from six projects undertaken between 1999 and 2004, the study reflects the changes and continuities in families' lives in differing types of locality in the north of England. Again, interviews allow for the close exploration of everyday practices and how these draw upon memories and anticipations. *Focus groups* are a further example of conversations used in research, but in this example a small group of people come together to debate a topic or issue. The researcher acts as a facilitator aiming to keep discussion and debate relevant, ongoing and inclusive (see, for example, the study by Birkett et al., 2004 on health and nutrition in families in which parents offered their experiences and reflected on those of others on parenting, family meals, food preparation, and physical activity. The advantage of the focus group approach was the debate among parents in which family practices were shared and opinions on a range of these, together with future options, were considered).

Sociologists have often observed how families interact and engage with other groups and services (Papini et al., 1988; Livingstone and Bovill, 2001). Sociological observers generally choose from three possible roles when engaging in *observation*. There is the complete participant who is active and involved, and records observations later; the participant-as-observer who is clearly known to all and records during and after engagement with the family; and finally the complete observer who, for example, sits in a room and observes what goes on. Each role has advantages and disadvantages, not least because of the artificial nature of being a participant and/or an observer. Nevertheless, observation continues to be a fruitful method in researching families.

In an important study by Charles and Kerr (1988) on families and food, the authors asked women to keep food *diaries* for a fortnight between a first and second interview. The method illuminated how interview and diary data were sometimes at odds with each other, or supported, and illustrated additional issues. This method has been used in a range of familial contexts including audio diaries on the topic of sleep (Arber et al., 2007). Other qualitative approaches to *participatory and creative methods* are:

- auto/biography or life history – in which people talk about their individual experiences and thoughts across their lives or specific topics

- physical participation – walking around a home or location to identify and discuss key points. See, for example, the work of Clark and Moss (2005) with children on the spaces in which they live with their families and play with friends. Walking and identification provides insightful information on how children live day to day. Further, this work provides insights to multimethod work, with what they have termed a 'mosaic approach'

- writing, drawing, visual techniques – these methods have been used by Clark and Moss (2005) and, among others, the work of Punch (2002), generally in combination with other ways of data gathering.

Documentary research incorporates the use of texts and documents, including source materials such as government publications, newspapers, census publications, novels, film and video, personal photographs, diaries and many other written, visual and pictorial sources. These can be in paper, electronic or other hard copy form. Documentary research provides a context for other data. For some researchers this is the main form of information in, for example, producing profiles of family composition and experiences through statistics and policy analysis.

In Box 3.3 we introduce longitudinal research and the idea that research may be collected at different points over years and decades to offer a longer-term profile of family structures and trends.

Box 3.3   Longitudinal research: timescapes

Longitudinal research is conducted over a period of time, generally longer than three years, drawing upon data collected through a number of methods. One notable project is that of *Timescapes* (see http://www.timescapes.leeds. ac.uk/), funded for five years by the UK Economic and Social Research Council (ESRC). The project is exploring how personal and family relationships develop and change over time. The focus is relationships with 'significant others', which includes parents, grandparents, siblings, children, partners, friends and lovers. One example of a project of longitudinal research is the work of MacLean et al. (2010). They undertook three waves of fieldwork with 14 families living in Scotland on the topic of negotiating issues between parents and primary-school aged children on working parenthood. When the project began in 2007 the outlook for jobs and income was brighter than in subsequent years when a severe economic recession hit in 2008. Thus the data illustrated how families experienced the outset and consequences of recession 'against the backdrop of their financial histories and anticipated futures' (MacLean et al., 2010: 159).

?   Looking back over the last five years, what has changed or remained the same in your family? How might a researcher document continuities and changes in your family?

SECONDARY ANALYSIS OF RESEARCH STUDIES

Sometimes researchers do not collect data but instead review the wealth of material available from completed projects. A critical review of other datasets and materials is commonly called secondary analysis. It is an important and growing way of providing evidence to inform theory, policy and service provision. However, secondary analysis does raise a number of issues too. To explore the advantages and disadvantages of this approach we open with the example of secondary analysis undertaken in the mid-twentieth century by Talcott Parsons. Subsequently, in Box 3.4 we draw attention to a recently established archive to facilitate secondary analysis, held by the Timescapes team.

Parsons (1953) was working over the 1940s, 1950s and 1960s to explore the adaptation of families to the post-war American free market economy. His analysis sought interlinkages between voluntaristic action and realism, or put more simply finding out what drives people to act as they do and why. The impetus for his research derived from a number of disciplines, including natural and social sciences. In an analysis of the relationship between economic systems and family activities, Parsons asserted that a 'partnership' was evident. The roles of husband and wife, inside and outside the home, were necessarily differentiated and gendered. These roles, Parsons suggested, were complementary and accepted in so far as this was clearly how many couples with children organized their family life. These observations have come in for a fair amount of criticism.

But how did Parsons develop these ideas? In contrast to sociologists who undertake research projects using some of the methods identified in the preceding section, Parsons conducted secondary research. He reanalysed data from other researchers or government sources. This search for data sources and analysis of material was based on his theories. Parsons assessed the role of family, education, culture, and their respective and combined contributions to social systems. For Parsons, families were considered to be key elements in 'pattern maintenance and tension management', critical to the development of moral education. Tensions became evident in his work. On the one hand, he recognized the role of kinship in generating and sustaining inequalities (through, for example, inheritance of income and property), and yet his work appears to sanction or confirm gender codes for the roles of women and men in the home and workplace:

> One mechanism which can serve to prevent the kind of 'invidious comparison' between husband and wife which might be disruptive of family solidarity is a clear separation of the sex roles such as to ensure that they do not come in competition with each other. (Parsons, 1953: 79–80)

These roles seemed obvious to Parsons and were reinforced by his concern for social order and norms as evident in his sociological theories. In summary, believing that the so-called nuclear family was best adapted to life in capitalist economies, Parsons received criticism for asserting that the least stable households were among the low-income and low-education households (Cheal, 2002: 30). The implications for government and service responses to social class, race and gender analysis were notable. Many argue that this work reinforced the idea of the nuclear family as a favoured family structure and the one best capable of serving the myriad economic needs of capitalist societies.

Debates on Parson's findings were heated and often polarized sociologists, politicians, policy makers and people. Was secondary analysis employed to find data to support explanations of family life? For example, in the secondary analysis undertaken by Parsons, he ignored a number of issues on which research data was available, including unpaid work, women's multiple roles and aspirations, the kinship links of families, single parents, ethnicity, and social and religious movements.

Many researchers, theorists and commentators grapple with this when considering any piece of research; is this work predicated on personal views with information sought to support these? People observe activities, become aware of social and economic structures, reflect upon the actions of individuals and groups, and interpret information. Thus any, and every, research study can be criticized for personal predilections. The work of Parsons' was located in capitalist and North American contexts. As noted above, this narrow database is interpreted without due attention to gender, power, social conflict (for example, domestic abuse or intergenerational conflict) and contexts; do people freely create nuclear families or are families a response to economic and social structures and factors such as the location of available jobs or dwellings? Keeping those points in mind, it remains the case that the secondary analysis work of Parsons was momentous in bringing families into the sociological realm as never before.

In Box 3.4 we draw attention to a developing resource for those interested in secondary analysis: the Timescapes archive managed at the University of Leeds, UK. This allows not only for secondary analysis of completed projects lodged in the archive but is also a resource for the details of projects and publications on families.

Box 3.4   The Timescapes archive

A core development within the Timescapes longitudinal project is the Timescapes archive. This involves the gathering together of data generated through qualitative empirical research. The core element of the archive is Timescapes projects (see Box 3.3) which have been brought into a composite resource for sharing and re-use. Related projects may also apply to have their data lodged in the archive.

Based at the University of Leeds, the archive offers exciting possibilities for analysing data through time, over the life course and across the generations. It is possible, for example, to bring together data on parenting across the generations, exploring young people's experiences of being parented and their aspirations for becoming parents, early and midlife transitions to parenthood and the shifting nature of parent–child relationships in early, mid and later life.

It is anticipated that this collation of projects completed over a number of years, on topics of relevance to family studies will offer opportunities for secondary analysis. Further analysis will generate new insights about the meaning and dynamics of lives and relationships through biographical, generational and historical time.

Potential users must register to access the archive and can do so by visiting www.timescapes.leeds.ac.uk/the-archive/.

HISTORICAL RESEARCH ON FAMILIES

Historical work on families and relationships has been central to documenting the changes and continuities in family structures and processes. There is a vast array of research work which generally uses the methods of ethnographic work with oral histories and biographical work, and documentary analysis of information charting daily life in previous centuries and decades. To offer insights into this genre or research we draw upon several studies, which have been chosen to reflect the challenges in gaining access to information to examine family structures and processes. Four sub-sections follow:

- Approaches to the history of families
- Better times for families?
- Documenting change in family processes
- Family and sex 1900–2000.

APPROACHES TO THE HISTORY OF THE FAMILY

Historians have long had an interest in families, especially in those that exercised power and wealth (Anderson, 1980; Hartman, 2004). The historical analysis of more ordinary families burgeoned from the 1960s, along with women's and gender studies. In this section we introduce a number of key studies which offer insights into the trends in formation and practices of families. At the outset of our discussion we note some general conclusions about historical work:

- First, as Anderson notes 'there is no simple history of *the* Western family since the sixteenth century, because there is not, nor ever has been, a single family system' (1980: 14, emphasis in original). Much of the available literature on the history of families is drawn from European and North American studies and offers a vibrant but potentially narrow base for any conclusions. Historical data on families in the majority world can be difficult to source (Leeder, 2004).

- Second, and drawn from the Anderson quote, even with the limitation to the available research base, diverse families are evident throughout history. The immigrant families arriving in Canada and the USA during the eighteenth century for example, Catholic Irish migrants arriving in New York, and the Amish German communities settling in rural areas of Pennsylvania, brought with them different belief systems and ideas on relationships, childrearing and marriage. The everyday lives of these families and communities will have stood in stark contrast to the lives of Native American communities.

- Third, data sources are partial. In previous centuries the recording of everyday life was a limited pursuit because literacy skills were not widely prevalent. Of course, recording took place through various methods including forms of illustrative, written and art work. Further, gaining access to sources may also be problematic;

for example, the daily lives of Native Americans may be best represented in pictorial ways but these communities are located in the rural American Midwest making them physically inaccessible to many.

Given these various limitations, what insights can historical work offer? Anderson's (1980) efforts have had a major impact. His book *Approaches to the History of the Western Family 1500–1914*, provided three approaches to the historical analysis of families, namely demographic, sentiments and household economics, and we shall consider each in turn. The demographic approach is based on the analysis of long-term trends in information collected through standardized research, most commonly census surveys (Box 3.5). This approach offers the possibility to identify and assess trends such as age at first marriage, age at birth of first child, and size and membership of families and households. In summary these data allow for the identification of trends over time. It also encourages reflection on the implications of trends for current and future policies and services.

Box 3.5   Four thousand years and counting: a brief history of the census

The first census is thought to have taken place in China during the Xia dynasty over 4,000 years ago. Censuses were also recorded in ancient Egypt, and in the Greek and Roman Empires. The modern form of the UK census has a forerunner in the Domesday Book of 1086, collated so William the First could organize taxation. Among the most famous surveys is the one referred to in the New Testament (of the Christian Bible) that required Mary and Joseph to travel to Bethlehem before the birth of Christ. Again, the reason for this was the taxation system of the then Roman Empire. Today most countries conduct a census every 10 years and the focus is less on taxation and much more on gaining data to plan welfare and public services such as health, housing, transport and education. Demographic approaches do, however, lead to presumptions being made about trends. Questions are open to interpretation by those responding, and respondents may neither always feel able nor want to be open about sensitive topics which could include intimate relationships in and outside families, parentage and illegitimacy, and finances and resource allocation. Also information collected through surveys cannot offer much on the reasons for certain behaviours. Thus the historical and contemporary demographic approach can provide a map of trends but allows for little in the way of understandings.

Documentation on social relationships provides the basis to the *sentiments* approach. Here documentation is broader than a census survey and includes interpretation of diaries and other writings or materials. Three examples of work that might be placed under this umbrella include Stone's (1977) *The Family, Sex and Marriage in England, 1500–1800*, Gillis's (1996) *A World of their Own Making: A History of Myth and Ritual in Family Life*, and Hartman's (2004) *The Household and the Making of History*. These and similar studies focus on individuals, partner selection and changing attitudes towards personal relationships. They emphasize meanings and attitudes and how practices of families are supported and challenged by wider economic, cultural and international contexts. Changes in economic systems and in living environments such as early industrialization and urbanization have had an impact on families and on everyday life, and these were documented by many. Engels (1845) conducted the ethnographic and documentary study *The Condition of the Working Class in England* in 1844. The findings of this study underpinned theoretical developments by Marx and Engels as well as offering key insights into the lives of families living through a period of major change. The sentiments approach draws upon limited sources, is rich in detail through the depth of analysis, and is drawn from the emphasis of the researcher. Bias in data selection and interpretation is a major criticism of this approach.

The household economics approach bridges and yet differs from the work of both demographic and sentiment historians. Economic behaviour of household members provides the main theme notably:

> ways in which, and the conditions under which, resources (including human resources) become available to the family and to its members, on strategies which can be employed to generate and exploit resources, and on the power relationships which arise as a by-product of these activities. (Anderson, 1980: 66)

Specific topics include inheritance, resource allocation among family members, and changes in work from peasant to industrial societies. While the approach offers insights into the ways in which families acquire, allocate, seek and exploit resources, the focus on economic data limits the potential to understand why and how these processes operate. Further, readers need to establish and assess the implications of the researchers' theoretical underpinnings and the conclusions offered.

BETTER TIMES FOR FAMILIES?

A major impact of the social history work about families has been to challenge the notion of better or golden periods for families. The idea that there have been better times for families is cited by commentators, politicians and policy makers as an antidote to contemporary social issues or problems. Examples include debates on births outside marriage, cohabitation, and the incidents of domestic violence and child abuse, where assertions are made that in previous centuries or decades these problems were less evident (Coontz, 1992).

In the historical analysis offered by Gillis this is addressed by arguing that it is 'imperative we disabuse ourselves of misconceptions ...' (1996: 18). Families of previous centuries suffered from deep levels of insecurity with wars, infectious diseases, precarious sources of income and family change. Deaths resulted in great levels of insecurity with children and women left destitute with no or limited access to welfare, and what was available was often delivered through religious groups rationing resources through criteria based on moral codes. Gillis makes an important point that while many consider the history of the family in a linear fashion, the memories and histories of families are cyclical and based on rituals, events important to members and how these are told and understood. This analysis points out how the myths that surround the family are often ideological, constructed from limited sources of evidence, and yet offer solace to those who consider diversity and change unsettling:

> if history has a lesson for us, it is that no one family form has ever been able to satisfy the human need for love, comfort and security. We must recognize that families are worlds of our own making and accept responsibility for our own creations. (Gillis, 1996: 240)

The experiences of what might be called 'ordinary' families as opposed to elite or powerful families were often ignored or were hard to document. In more recent years, families have been the focal point in studies which make claims to their centrality in historical processes. One such study is that of Hartman (2004) in her book *The Household and the Making of History*. The subtitle, *A Subversive View of the Western Past* alerts the reader to what some may consider to being its controversial content. In brief, Hartman asserts that the unique late-marriage patterns in western Europe proved critical to the birth of the modern world from 1500 onwards. The historical analysis by Hartman found that daughters of peasant families began to marry at a similar age to men (Box 3.6). Marriage took place at an older age than in other countries and continents and thus she asserted this change was a trigger to family formation and processes.

With the development of later marriage, however, and such key changes in beliefs and practices, young adults were encouraged to accept a large measure of personal responsibility. Nuclear families, Hartman asserts, were an unintended consequence of late marriage with the newly married couple considered capable of greater independence in economic and emotional aspects of family life. These smaller families created boundaries between private and public spaces. Without an extended family and with two adults to undertake domestic labour, gendered roles were ensured and a hierarchy evolved which favoured men.

Box 3.6   Age at first marriage

Hartman (2004) blends the approaches of demography and women's history. She notes how in medieval times early marriage from the age of seven to ten years was an accepted practice in a number of countries and cultures, including parts of Africa, China and the Middle East. Multifamily households were common as newlyweds moved into the home of the husband's family. However, in regions of Scandinavia, northern France and areas of what are now called the Netherlands, a significant number of people, between 10% to 20%, did not marry, and in this figure there were more women than men. While wealthy and powerful families continued to organize arranged marriages, other families grew to accept that young people could select a partner. Further, one-partnership households grew in number.

This coincided with changes in religious belief systems and the rise of the philosophical movement of the Enlightenment and Protestantism in northern Europe. These trends took centuries to evolve, but even at the outset this pattern of late marriage allowed for greater stability through delaying childbirth and related risks, and through the establishment of one-partnership households. Urbanization in west and north Europe further reinforced these trends with housing provision and employment patterns underpinning later marriage. Drawing on the historical work of Peter Laslett (1965), who concluded that for centuries the average size of households in England was four to six persons, Hartman proposes a historical global 'anomaly', namely the trend to later marriage for women and nuclear households in Western households that created new levels of household independence and partner interdependence.

DOCUMENTING CHANGE IN FAMILY PROCESSES

The exploration of familial relationships around children and childhood, and of those around death and inheritance, brought into the research arena groups often silenced in historical and sociological studies. The oral history work of Hareven (2000), along with her secondary analysis of documentation and data from a range of historical studies, offers insights on the processes of change. The home, for example, was a site for 'a broad array of functions and activities that transcended the more restricted circle of the nuclear family' (2000: 303). These activities could include the production of food or of goods to consume and sell, and child and elder care as well as such classic domestic tasks as preparing meals and leisure.

In many cultures the home might be viewed more as a retreat and a place for consumption of goods and services and less a site for activities of production. Exchanges between family members, neighbours and friends remain important, but in the past they had significance related to survival. These trends may return under the pressures of economic recession. The rationing of welfare services and benefits is likely to increase mutual interdependencies and return us to practices of previous centuries. This is likely to happen in an uneven and unequal way. Those individuals and families that are embedded in supportive social networks, have communication and social skills, are articulate and possess resources, are better placed to take advantage of any return to self-sufficiency or familial sufficiency.

As Hareven points out, families do not change in unison; change is a complex process with some changing and others resisting. An example would include a daughter who decided to divorce in the 1960s and was ostracized by her parents who view marriage as a lifelong commitment. Years later she remarried and the parents accepted the new partner, embraced the changes and attended the wedding. They also welcomed step-children into the family, something their own parents would never have agreed to. This example illuminates how children can also be innovators and promote change. This may be through education and languages they bring into households. Literacy skills and local cultures may also be transmitted by those moving in and out of households and studying or working. Again these shifts between the private world of the home and public arenas of work and school may cause tensions and will provoke reaction and responses. The porous boundaries between families and their contexts may also be considered through the concept of 'structural lag', a term used to describe how change may evolve within families, and institutions may take time to catch up. In contemporary terms one example from the minority world is the provision of care services for young and old. In many countries this fails to keep pace with changes in the labour market participation among women and demographic trends. Hareven comments:

> The mismatch between changing lives and changing social structures is remarkably applicable to understanding the social changes involving the family and the anxieties surrounded its future. (2000: 301)

Noting the paucity of transnational and cultural social history studies, Hareven emphasizes the importance of the local when she concludes that 'grand social changes are mediated through local cultures' (2000: 334).

FAMILY AND SEX 1900–2000

Exploring the broad theme of family and sex from 1900 to 2000, Therborn considers male domination in families and relationships, marriage and the social sexual order, relationships and fertility, and state responses to changing trends. The range of materials drawn upon is vast and the bibliography covers 41 pages! We cannot do justice to the depth and breadth of Therborn's work but would note how he draws upon a wealth of historical data to reflect upon the future. Therborn's study (2004) offers insights into families and relationships.

> ➜ In Chapter 1 we quote from Therborn (2004: 1) that: 'A family is always an outcome of sexual relations past or current: no sex, no family.' Also in Chapter 1 we drew attention to the key characteristics of families regardless of location and context. These include a sense of common identity, economic co-operation and ownership, reproduction of the next generation, carework and domestic labour and co-residence.

Examining data sources from across the world, Therborn offers a geographical and cultural road map to enable readers to:

> view family systems as ... institutions or structures taking their colouring from the customs and traditions, from the history of a particular area, a cultural wrapping which may remain after structural, institutional change, leaving imprints on the new institution. (2004: 10)

Patriarchy (male domination) remains evident but has waned in some continents, including Europe and North America, remains conspicuous in other places, such as Asia and Africa, and has come under severe pressure from many sources including supranational organizations such as the UN, with the Declaration of Human Rights and the Doha Declaration on Families. Trends in marriage have shown a rise and fall in industrialized countries, but have remained relatively stable in Asia and Africa. Fertility rates have declined in many countries with better access to safer forms of contraception and abortion, increased survival rates of children and increased familial resources. Wars and political, economic and social changes have had an impact on the rate and age of marriage, on patterns of cohabitation and on fertility. A key conclusion, as Jamieson notes is that:

> differences in the pacing of the change and in the detail of the nature of the changes are structured by the family systems and these family systems endure and continue to be anchored by regionally specific norms and institutions. (2010a: 3)

This quote from Jamieson echoes the findings of Hareven (2000) on the complex process of change in family structures and processes and the ways in which these often mediated through local cultures. In contrast, Therborn (2004) concentrates on change to family systems largely through economic forces. Much of the data he draws upon are statistical, including demographic data, figures on employment and on use of welfare benefits, and housing statistics. He includes a review of family law. His data sources and analyses differ from those of Hartman (2004) and of Hareven (2000), who draw upon oral histories and archive work as well as statistical material.

PRIVATE TROUBLES AND PUBLIC ISSUES

Social research can claim to illuminate how individual and collective experiences are shaped by social context and, by contrast, how families create their way of life by drawing upon, ignoring or challenging structures, norms and values. The idea of the 'sociological imagination' is helpful in examining the role of research. C. Wright Mills (1959) coined the term the sociological imagination to describe how individual troubles and public issues can come together. For example, a middle-class Italian couple discussing whether or not to have a baby may consider the potential impact on their personal, work and family lives. Their conversation may include the joy, the tiredness and frustrations a baby can generate. Alongside a discussion of these issues will be practical considerations; the need for a bigger flat, a reduction in income due to time away from work coupled with increased living costs, and organizing the day-to-day domestic and care tasks. Changes in the provision of childcare, the possibility of support from grandparents who live some distance away, and the provision of education and healthcare may also be factors raised during the conversation. It may not, however, be possible to plan a pregnancy or assume the arrival of a healthy baby.

The private issue of whether or not to have a baby becomes a public one as a range of policies (taxation, childcare, maternity and parental leave) and services (benefits, health, education and housing) come into the decision-making process. Historical and biographical perspectives might also be discussed. Familial and personal experiences of childbearing and childrearing are likely to be drawn upon, as too are the changes in the role of women, and the emphasis upon engagement in paid employment for adults, regardless of care responsibilities. Further, in previous decades there may have been little discussion on whether or not to try to have a baby if the couple were practising Roman Catholics, as the teachings of this church do not condone the use of artificial contraception. In contemporary Italian society, this teaching is largely ignored – Italy has one of the lowest fertility levels in the EU. If there is a low fertility rate, governments may encourage procreation through incentives in taxation, welfare benefits and services and social policies.

Likewise governments may seek to control their populations, as with for example, the one-child policy in China introduced in the 1970s. Outlawing a second child drew upon demographic research and involved a range of legal, health and social and welfare services. However, the cultural preference for boys resulted in an increase in the abortion and infanticide of girl children. The impact of this policy is stark with recent research demonstrating the implications for social cohesion, including reduced opportunities for marriage for men, growth in the sex trade and the trafficking of women for marriage, and violence and aggression among men competing for female partners and towards women who dismiss their advances. Researchers could argue that evidence on the impact of the one-child policy was not addressed. The key goal of the policy was to limit population growth and resultant demand for services, and a reduction in population growth has been achieved. The longer-term implications, however, are stark, and the Chinese government has now relaxed restrictions (*The Economist*, 2010).

These examples illustrate how the sociological imagination takes us across the broad personal sweep of history, socioeconomic structures, biographies and the potential for individual choice. These intermingle in ways we rarely interrogate. This complex interweaving of the personal and the public, and the historical and biographical, presents challenges for researchers and policy makers alike. What is the best way to document and assess personal issues and public responses? The social sciences offer a range of tools to document and assess aspects of family life. The research design and combination of methods chosen to collect data reflect the researcher's standpoint on the topic in question:

> every research tool or procedure is inextricably embedded in commitments to particular versions of the world and to knowing that world.

To use a questionnaire, … to take the role of participant observer, … to measure population growth, and so on, is to be involved in conceptions of the world that allow these [*methods*] to be used for the purposes conceived. (Hughes, 1990: 11).

Alternatively there may be a lack of a sociological imagination among people, institutions and governments. As a result of belief systems there remains an unwillingness and a failure to adequately address how personal decisions lead in the longer term to public and personal problems, including tensions and exploitation. Historical work identifies and illuminates how contradictions abound across cultures and remain evident in different attitudes to same-sex relationships, marriage, childbearing, parenting, elder care and death. The core of human existence remains for most a search for the emotional bonds between two or more people, be that through intimate, friendship or familial relationships.

> **?** What do you consider to be private troubles that are public issues in your life and that of your family?

RESEARCHING CHANGE AND CONTINUITY

Identifying and exploring changes and continuities is a key goal of much social research on families. In this final section of the chapter we have selected three research topics that document and seek to explain change and continuity in structures and processes of families and relationships: solo living, talking about sexual activities and single parenting. Our aim in this section is to illustrate how research can explore ideas from theories in greater depth or further investigate results from previous projects, such as large-scale social surveys. A theme that runs through the topics we have chosen is that of individualism. We have chosen this because the notion of the individual creating and gaining self-affirmation has been the cause of some debate on roles and relationships among family members and networks (Box 3.7), especially in North America and Europe.

> → In Chapter 2 we introduced the theme of individualization, noting the assertion by a number of theorists that the search for self-affirmation was creating intense and highly personalized relationships (see among others, Giddens, 1992; Beck and Beck-Gernsheim, 1995; Bauman, 2005). Collectively these ideas and related studies have forged explanations about families, and relationships and challenge what have been termed the individualization or detraditionalization thesis.

Claims to individualism and, to varying degrees, selfishness in families and relationships, particularly on the part of women, remain popular among some researchers, commentators, politicians and journalists. One key claim made was that women would be at the forefront of change, not least through a search for more equal forms of relationships; gender roles would be challenged, leading to changes in family processes with more equal engagement in unpaid work and for some the ending of family structures in the search for self-affirmation (Woodward and Woodward, 2009).

The growth in solo living among adults was also cited as a trend undermining family formation and sustainability as well as exemplifying the individualistic nature of contemporary social change. As we explore below, however, research illustrates that these explanations might misinterpret or over-interpret trends in family structures and processes.

Box 3.7   Individuals, networks and structures

The work of Bott (1968) is recognized as ground-breaking. Interview data with families in London indicated that adults in intimate family relationships seek a companionate relationship with a deeper sense of fulfilment than merely undertaking roles generated by economic necessity, as suggested by Parsons among others. Further, in these urban families, members could operate in an 'individuated' manner in so far as they were freer to develop their social networks and own affairs. As Leeder (2004: 46) points out this form of 'networking' is less likely in rural families in the majority world where interconnections and organized activities are imperative to everyday survival. Further, roles and role function may be more keenly delineated, again due to necessity.

➜ In Chapter 5 we consider marriage and companionship in greater depth.

Individualism is not a new phenomenon. There have long been debates about the ideology of the individual and individualism, with arguments pre-dating capitalism (see, for example, Macpherson, 1962). In more recent decades the idea of the individual asserting themselves is one which is regularly drawn upon to explain changes in families and relationships, especially in the minority world. The recent call to re-examine individualism in more detail took place alongside changes in longevity, in the role of women, in the formation and re-formation of intimate relationships, in attitudes to children and young people, and in education, training and employment. As Jamieson (1998) has pointed out, the notion of individualism became shorthand among some for superficial and inadequate explanations for changes in families and relationships. This was especially so among those concerned with a perceived demise of what was assumed to be the 'traditional' patterns of families and family life. Nevertheless, families in all their diverse forms remain strong and we note the continued need to place family processes or practices in the wider context of family structures and socioeconomic contexts.

SOLO LIVING

Major social surveys demonstrate a growth in the incidence of solo living, that is, people living on their own (Box 3.8). The European Social Survey (ESS) found that among working-age adults the percentage living alone is approaching 20% in some countries, although across studied countries the composite figure is 10%.[1] The greatest growth is among men. This is particularly marked among men aged between 18 and 59 in countries grouped under the umbrella of north-western Europe, to include among others Sweden, Norway, Finland, Denmark, France, Germany and the UK (Jamieson et al., 2009). Men in this age group might be expected to be in intimate partnerships and active in families with children. This trend may be explained by delays in forging partnerships, increased periods out of relationships, or being in a relationship but not in co-residence (commonly termed 'living apart together' and discussed in Chapter 5). This latter point draws attention to the need to consider solo living as distinct from being single. So far these explanations could refer to men and women equally, so why the marked growth in solo living among men? Jamieson et al. (2009: 6.3) describe how higher rates of solo living among men can:

> in part be explained by widespread and persistent gender differences that resonate more with traditional behaviour and gender inequalities than women's ability to drive social change.

Thus while in some countries a period of independent living is a precursor to relationship formation for both genders, women, for example continue to look after children after separation from a partner, earn less in general over their lifetimes, and seem less inclined to solo living given the financial and care issues. These potential explanations are drawn from secondary analysis of data from the ESS and also of data from a two-year study conducted by Jamieson and Simpson (2010) in which 140 telephone and 35 face-to-face interviews were conducted with women and men living in rural and urban locations in Scotland. The consequences of solo living were also explored, and it would seem that for many women in solo living, rather than reducing social networks and interaction, they maintain kin and friendship ties. Technologies play a role in this as these allow for easier communication among

1   The ESS 'is an academically-driven social survey designed to chart and explain the interaction between Europe's changing institutions and the attitudes, beliefs and behaviour patterns of its diverse populations'. Started in 2001, it is now in its fifth round and will report in autumn 2011. This repeat cross-sectional survey covers more than 30 nations and has been funded through the European Commission's Framework Programmes, the European Science Foundation and national funding bodies in each country.

those with emotional or familial attachments. Solo living women constituted a higher proportion of above-average earners than others in this study. This indicates that income levels are a factor in making solo living an option. For many women, however, the conflict between caring roles and, in some aspects of the labour market, their restricted earning potential, makes solo living an improbable or impossible option.

Box 3.8   Explaining and questioning changes in solo living

How can research aid the exploration of family structures and processes? First, there may be the identification of a trend in a survey such as solo living, which is further explored through secondary analysis. Or there may be an idea or theory which suggests there is an assertion worthy of deeper examination. Whatever methods are chosen, research promotes reflection, investigation and assessment of findings and conclusions. In the case of solo living, a team of researchers undertook secondary analysis of a large comparative social survey and then followed this up with interviews to explore issues in greater depth. But is solo living a choice? What are the implications for families and lifestyle? The combination of projects and the use of different research methods offered data which challenged key elements of the individualization thesis, not least of which are assertions on the demise of kin and friendship networks and gender roles. It would seem that traditional ways of connecting and living are evolving while key elements are maintained, notably gender differences in life experiences and choices.

TALKING ABOUT SEX

Researching sexual behaviours and sexualities more generally can be fraught with a host of difficulties. After all, sexual activity is one of the most intimate and private areas of our lives. Sex is also a driver of public policies, including demographic, family, health and education policies, and is central in media portrayals of relationships. Views on what is appropriate differ widely between societies, across belief and ethnic groups and over the lifecourse. This is a controversial topic and one that elicits much debate among politicians, policy makers, friends, families and communities.

Questionnaire surveys have been used to document the number and key characteristics of partners as well as sexual experiences and preferences (Bryman, 2008). This research method can offer a map or profile of activities around which services and policy may evolve. It has also been heavily criticized, not least because respondents may be embarrassed or offer answers that they think place them in a favourable light. For example, a young man may feel it is appropriate to add additional partners to any request for numbers as a means of enhancing status and bolstering his sense of masculinity.

A young woman, however, may do the exact opposite as she is keen to avoid any sense of being labelled 'easy'. The sexual 'double standard' for men and women is just one example of factors which have implications for research. Likewise, individuals who have preferences that some may consider inappropriate or be deemed illegal pose particular issues for the researcher.

In a study conducted on two continents and over a decade, Ken Plummer (1995) recounts how he collected, analysed and shared sexual stories from diverse perspectives. The study took a story-telling approach to data collection in an attempt to address the criticisms of other methods used in researching sexual activity. Plummer asserts that while a number of disciplines, including anthropology, history and psychology, have valued stories and story-telling to explore events, beliefs and identities, sociology has been slow to grasp the potential. Today, narrative research is a valued approach in social sciences and its topic is 'the personal experience narratives of the intimate' (Plummer, 1995: 19), and Plummer goes beyond the story as told to the researcher. He explored the ways stories are produced, what role they play in people's lives, in political processes, and how in putting them together and telling them, people change and diverge. Stories perform a social function as well as providing a rich portrayal of actions, roles and contexts.

A phenomenon Plummer is able to develop through story-telling is that of power in sexual and personal relationships and experiences. Power is evident as 'a flow of negotiations and shifting outcomes' (1995: 26), and Plummer notes the following:

> Sexual stories live in this flow of power. The power to tell a story, or indeed not to tell a story, under the conditions of one's own choosing, is part of the political process. (Plummer, 1995: 26)

Silences and secrecy inhabit the world of sex and sexual story-telling, and this presents the potential for bias and a flow of power between the story-teller and the researcher. Deciding what to tell or not, and when and how will be partly determined by the response, both verbal and non-verbal, to the story-teller. In the case of sexual stories, how the topic is introduced, how an interview is set up, in which location and how it is recorded also have a bearing. The issues presented for research design, conduct, analysis and presentation are myriad.

One interesting topic Plummer draws attention to is how stories are 'consumed'. For the story-teller, he asserts, there is not only potential for deeper understanding and discovery but also to situate themselves as scriptwriters, producers and even myth makers about their sexual lives. Stories are shaped and organized according to cultural and situational contexts, as well as personal preferences. Commonly they have a beginning, middle and end, but in the case of sexual stories the 'beginning' may draw upon earlier personal biographies. Silences too shape the stories as do changes in tone, intonation and physical movement. Stories give voice to those 'from below' (Plummer, 1995: 60) and stand counter-posed or alongside those of the experts or presumptions of other people, practitioners and policy makers. To tell sexual stories can lead to stigma and the fear of rebuke, but without these the potential to research and explore the world of intimate relationships is all the poorer.

> → We discuss relationships and sexualities in more depth in Chapter 5.

In conclusion, Plummer draws attention to the workings and practices of 'gendered heterosexism' (sexual preference for those of the opposite sex), prevalent in all stories, whether these were about same-sex, violent or consensual relationships (1995: 31). Drawing upon data and relevant theories, Plummer (1995) offers the notion of 'intimate citizenship' to aid understandings of who has the power, will or ability to express their sexual lives in an open and validating manner. This is particularity drawn out when reflecting on 'family' stories and the ways in which 'family values' and ideologies can dictate, marginalize and dismiss sexual experiences. Plummer comments:

> The future may well lie in the proliferation of more and more stories of differing ways of living together that help provide new understandings and communities of citizenship. (1995: 154)

SINGLE PARENTING

Single parenting is another topic which is viewed by some as a challenge to family formation (Box 3.9). The topic has also generated claims that duty and responsibility have given way to the values of self-realization and autonomy, resulting in relationship breakdown and re-formation on a recurring and increasing basis among a notable number of adults. The trends in single parenting are demonstrated by an examination of statistics taken from two census surveys. In the UK in 1971 90% of dependent children lived with married parents. By 2001 this percentage had fallen to 64%. Single parents accounted for 7% of all households with dependent children in 1971, and by 2001 had risen to 23%. Single parents, who were never married or cohabited, rose from 1% to 10% over that period with divorce accounting for a rise from 2% to 9%. Single, separated or widowed stayed the same at a combined figure of 4% (Williams, 2004). Of course, family formations change over the years, as do relationships. But even a cursory glance at these statistical data illustrates the depth and breadth of the changes. A review of the social, economic and demographic profile of single parents by Rowlingson (2001) demonstrated how policies, especially those linked to welfare services and benefit payments, impact on behaviours. Here we note and illustrate the relationship between policy and research done on and about families.

Box 3.9   Women, men and single parenting

Across the world survey research has demonstrated that single parents are predominately female – over 90% in most countries. Children nearly always stay with their mothers. A man as a single parent remains an exceptional case and is often the result of the death of a partner. Women can find themselves as single parents due to the breakdown of marriage or cohabiting relationships, due to divorce or death, due to having never married or cohabited. The reasons for female single parenthood vary between countries, cultures and religious communities. Census and survey data demonstrate differences within the UK. For example, the never married, never cohabited group is dominated by women aged 21 or under of low-income origins. This does not mean, however, that women in this group might not be parents. Further, cultural beliefs impact. For example, as a proportion of their community African-Caribbean women are more likely to be single parents than those of any other ethnic group. By contrast women of South Asian origin of the first or second generation are least likely.

Economic, ethnic and cultural contexts to single parenthood are evident in all countries. When figures are aggregated for a country and then these are compared with figures for other countries differences are also apparent. Japan, for example, has a very low rate of single parenthood while the USA has the highest. Of course it matters how single parenting is defined and categorized and this will differ within and between countries. With this proviso in mind, the contrasts are obvious and worthy of further investigation for a host of reasons. Do women actively choose single parenthood? Are they left with little choice? Or is this an option not open to all women for economic, social and cultural reasons?

Rowlingson (2001) examined available data on single parents and from her review noted that demographic factors have an impact on social and economic well-being. Routes into single parenthood are a key predictor of economic fortunes. Younger, never married or cohabited single mothers are least likely to work. This is reinforced by the likelihood they have fewer qualifications and limited or no work experience due to their age at motherhood. By contrast those entering single parenting on the death of a partner are often older, with greater income and experience, albeit that the family income as a whole is likely to drop post-bereavement. These broad trends have implications for social and public policies, including childcare and employment services. Likewise the existence and level of relevant services and policies will have an effect on choices. In some countries, for example, southern European countries, welfare services for single parents are limited and are offered through a combination of church and state. Limited access combined with stigma due to religious beliefs and cultural values may close off the option of separation and single parenthood, in addition to pregnancy in teenage years or outside marriage.

The choices people make can seem to be open to the individual. Do they choose single parenthood for self-affirmation? Or is it a result of bereavement or abandonment? If it is a choice is it a forced choice due to violence or abusive behaviour, or infidelity? Relationships break down for a range of reasons. The availability of support networks, employment opportunities and policies, and public services and benefits will also be factors. Thus the route to single parenthood is not a straightforward or linear one but likely to involve a range of people and factors to be considered over a period of time, which may be years.

How do we research this? Asking people would seem the obvious method, but how, in what way, and when? The theoretical underpinnings of any project have implications for the approach and content of research design. For example, a researcher choosing to explore individualization or detraditionalization might examine statistical data further by asking people who are single parents to talk about their personal biographies, or instead pose a series of semi-structured questions as part of a more formal interview approach. In the former, the person has more control over how and what they say and can offer a narrative or story. This will be more time consuming and resource demanding than, for example, an interview which asks participants the same five questions. Whether one approach is more valuable or useful than another is open to debate and depends upon the potential use of information.

> ➜ In Chapter 2 we discussed a range of explanations for family structures and processes. Among these is the work of Karl Marx (Marx and McLellan, 2008), a key proponent of the role of economic systems in shaping social and familial life.

Finally, researchers, theorists and commentators would do well do keep in mind the observation of Ribbens McCarthy and Edwards:

> Actual family experiences may be equivocal and shifting, involving deep paradoxes around such issues as power and love, or care and oppression, and the related feelings may hold ambivalence. The same act, say of cooking a meal, may feel like a practical expression of caring for someone on one occasion (or even at one moment), a form of sociable leisure activity on another occasion, and an exploitative form of labour on yet another. (2010b: 6)

The interpretation of activities, words, ideas and other forms of information (for example, statistics or policy statements) could also be likened to the composition of a mosaic. Nevertheless we have to start somewhere! Being honest about the underpinnings of a project, and noting the drawbacks and the process of collection and analysis allow readers to assess the potential quality of a project. No one source of information – or ideas – offers all the answers. We would encourage readers to avoid viewing the drivers of changes in families as always being external and promoted by economic systems. Of course these matter, but never underestimate the everyday workings of families; how individuals, families, policies and networks interweave and forge an ever-changing mosaic.

SUMMARY

In recent decades there has been a notable growth in the range and amount of socio-logical research. The challenges for the future are aptly demonstrated through an analy-sis of historical data and contemporary trends. Findings from research projects, both historical and contemporary, are regularly considered in policy work, the development of services and by the media. Governments and supranational organizations, such as the UN, place a high level of significance upon studies that offer insights into the ways in which families are formed, change and dissolve, and how we live our daily lives in the context of the family.

The topics and issues considered in research do vary but frequently contribute to the analysis of family structures and processes such as the composition of households, paid and unpaid work, how resources are distributed across families, and care for the young, older and sick.

This chapter has considered how sociological research on families can help us to identify, examine and explain family structures and processes. At the outset of the chap-ter we offered an overview of research methods and considered survey and ethno-graphic methods as well as the secondary analysis of existing studies and data sources. In examining research on families we looked at historical and contemporary work which considered change and continuities. Anderson (1980) drew attention to the three approaches to the historical analysis of families, namely demographic trends, sen-timents among family members and communities and the role of household economics in determining and explaining family structures and processes.

Considering historical studies in more detail, we chose to highlight social historical research on 'ordinary' families and their everyday practices. The work of Gillis (1996) offers a reminder that we can idealize the past, ignoring the challenges and tensions in family processes. Hartman (2004) offers historical analysis of the age at first marriage, asserting that postponing marriage has had longer-term implications for family struc-tures and gender roles in the minority world, including the growth in nuclear families. The work of Hareven (2000) suggests that change is complex and is evident in differing ways in various families. Change is not uniform and can take place alongside adherence to familiar and traditional patterns and activities. The sweep of data studied by Therborn (2004) over the twentieth century demonstrates the ways in which change can take place at a differing pace and in a range of ways across the world. Change is not uniform and trends in marriage, for example, illustrate how the popularity of marriage has risen and fallen in the minority world but remained relatively stable in much of the majority world. Explanations for trends note the impact of economic systems, societal norms, religious and cultural beliefs, and the impact of science and technology with safer forms of contraception and fertility control. The economic imperative to marry or form inti-mate long-term partnerships varies across the world as well as among individuals.

In considering contemporary research we chose to examine three notable trends, namely the growth in solo living, how people talk about sexual activity and the changing experience of single parenthood. Prior to introducing these topics we introduced the idea of the sociological imagination (Mills, 1959). This reminds us that what is concerning for family members is also a public issue; for example, family illness, unemployment and breakdown are among the family processes that have wider implications for society, policy and service provision. In conclusion, how we engage with others in families and live our lives through families is the subject of much sociological research.

EXPLORE FURTHER

Gabb, J. (2008) *Researching Intimacy in Families*. Basingstoke: Palgrave Macmillan.
Greenstein, T. (2006) *Methods of Family Research*. New York: Sage (1st edn 2001).
Hunt, S. (ed.) (2010) *Family Trends Since 1950*. Bristol: Policy Press.

USEFUL WEBSITES

The ESRC is the UK's largest organization for funding research on economic and social issues. The database on its website holds the final reports and listings of outputs from completed projects. See www.esrc.ac.uk.

The Joseph Rowntree Foundation funds research on social problems, the family, gender, ethnicity, class and the welfare state – among other topics. This website contains a summary of a range of recent research. See www.jrf.org.uk. Choose 'Findings', and enter your topic in the search box.

The website of the Office for National Statistics contains a vast amount of secondary data for any topic on which the government collects information and has a searchable database to find data on specific topics. It is essential for teachers and is also very useful for students. You can find summaries, or search for more detailed downloadable datasets. See www.statistics.gov.uk/default.asp.

The UN Millennium Development Goals website offers insights into how research from across the world can inform initiatives. The composition of the goals and research that they drawn upon and progress is charted at www.un.org/millenniumgoals/

4 Politics, Policies and Practices

Keywords: policy, family policies, politics, addressing change, transnational labour migration, service provision

INTRODUCTION

Families and their practices are of pressing importance to politics and the development of policies because, however constituted, they are the setting in which most of us find our emotional and material needs met. The family context is the base out of which the majority of adults and children are enabled to work, be educated and contribute to society. Unsurprisingly therefore, every country's government has a vital interest in the welfare and practices of families in its jurisdiction: they are concerned with how families are constituted (family structure) and with what goes on inside families (family process). Families are treated as both the problem and the solution to a wide variety of social ills. For example, children growing up in poorly functioning family backgrounds are perceived to be at risk of engaging in criminal activity during adolescence and later in life, while a supportive family is seen as a protective factor against such an outcome (Farrington and Welsh, 2007). Pervasive family breakdown is seen as symptomatic or even to a certain extent as causal of wider social breakdown (Murray, 2006) whereas 'well-functioning' families which may, or may not, be associated with a particular form or structure, are seen as the bedrock or foundation of a cohesive society. Such perspectives provide a rationale for government intervention in families. In an environment constrained by politics, policies are formulated and implemented with the intention of influencing either family structure or everyday family processes or both.

In this chapter we begin by defining what we mean by politics, policy and practices, and then look at how governments across the world support the family as an institution, which necessitates grappling with the realities of family change. We then consider influences on the formation of policy, ranging widely from national and international politics to the findings of social science research.

> ➜ As we noted in Chapter 2, sociological explanations and ideas about families have an impact on policy development and implementation. However, theories and concepts have to be grounded in findings from research on issues such as the composition of households; employment and care (for the young, older and sick); and how resources are distributed across families (emphasized in Chapter 3). Local and national governments and supranational organizations, such as the United Nations (UN), pay close attention to studies which offer insights into the ways family structures form, change and dissolve, and how citizens carry out their daily lives in the context of the family.

Following on from observations made in Chapter 2 about family ideology, we look at ways in which the notion of the family can be simplified and even idealized by politicians and by the broad range of policy actors who influence the formation and implementation of policy in this area and we consider the need to go beyond implicit stereotypes. Finally we look at the important role played by welfare states, how services are developed to aid families and how the delivery of these services is made possible or legitimized through policy.

DEFINITIONS

Harold Lasswell (1935), the American political scientist, defined *politics* as who gets what, when, and how. Expanding on this, politics is the art or science of government or governing, especially the governing of an entity, such as a nation, and the administration and control of its internal and external affairs. 'Politics' also refers to the opinion an individual or group holds with respect to questions that may be termed politicial (American Heritage Dictionary, 2000).

Policies can be defined as courses of action selected from (a number of) alternatives, which take into account various different conditions and are meant to guide and determine present and future decisions. A policy can also be seen as a high-level overall plan which uses political, managerial, financial and administrative mechanisms to express the general goals and acceptable procedures of a government, organization or group, or even of an individual.

Policy is different from rules or laws. Laws can compel or forbid certain practices, but a policy acts more as a guide to the action(s) believed to be most likely to achieve a desired outcome. In practice, the dividing line between law and policy is more blurred. Sometimes a law has to be enacted to enable a government to implement a policy.

This chapter will maintain a global perspective and focus on social policies affecting family life that have been formulated at a governmental level. Social policies have been defined as

- purposive courses of action taken by
- actors or sets of actors to address
- particular issues or problems of concern (Bengtson et al., 2004: 543).

Definitions relating to different understandings of the scope of family policy, a sub-category of social policy, are offered in Box 4.1.

Box 4.1   Defining family policy

Family policy is the branch of social policy that is particularly focused on supporting or strengthening the functions that families carry out. These are, according to the UN Programme on the Family (2009), reproduction, care, emotional support and intergenerational solidarity (the close interpersonal ties seen across two or more generations within families, characterized by interdependence and mutual support).

Definitions of family policy offered in the academic literature differ according to their intended scope. Some are provided here in order to draw out important

(Continued)

(Continued)

perspectives on what is considered to be the legitimate remit of this branch of policy. Moen and Schorr define family policy as 'a widely agreed-on set of objectives for families, toward the realization of which the state (and other major social institutions) deliberately shapes programmes and policies' (1987: 795), whereas Kamerman and Kahn include within family policy 'everything that government does to and for the family' (1978: 3).

Kamerman and Kahn also separate out explicit policies designed to achieve specific goals regarding families from the more implicit 'family perspective in policy making' (Kamerman and Kahn, 1978). Explicit policies focus on four aspects of family (Consortium of Family Organizations, 1990; Ooms, 1990):

- family creation
- economic support
- childrearing
- family caregiving.

A family perspective in policy making is concerned with the impact on family well-being (e.g. family stability, family relationships and the family's ability to carry out its responsibilities) of any policy or programme regardless of whether it was specifically or primarily intended to affect families.

So family policy would include issues concerned with the four aspects of family cited above, for example, childcare, child maintenance after parental separation, divorce, domestic violence, underage crime, elder care, child protection and teenage pregnancy. Tax and benefit reforms that help parents with childcare costs or that remove disincentives for couples to live together openly would also be categorized as family policy, whereas tax reductions for individuals, even though many or most live in families, would not. Similarly, healthcare, housing, poverty, substance abuse, and unemployment are not aimed specifically at families and would not be treated as family policies. Nevertheless, a rounded consideration of these issues requires a family perspective and an understanding of how families contribute to problems, how families are affected by problems, and whether they need to be involved in solutions (Ooms, 1990).

Policy *actors*, those involved in the formation and implementation of policy, are divided by Appleton and Byrne (2003) into political and civil society categories. Political actors include politicians and civil servants from central and local government, whereas civil society actors include service providers, non-profit/non-governmental organizations (NGOs), research institutions and policy thinktanks.

When we talk about *practices* in relation to family this refers to the things families *do* (Morgan, 1996), the most relevant in this chapter being those provoking a political or policy response. To reiterate what was said in Chapter 2, family practices include the ways families are constituted, their structure, as well as how they function, the internal processes that will also have an external effect. Policy responses may be forthcoming because a family practice is considered by policy actors to be dysfunctional and ultimately harmful to family members, or because a practice is to be encouraged. For example, historically parents were largely unrestricted by governments in terms of the forms of discipline they used with their children. Now, however, the practice of smacking has been banned by some governments including those in Austria, Croatia, Cyprus, Germany, Israel and all the Nordic countries. Other countries have changed their laws to restrict the rights of parents to use corporal punishment but have not made it comprehensively illegal.

More positively, the family practice of parents reading to their children and generally supporting their children's education has become the focus of various government initiatives to improve literacy skills. These initiatives encourage and enable parents who would not otherwise do so to engage in beneficial practices in which others already engage. For example, in Romania in 2005, the Ministry of Education agreed to invest in family literacy programmes (UN Educational Scientific and Cultural Organization, 2009) which help parents develop and strengthen their own literacy and social skills so they can support their children's education and complement school-based learning processes.

> **?** While very few people would argue against supporting parents in ways that better enable them to educate their child(ren), the first example given above of smacking sparks much disagreement about the appropriate limits of government intervention (some would say 'interference') in family life and raises more general questions: when and under what circumstances do you think intervention is valid?

POLICIES AND FAMILIES' FORMS AND FUNCTIONS

Changes in family forms (structure) and functions (processes) are increasingly seen as something to which governments at local, national and supranational levels should respond. Even in countries that provide very little publicly delivered welfare, governments are concerned when the ability of individuals to rely on family support becomes tenuous because of the negative implications for that society's cohesion, economic productivity and, ultimately, global competitiveness.

> **➜** In Chapter 1 we explained that economic changes can themselves provoke shifts in norms of family support which will in turn necessitate a policy response. In developed countries that have seen a decline in their manufacturing base and a fall in the numbers of unskilled and semi-skilled jobs, many men in low-income communities unable to find work are considered by women to be less 'marriageable' than before. This has contributed to a move away from marriage as the majority setting for childbearing (Edin and Kefalas, 2005).

The UN, the supranational institution influencing the widest range of countries, considers the family to be a vital partner for the achievement of its Millennium Development Goals. The overarching aim of these goals was to halve absolute global poverty by 2015. The Millennium Development Goals include measurable, time-bound targets addressing poverty and hunger, education, maternal and child health, the prevalence of diseases including human immunodeficiency virus HIV/AIDS, gender equality, the environment, debt, trade justice and aid. A central tenet of the UN Programme on the Family (the focal point within the UN system on matters related to family) is the importance of coordinating family policies and programmes within national governments and the UN itself.

> ➡ In Chapter 6 we describe how the increased provision of paid work and improved terms and conditions for workers are central to a number of global programmes including the UN Millennium Development Goals. Particularly noteworthy is the campaign for decent work, established in 1999 by the International Labour Organization (ILO), and endorsed by the international community.

FAMILY POLICY – NEW KID ON THE BLOCK?

The relative newness of this *explicit* focus of policy defined earlier in Box 4.1 is described by the American policy theorist Karen Bogenschneider. She states that 'the field of family policy was conceived in the 1970s and has come of age in the 1990s. At the dawn of [that] decade, family policy was a concept without a consistent definition, a perspective lacking a solid rationale, a field in need of legitimization, and a rhetoric in search of grounding and guidance from theory and practice' (Bogenschneider, 2000: 1).

However, this observation has to be seen in the broader historical and geographical context of state support for families. For example, early in the First World War (1914–1918), the British government agreed to set a precedent in paying tax-funded allowances to all 'dependants' of servicemen, a term that included, under certain criteria, mothers of serving military and 'unmarried wives', as well as legal wives and children (Departments of State and Official Bodies, 1915). This was foreshadowed by Lloyd George's 1911 National Insurance Act, which had led to the first contributory system of insurance against illness and unemployment. With all wage-earners between 16 and 70 required to join the health scheme, this had a significant impact on families. State support for families took a further step forward in many European countries around the time of the end of the Second World War with an example from the UK given in Box 4.2. Prior to that period, any cash support for families provided by governments was mainly limited to low-income and large families (Gauthier, 1999).

Box 4.2 Supporting a nation's families – the post-war Beveridge reforms in the UK

Sir William Beveridge is credited with much of the design in the UK of the welfare settlement after the Second World War, a set of arrangements aimed at addressing what he termed the five giants of 'want, disease, ignorance, squalor and idleness'. Nearly 70 years later many of its elements are still evident. Public services, such as education, healthcare and dental care, were made universally available, largely free of charge and funded primarily by general taxation in contrast with a system originating in nineteenth-century Germany, funded predominantly by social insurance contributions which became known as the 'Bismarck model' (named after the German chancellor who introduced this system). Other services, such as social care, were rationed according to need.

Family allowances were introduced (reducing the tax levied on incomes which had to be shared among several family members), and included a universal family payment which supplemented the incomes of all families, irrespective of their financial circumstances. The national insurance scheme strengthened families' protection against poverty in the event of sickness, widowhood, old age or unemployment, with financial benefits such as pensions paid according to contributions made by individuals throughout their lifetime.

In many ways this welfare settlement transformed UK society and impacted families in a positive way. Significant improvements were achieved in levels of education, health outcomes, life expectancy, social mobility, employment opportunities and prosperity. Many aspects of Beveridge's model have influenced the design of other welfare states, especially in northern Europe (e.g. Denmark, Ireland and Norway) whereas elements more in common with the original Bismarck model tend to predominate in countries in central and eastern Europe (e.g. Austria, Belgium, Estonia, France and Slovenia) (CESifo, 2008).

As time passed, more comprehensive programmes considerably expanded the proportion of families in receipt of state support. These included family allowances (also called child allowances or child benefits) and tax relief for those with children. Benefits in kind, such as paid maternity leave schemes for working parents, were introduced in most European countries much earlier than family allowance schemes, as early as 1883 (Gauthier, 1999). So while family policy has gained a new prominence in the planning and work of governments, there is a much longer history of state support for families, evidence that the recognition of the key role of families in social cohesion has significant historical antecedents.

HOW DO POLICIES DELIVER BENEFITS TO FAMILIES?

A key area of difference between how welfare states meet families' needs lies in whether cash transfers or services are relied upon (Sainsbury, 1996). Financial subsidies enable families to make decisions about the form assistance will take, although there are fewer guarantees that the money will actually be spent in a way that benefits the family. Offering pre-existing services restricts choice but may be easier for families who do not have to source a provider (see the discussion on individual budgets in the next paragraph). Whereas in the UK and Sweden the provision of services has traditionally been favoured, cash transfers are more typical in the Netherlands. Policy decisions determine the types of service offered and the level to which cash transfers are set. Although it is possible for a complete change in approach to be adopted, for example a switch from services to cash transfers, this requires building a consensus that old strategies for dealing with enduring problems have failed or are far less effective than they could be. 'Institutional lock-in', where longstanding traditions and institutional practices become embedded, makes radical change difficult to achieve (Hudson and Lowe, 2009).

Such a policy shift has, however, been effected in certain areas of social care in the UK. A move towards cash transfers or 'individual budgets' is enabling parents of disabled children to become commissioners of their own services. This follows other European countries such as Austria, which introduced care allowances (termed *pflegegeld* or 'care money') in 1993, funded from general taxation. The services people buy are, ideally, highly tailored to their own particular needs, so they are not reliant on services commissioned by local government which are often criticized on the grounds that they assume that 'one size fits all'. This trend towards the reduction of the role of the state as a direct provider of social care and the establishment of commercialism and individualism in the field of social policy has been described as the 'individualisation of the social' (Ferge, 1997: 20).

POLICY APPROACHES TO DIFFERENT FAMILY FORMS

As we noted in Chapter 1, much sociological work on families 'revolves around the theme of social change' (Gillies, 2003: 2) and there is a consensus that family forms or structures have changed markedly over the past 40 years (although family change in itself is not a new phenomenon) and this has implications for governments and therefore for policy. We also referred to the fact that, while some commentators are ambivalent about these changes, somewhat polarized 'optimistic' and 'pessimistic' perspectives have been identified (Williams, 2004; Walker, 2006). When family change and particularly family instability is associated more broadly with societal demoralization, alienation and fragmentation, this can be perceived to be threatening to the well-being of children and thus society in general (Fukuyama, 1999; Bauman, 2003). Alternatively, family change can be perceived in different ways as the embracing of greater diversity in family relationships (an example of types of partnerships is found in Box 4.3), or as a welcome loosening of family ties if these free adults and children from potentially oppressive and conflict situations (Smart and Shipman, 2004).

The policy response advocated by the latter 'optimistic' perspective is one of providing greater support for parents and children to enable them to exercise their choices and rights responsibly as circumstances change. Family breakdown (in the form of divorce or separation), for example, is perceived to be something over which families (adults) and the policy community have relatively little control. Hence the onus lies with welfare states to mitigate its consequences. Policy assistance concentrates on helping families to deal with the consequences of breakdown, in particular on mitigating the effects of parental separation on children, rather than on preventing its occurrence in the first place. In Australia it has become compulsory for separating parents to attend mediation before filing for legal proceedings (and in the UK, the provision of information about mediation is becoming mandatory). The government has set up family relationship centres in Australia, described in the section 'Types of Service' later in this chapter, which offer free mediation.

An example of prioritizing the financial needs of children after their parents part can be seen in the UK government's recent announcement that any money paid by non-resident parents to support their children will no longer be taken into account when calculating the state benefit entitlement of the parent with whom the children live (unless it increases the savings of the care-providing parent above a fairly modest threshold). This means that more money goes directly towards supporting the child, although it could be argued that couples experiencing some relationship difficulties might be slightly more incentivized to separate as a result of the policy, which could thus have had an unintended effect on family practices. Prior to this announcement parents caring for their children were allowed to keep only the first £20 of child maintenance per week before their benefits were reduced (Department of Work and Pensions, 2010).

Box 4.3   Alternative partnership forms

Policy approaches which institutionalize or give official recognition to alternative partnership forms might also be interpreted as embracing of family diversity. For example, in Canada under the Modernization of Benefits and Obligations Act of 2000, legal distinctions between married and unmarried same-sex and opposite-sex couples were eliminated for couples who have lived together for at least a year. In France, unmarried couples may enter into civil solidarity pacts, which give them most of the rights and responsibilities of married couples after the pact has existed for three years. Several other countries, including the UK, have instituted registered partnerships for same-sex couples. At the same time, in other parts of the world, particularly in several Islamic and African states, sanctions against homosexuality are severe and can include judicial execution.

See Chapter 5, 'Same-Sex Couples and Families' on page 144, for further discussion of this subject.

The pessimistic perspective, linking changing family forms and instability with social decline, is evident in the efforts taken by the US federal government to make an explicit connection in welfare reform with decreasing the number of children born outside wedlock. In order for poor families to obtain self-sufficiency, one of the objectives of the Personal Responsibility and Work Opportunity Reconciliation Act of 1996 (also known as the Welfare Reform Act) was to encourage marriages and two-parent married families. Policy was thus explicitly focused on influencing family structure. Graefe and Lichter (2008), who analysed the effect of this policy on poor women's marriage patterns, explain that marriage is purported to reduce welfare dependency which is associated with poorer child well-being. However, women need to marry men with earnings sufficient to lift them and their children out of poverty and entitlement to welfare for this to be the case.

> **?** To what extent do you think governments have the means and legitimacy to influence personal decisions about whether or not to marry? What justification might they give for exercising those means?

Perhaps some middle ground can be seen in the policies of countries such as Norway and Australia, which acknowledge the realities and disadvantages of family breakdown but have policies aimed at preventing couples who are experiencing relationship problems from splitting up or, at the very least, from separating acrimoniously. (The national services provided through these policies are described in the section 'Types of Service' later in the chapter.)

EVIDENCE-BASED POLICY

One further development in policy formation and implementation now increasingly prevalent in many Western countries is a reliance on social science research. Solesbury noted in 2001 that this appeared to be a peculiarly British phenomenon and there has been a long tradition in the UK of research guiding policy. For example, the Fabian Society, a socialist intellectual movement, influenced policy formation at home and abroad through published research from the early 1900s, and the Beveridge reforms noted in Box 4.2 were based on a comprehensive report on social policy presented to the British Parliament in 1942.

However, later on in the decade other countries in Europe were establishing links between policy and practice, measuring the impacts of policy on family life and assessing beneficiaries' perceptions of the influence of policy on decision-making processes concerning family formation and living arrangements (Hantrais, 2004).

> → Chapter 3 describes how research is used to aid understanding families in many minority world governments and supranational institutions such as the UN try to use research to inform policy.

The policy community in the USA has quickly moved beyond simply insisting that policy formation be informed by solid research. It is leading the world in producing detailed comparative studies determining best options *between* evidence-based approaches in terms of cost–benefit analysis. For example, the Washington State Institute for Public Policy study on benefits and costs of prevention and early intervention programmes for youth quantifies return on taxpayers' dollars for a wide range of different policy approaches which have a bearing on family life (Aos et al., 2004). These include very early intervention with vulnerable pregnant women and pre-kindergarten education as well as youth substance abuse programmes and mentoring schemes. The study then quantifies the effectiveness of individual programmes so that government commissioners of services can make fiscally informed choices between them. Effectiveness can be bound up with the quality of emotional support offered to parents and not just with economic support in the form of, for example, free or subsidized childcare.

FAMILIES IN ACTION

In this section we will look at specific aspects of family practices, both structure and process, which are of interest to governments and why they choose or are compelled to intervene (usually by developing and implementing policy) when families are unable to function in a way that is beneficial to the wider society. As we said earlier in the chapter, governments have to take note when individuals' ability to rely on family support becomes tenuous because of the effect on social cohesion, economic productivity and the country's ability to compete in the global marketplace.

> → Chapter 6 describes the effects on children and the social fabric when large numbers of parents are forced to migrate for work and we describe how governments are responding to these families' needs in the section 'Types of Service' later in this chapter. It is also important to note that families can be negatively affected when governments withdraw support that was formerly available. See Topic 1 in Chapter 1 for a discussion of the effects on families of the withdrawal of state benefits which accompanied the dismantling of communism in the early 1990s.

FAMILIES AND SOCIAL COHESION

Social scientists of different political orientations agree about the importance of families for social cohesion. While Brenda Almond (2006:1) states that 'The family is and always has been the foundation of communities in which the cherishing of each individual can flourish', Anthony Giddens emphasizes that strong family ties, 'part of the wider fabric of social life' (1998: 98), can be an effective source of civic cohesion. This broad consensus also tends to be taken as the starting point for many governing bodies. For example, a consultation paper from the UK government in 2010 states that 'Strong families give children love, identity, a personal history and a secure base from which to explore and enjoy life as they grow up. Strong families also help build strong communities, so they are crucial for a successful society' (Department for Children, Schools and Families, 2010: 4). Similar sentiments have been voiced by supranational institutions such as the UN as we highlight in Box 4.4.

Box 4.4   A reaffirmation of the UN commitment to protect the family

In New York in 2004 the UN formally adopted General Assembly Resolution 59/111, calling for protection of the family as the 'natural and fundamental group unit of society', reaffirming what was originally stated in article 16 (3) of the 1948 Universal Declaration of Human Rights. The full Article is reproduced below:

Article 16

(1) Men and women of full age, without any limitation due to race, nationality or religion, have the right to marry and to found a family. They are entitled to equal rights as to marriage, during marriage and at its dissolution.
(2) Marriage shall be entered into only with the free and full consent of the intending spouses.
(3) The family is the natural and fundamental group unit of society and is entitled to protection by society and the State.

For the full text, see www.un.org/en/documents/udhr/index.shtml.

Social cohesion is important for national and local governments because its presence or lack determines a country's or community's ability to collaborate to make progress (Ritzen, 2000) and the level of trust that exists between people. According to Judith Maxwell, 'Social cohesion refers to the processes of building shared values and communities of interpretation, reducing disparities in wealth and income, and generally enabling people to have a sense that they are engaged in a common enterprise, facing shared challenges, and that they are members of the same community' (1996: 13).

Family cohesion, defined as 'the emotional bonding that family members have toward one another' (Olson et al., 1984: 60), can facilitate key processes perceived as contributing to social cohesion. Important examples of these key processes such as the development of 'character', the provision of mutual support and care, and the generation of a sense of personal and group identity, are outlined below.

- **Development of character**. In his classic work on democracy in the USA in the 1830s, Alexis de Tocqueville (1945) described the family as the first institution to teach 'habits of the heart' and expounded upon its important role in discouraging the worst excesses of individualism by emphasizing responsibilities to others. Ideally, children develop a sense of how relationships, rights and duties function by seeing how their parents react to them, to any siblings and to each other.

- Many children across the world are growing up apart from their families and in contexts that are antithetical to the development of these character traits. For example, children have been drawn into conflicts as armed soldiers in many countries including Burma, the Democratic Republic of Congo, Liberia, Uganda, Somalia and Sri Lanka. This is in spite of many of these nations being signatories to the United Nations Convention on the Rights of the Child (UNCRC), adopted in 1989 (see Box 4.5). Article 38 of the UNCRC requires governments to take all feasible measures to ensure that persons below the age of 15 years do not take a direct part in hostilities.

- The exposure of youth to acts of extreme violence can desensitize them to suffering, increase the likelihood of them committing violent acts themselves and otherwise alienate them from mainstream society. International treaties and advocacy from within countries can exert pressure on governments to rehabilitate such young people. Policies are thus developed and implemented to mitigate some of the harm that has been done to these young people as a result of them losing the protection of their families. In Sri Lanka, some (but by no means all) former combatants in civil war/unrest are given vocational training, education and access to sporting and other cultural events in a government-run protection and rehabilitation centre (Clifford, 2010).

Box 4.5   The United Nations Convention on the Rights of the Child (UNCRC)

The UNCRC, ratified by General Assembly resolution 44/25 of 20 November 1989 makes reference to the Universal Declaration of Human Rights (see Box 4.4) and includes the following phrases in its Preamble:

Recognizing that the child, for the full and harmonious development of his or her personality, should grow up in a family environment, in an atmosphere of happiness, love and understanding,

Considering that the child should be fully prepared to live an individual life in society, and brought up in the spirit of the ideals proclaimed in the Charter of the United Nations, and in particular in the spirit of peace, dignity, tolerance, freedom, equality and solidarity,

Bearing in mind that... 'the child, by reason of his physical and mental immaturity, needs special safeguards and care, including appropriate legal protection, before as well as after birth...'

For the full text, see www2.ohchr.org/english/law/crc.htm.

- **Provision of mutual support and care**. The family has been described as one of the welfare 'pillars' of society (Esping-Andersen, 2002). Family members provide informal support for each other based on two strong principles: a sense of moral responsibility, meaning the feeling that it is right to help each other, and an awareness of reciprocity, referring to the need for help to be given and received in a reasonably balanced way (Quinton, 2004). Such informal support can extend beyond the nuclear family to a wider circle of kin.

• The way extended families share interests and pool risks was highlighted by sociologists such as Michael Young who described to British social planners in the 1950s how 'many working class families operate continuously as agencies for mutual aid of all kinds' (1954: 136). He criticized government housing policy which paid insufficient attention to the importance of extended family networks in setting criteria for housing allocation. When adult children married and were unable to find housing near family, key social support mechanisms were jeopardized.

• Although similar support mechanisms can also operate between friends and neighbours, some research indicates that specifically *family* support makes a difference. For example, one study of elderly women found that where family support was perceived to be low, subjects' psychological well-being was poor, regardless of support from friends and their membership in a social network (Thompson and Heller, 1990). Other, more recent studies also point to the effects of relationships with children and other relatives on health and well-being (Antonucci et al., 2003; Barefoot et al., 2005). Such findings suggest that where policy seeks to replicate the processes and benefits of actual family care (where it is unavailable) there is a limit to the extent that it can successfully do that. It is important, however, not to assume that all extended family relationships are supportive, and to be aware that many family relationships are subject to negotiation as well as obligation (see Box 4.6).

Box 4.6   Negotiation and obligation in family relationships

Finch and Mason have described how people 'work out' how to treat their relatives 'in a two- (or more) way process of negotiation in which people are giving and receiving, balancing out one kind of assistance for another ... responsibilities are thus created rather than flowing automatically from specific relationships' (1993: 167). Support increasingly depends on the quality of relationships forged, the forming of what Finch (1989) termed 'cumulative commitments'.

Equally, there are many contexts, such as in transnational care, where family relations operate at 'long-distance' but feelings of obligation to provide care remain important and are linked to cultural constructions of duty and responsibility. Baldassar (2007) describes how families' members respond to each others' care needs according to perceptions of what it means to behave like a 'good' or 'proper' family which, in the transnational family context, can require the significant upheaval of migration.

Recent policy discussions across Europe and further afield are paying particular attention to the role played by the extended family and specifically by grandparents (whose importance to families was described in Chapter 1), such as the care they may provide for young children while their parents work. In Hungary, in lieu of the parents, grandparents can claim certain types of child benefit and childcare allowances if the child is looked after in the grandparent's home, and they are also entitled to take associated leave (Hemmings, 2007).

However, grandparents' roles can become stretched beyond desirable limits when they are forced to take on full-time care and financial support of their grandchildren. Advocacy groups speaking on behalf of such 'kinship carers' lobby minority world governments and demand changes in policy which will increase financial and other support to improve their position. In majority world regions most affected by the HIV/AIDS epidemic (such as India, other parts of Asia and sub-Saharan Africa), grandparental care has increased markedly. When children's parents die not just from AIDS related causes, grandparents often have to step in to become primary carers and providers despite meagre financial resources and declining stamina. Approximately 12 million children (under age 18) have lost one or both parents to AIDS in sub-Saharan Africa. Although policy responses are forthcoming, the Joint United Nations Programme on HIV/AIDS (UNAIDS; 2008), notes that while most high-prevalence countries have government strategies in place to support children orphaned by the disease, few national programmes reach more than a small minority.

→ In Chapter 6 we describe the consequences of parents being forced to live and work at a significant distance to their children as migrant labourers, and how this impacts on *their* parents' generation.

In many societies and contexts, the wider family unit may be the first or only port of call when tragedy strikes, or in contexts of poverty and deprivation. However, family membership provides not just a safety net but potentially also advantages through access to wider networks, wealth and education and is thus associated with social inequality. Many government policies seek to 'level the playing field' and compensate for what is referred to as the intergenerational transmission of disadvantage, where children are subject to the same barriers to achievement as their parents (see Box 4.7). These disadvantages are usually financial but they are also related to family practices flowing from the extent to which education and paid work are valued within the family – and attainable.

Box 4.7   A 'pipeline of programmes' enabling parents to impart better life skills

Harlem Children's Zone (see www.hcz.org) has been set up in one of the impoverished neighbourhoods of New York, where social mobility had more or less completely stalled. The aim has been to provide a 'pipeline' of programmes 'from cradle to college to community' to enable parents and their children to acquire the skills they will need to succeed in twenty-first century society, which were not typically present in these families. Early in the 'pipeline' is a Baby College that aims to teach (often teenage) parents how to provide the care and nurture their very young children need (Tough, 2009). It is followed by school-based programmes from elementary through middle school and high school to college and is accompanied by family, social service and health programmes and community-building programmes. The early signs of success of Harlem Children's Zone have produced a policy response in the form of a promise by President Barack Obama to reproduce its approach in 20 more cities in the USA.

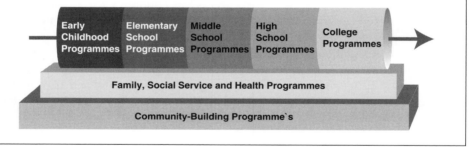

- **Sense of personal and group identity**. The association between psychological well-being and family support mentioned in the previous section may be due to the sense of identity which individuals derive from belonging to a family, and this in turn shapes relationships with non-related others. Chapter 1 described how our genealogy can give us meaning, and described the importance of kinship and lineage as organizing principles for social life. As well as providing care, older members of the extended family also educate growing children in 'the language of the group' (Bloch, 1953: 41), function as the repositories and transmitters of culture (Dench, 2000), and communicate distinctive aspects of wider group identity to children as new members.

- Contemporary governments and other policy actors draw on these principles when searching for successful solutions to social problems. For example, in traditional Maori culture, family identity is implicit in notions of *whanaunatanga*, of knowing one's lineage and ancestors. Determining the place of each individual in wider Maori society entails understanding how someone is related to the other members of their *whanau* (family), *hapu* (subtribe) or *iwi* (tribe) (Munro et al., 1989). This remains important when Maori are in treatment for alcohol and drug misuse. Programmes that draw the extended family into the process have been shown to enhance addicts' sense of belonging and relatedness and to contribute to recovery (Huriwai et al., 2001).

- The principle of drawing in as many family members as possible into a problem-solving process to meet welfare needs of an individual has been extended to other areas of social policy in other countries through the Family Group Conferencing model (Love, 1999). For example, it is also used in New Zealand's youth justice system to divert young offenders away from the courts, and it is used in Canadian, British and many other countries' child protection proceedings to explore family-based alternatives to taking children into local authority care (Nixon et al., 2005).

In summary, many governments work on the principle that society is largely held together by families; families are a society's building blocks, and the functions performed within and by families — what families *do* — are essential for society's successful functioning. The corollary of this, considered in the next section, is that if families are fissive or dysfunctional, this may compromise the integrity of society itself.

FAMILIES AND SOCIAL BREAKDOWN

Governments of every political persuasion, and across the globe, have to grapple with the far-reaching implications of change in families, especially where it threatens to undermine the social and economic well-being of wider society. The challenges that changing families present to governments differ within and between global regions and political groupings. We have already touched on the ways in which family dynamics or processes alter in contexts of high prevalence of disease and war, but many of the more advantaged Organisation for Economic Co-operation and Development (OECD) countries have also seen profound changes in families, especially over the past 40 years.

These include changes in family structure and the greater instability of the family as a unit, but also shifts associated with family processes, such as the need to reconcile family and employment responsibilities, alterations and imbalances in the contributions men and women make in the home and workplace, changing obligations and responsibilities between generations, and changing education and employment needs. Similar changes have taken place at different times in different countries. For example, although the UK, Sweden and Greece have some of the lowest first marriage rates in the EU, eastern European countries such as Estonia and Hungary have seen their rates fall more steeply from a former higher base (Letablier et al., 2003). Marital breakdown in Spain increased by 290% between 1996 and 2006 although prior to this the divorce rate was very low in comparison with those of other European societies (Institute for Family Policies, 2008).

➜ The introduction of Chapter 1, describes how family change, sometimes referred to as 'families in flux' (Giddens, 1992) is not new. Historical studies demonstrate how families across the world are always changing in response to a range of opportunities and challenges (Hareven, 1994).

The significant increase, especially in *parental* separation and divorce, is the cause of widespread international concern on the part of governments, other policy actors and civil society, because such trends are taken by some to imply the breakdown of the family and, to some extent, of society itself. Professor Linda Hantrais, an expert on European social policy, states that 'the main question raised by changes in patterns of family formation and dissolution concerns their impact on the future of the family as a basic social institution and the role the state can and should play in shaping family structure through its economic and social policies' (2004: 67). Governments are particularly concerned about the extent to which these changes in structure have challenged families' functions such as their ability to care for their vulnerable members, most notably members who are very young, very old or chronically ill. As a result, family policy often focuses on improving outcomes for children, not least because of the potential savings to be made if they grow into independent adults able to contribute to society. The increase in numbers of elderly people who are, or will be, lacking in family support is another focus for policy, one where governments are in many ways struggling to catch up with demographic realities.

BEYOND STEREOTYPES

It is important to reiterate that the shifts mentioned above are interpreted very differently by academics, commentators and policy makers, and policy responses differ according to whether an optimistic or pessimistic approach to family change is adopted.

Responses to change in terms of government action or policies can attempt either to maintain 'traditional' family forms (headed by heterosexual married couples), or to meet families' needs in the context of new realities. Hantrais (2007) describes how, in governments across the EU, policy makers had to decide whether or not to recognize alternative family forms in fiscal and social policy, and if and how they should support families through periods of transition, such as before, during and after divorce or separation. Approaches that governments take towards strengthening families are partly shaped by the type of welfare state operating in the country, discussed later in this section.

At the turn of the century, in many European countries, where 'traditional' family forms were still overwhelmingly prevalent, political rhetoric (see Box 4.8) emphasized the threat to the status quo posed by recognition of family diversity. Governments in Greece, Italy, Poland and Ireland typified this approach, reflecting the ongoing influence of religion in society and in these cases the close relationship between the Catholic Church and institutions of the state. In Poland the traditional married couple was supported in policy to the extent that laws were passed to restrict abortion and divorce. In Ireland, concern about high rates of extramarital birth led to the promotion of the married, two-parent family as the ideal (Hantrais, 2004). In Islamic countries religious values and the influence of members of the religious hierarchy similarly exert a strong pressure on governments' approaches to issues concerning the family.

Box 4.8   'The politics of the family'

The phrase 'the politics of the family' refers to the many ways in which national and local governments of the day and other politicians (including those in opposing political parties) talk about the family or families, and if, and how they consider it legitimate to intervene to support and strengthen them. The phrase also refers to the attitudes and ways of thinking about the family that drive those words and actions: 'Political debates include disagreements about what legitimately constitutes a family, what type of family practices, personal and domestic arrangements over a lifetime should be promoted, celebrated or otherwise given support and what should be censured and proscribed' (Cunningham-Burley and Jamieson, 2003: 1).

Treating the family as centrally important to social cohesion or as the source of social breakdown may be accompanied by a rigid approach to families in general, the favouring of one form of family over another and the working out of assumptions about families not conforming to this norm.

For example, it may be assumed that the optimal development of young children requires daycare to take place within the family (whether nuclear or extended). Where this is combined with an expectation that men will be the main or only financial provider government policy will not tend to cater for parents who both work a significant number of hours outside the home.

Spain has relatively few policy initiatives to support working mothers (although a family leave policy was introduced in 1999), and state welfare or support for families has been based on the continuation of what is termed 'the male breadwinner norm' (Millar and Warman, 1996; Glaser et al., 2010). On the other hand, countries such as Finland allow very long periods, up to three years, of paid leave from work when children are born and, in comparison with some of the other Nordic countries, provide significantly less publicly funded childcare before the child is three years old (Gupta et al., 2006; Hiilamo and Kangas, 2006). Such policy may make certain assumptions but not cater for parents' (particularly mothers') *actual* working patterns. According to Esping-Andersen (2009), this reflects the failure of welfare states (described later in the chapter) to engage with women's changing participation in the labour market.

> ➜ See Chapters 1 and 6 for more examples of the 'gender coding' of care work. The interaction of working and caring is examined in greater detail in Chapter 6.

Similarly, governments may assume that family members are available to take care of the elderly and thus do little to provide elder care services or give employees rights to take leave in order to provide care. In other words, certain family processes are taken for granted. Other countries make fewer assumptions about families' abilities to care for the elderly. Research in Sweden has shown the prevailing attitude to be that 'we do what we can for elderly people in the family but the main responsibility lies with the municipality and the state' (Hantrais, 2004: 181).

FAMILIES AND THE WELFARE STATE

We have said several times that the approaches governments take towards providing services, financial benefits or leave arrangements depends on the kind of welfare state prevailing in the country. Western or OECD countries are welfare states, which are political systems 'committed to modifying the play of social or market forces in order to achieve greater equality' (Ruggie, 1984: 11). As such they all, to a greater or lesser degree, enable individuals (where necessary) to 'uphold a socially acceptable standard of living independent of family relationships' (Cunningham-Burley and Jamieson, 2003: 13). The corollary of this is that as the number of individuals (e.g. elderly people and single parents) who are not financially dependent on other family members grows, the greater the economic load on the state. The politics of the welfare state is therefore tightly connected to the 'politics of the family', as described in Box 4.8.

> ➜ Topic 1 in Chapter 1 looks in detail at the impact of welfare regimes on families in France, the Russian Federation, and East and West Germany.

The 'welfare state' is the generic term that applies to minority world countries in which the state (that is, governing institutions) plays a principal part in the material welfare of all of its citizens. This complements to a greater or lesser extent what people earn for themselves as well as financial and other support from family, friends, neighbours and the voluntary sector. Esping-Andersen (1990) grouped such nations together into three distinct subclasses. Each of these three types are identified by him with a deep political tradition and philosophy (conservatism, liberalism and socialism) which correspond in turn to particular features of contemporary social policy (see Box 4.9). Principles concerning the nature and extent of state intervention and the acceptable relationship between the state and the individual differ in each subclass and influence the kinds of policies governments tend to implement.

Box 4.9   Grouping nations into three different welfare subclasses

Liberal regimes have high levels of social inequality and weak social rights and are best represented by the USA.

Conservative/corporatist regimes have strong social rights but the state plays a limited role in addressing inequalities, for example, Germany.

Social democratic regimes have strong social rights and explicitly pursue egalitarian goals, particularly as exemplified by Sweden.

Esping-Andersen's typology has been modified and extended in many ways (Arts and Gelissen, 2002), and others have looked more globally and beyond the minority world. Gough et al. (2004) have examined the extent to which governing bodies do or do not look after citizens in developing nations in terms of personal and family safety and welfare. They identify three broad global 'ideal types' of welfare regime:

- welfare state regimes (characteristic of prosperous capitalist countries)

- informal security regimes (characteristic of many parts of Latin America and Asia)

- insecurity regimes (characteristic of many African countries).

In the final category the state is weak, resulting in a precarious livelihood and security situation for many people. Esping-Andersen (2002, 2009) has further developed his thinking on the nature of welfare states. He contends that major change is going to be necessary across all types given the challenges presented by social and family change already described.

THE RELATIONSHIP BETWEEN POLITICS AND POLICIES

Political parties favouring a small role for the state historically saw the family as the sphere of private action *par excellence*, while those favouring a more redistributive approach requiring a larger state have also instinctively steered clear of the family (where disadvantage tends to be reproduced, as we illustrated in Box 4.6) by focusing on the individual. So policies favouring state-provided childcare might, for those in the first category, be seen as usurping the role of parents, usually mothers, as opposed to flattening out inequalities by ensuring all children receive a good start in life through early education. However, changes in family life are blurring political dividing lines. Where increasing numbers of elderly people, single parents and vulnerable people such as those with long-term sickness or disabilities are unable to depend on their family of origin, policies may be developed whatever political party is in power, to meet their needs. Similarly, helping the individual in an effective way often requires working with the family.

Yet despite this convergence, rhetoric concerning the family is frequently used as a political tool. Competing narratives concerning the family are constructed to communicate markers of difference between political parties' family policies. These markers of difference can be perceived as emblematic of profound philosophical differences between parties, despite the fact that individual politicians may strongly disagree with their party's position on certain family issues. This helps to explain why family policy is often particularly contested, with an example provided in Box 4.10 below. It is also important to be aware of the complexity of the policy-making process (whether it is concerned with family or any other area of concern), the many significant factors that influence it and the frequent need for compromise; according to Lindblom (1959), the essence of policy making is 'muddle'.

Box 4.10   Divorce in Malta

Although the official positions of the Labour and Nationalist (conservative) parties appeared to be somewhat polarized in the debate in 2010 over whether or not divorce should be legalized in Malta, within each party there was a lack of genuine consensus on the issue. While the Labour leader said that he was prepared to propose a law on the introduction of divorce and give his fellow Labour MPs a free vote, the Nationalist Prime Minister talked instead about the government's determination to strengthen the family before 'giving up' and introducing divorce. However, it was not the case that all Labour MPs and senior officials agreed with the approach of their leader, and some Nationalist MPs were privately in favour of making divorce possible where marriages have irretrievably broken down.

In many countries, conservative parties have historically tended to emphasize the importance of a particular family structure, what is termed the 'traditional' (two-parent heterosexual married) family because it is seen as an institution that can insulate the individual from any need for direct interference of the state. Labour parties, on the other hand (not least because they tend to be more strongly influenced by Marxist theories described in Chapter 2) see the state through a more benign lens, as a leveller of the disadvantage that can come from family membership. They will tend to emphasize family processes as a more important focus of concern. Philosophically therefore, conservative parties will favour approaches to the family that uphold what are perceived to be its 'traditional' functions (particularly the financial support of members). Labour parties, however, will be much more willing to acknowledge the shortcomings of this traditional model, allowing government to take on financial and other responsibilities previously seen as the preserve of the family and not, therefore, seek to uphold any particular family form.

In May 2011, a referendum was held in Malta over the issue of whether or not divorce should be introduced on the island, in what was described as 'one of the most notable episodes for the Maltese since independence was gained from the British in 1964' (http://www.bbc.co.uk/news/world-europe-13589320), not least because the result was no foregone conclusion. This was a highly contested issue that split political parties and went to the heart of the relationship between the Catholic church and the state. Just over 50% of the votes cast were in favour of divorce.

As stated earlier, politicians may also avoid talking about families *per se* and frame policies in terms of benefits to children. Indeed children's rights and the need to invest in children seem, at least at the symbolic level, to be the most salient aspect of family policy in some but not all European countries. In Italy, for example, such a narrative barely features (Naldini and Saraceno, 2008).

?   Think about how the current government talks about family and look for references to particular forms or what kinds of practices are socially approved. How much are children mentioned rather than parents and grandparents?

SERVICES AND PRACTICES

Programmes and services are often designed to meet the requirements of policies once the latter have matured into priorities for government. Alternatively, programmes and services may have existed prior to this happening and then provided some of the impetus for the adoption of a particular approach in preference to another. In other words they were presented as solutions to a problem that had not yet been properly articulated.

➜ See Topic 1 in Chapter 1 for international examples of how service provision has changed as a result of political shifts.

Statutory services are those funded and delivered by local and national governments to fulfil legal obligations placed on them. A very wide range of services impacting the family are provided by welfare states, most notably those concerned with health (including mental health and assistance for those with disabilities), education and social services (such as child protection and other social work functions).

However, a focus on governing institutions (at whatever level) and on welfare states can lead to an assumption that statutory services are the main delivery mechanism, with inadequate attention paid to the important role of what are termed 'civil society actors', particularly NGOs. Examples of NGOs include Save the Children, Barnardos, Age UK and the International Committee of the Red Cross (more usually referred to as the Red Cross), which is part of a wider movement with Red Crescent societies that tend to operate in Islamic countries.

At a supranational level, the European Commission has argued for the strengthening of relationships between EU institutions and NGOs, defined by the commission as organizations that are not profit distributing; voluntary; independent of government, political parties or commercial organisations; and not self-serving in aims and related values or pursuing the commercial or professional interests of its members, but acting in the public arena at large, on concerns and issues related to the well-being of people, specific groups of people or society as a whole (European Commission, 1997).

Dialogue between the political and civil society sector is, the commission argues, 'an important complement to the institutional process of policy shaping ... [which will] improve policy design and ... increase efficacy' (Prodi and Kinnock, 2000: 7) not least at the implementation and delivery stages. The role of civil society still varies greatly between EU countries (Appleton and Byrne, 2003), but what tends to be common to voluntary sector organizations is their work 'at the coalface', in direct contact with individuals and families themselves, and their involvement in what is referred to as the welfare *society*. The welfare society has been defined by Robertson as 'a social system in which welfare assumptions are an organic part of everyday life' (1988: 222). It might also be thought of, more colloquially, as a society characterized by people providing care to others beyond the boundaries of friends and family.

The voluntary sector or NGOs deliver many services as part of the welfare society, and they are also commissioned by bodies acting on behalf of the welfare state such as family or children's centres, social work departments and education authorities. As they receive payment from the state through these bodies and need to be accountable, ultimately to the taxpayer, for that funding, there is a significant degree of scrutiny of finances, procedures and outcomes. Rodger describes this relationship aptly: 'the boundaries are beginning to blur as the state divests itself of welfare obligations but retains an "at arms' length" interest in the supervision of the welfare field' (2003: 48).

> **?** Think about who provides services to people in your family and to others you know now and in the past. To what extent is the voluntary sector involved?

TYPES OF SERVICES

An enormous variety of services exists within and between countries, precluding an exhaustive typology. Many of these services assist families by carrying out functions that might previously have been considered the sole responsibility of family members, e.g. care giving for children and for elderly and vulnerable adults. Service provision has the potential to commodify and deprivatize care: care becomes something that can be 'bought in' rather than physically provided by family members. It is important to be aware that not only does the provision of services *modify* family practices, but changes in these practices, such as women's greater involvement in paid work outside the home, can generate a demand for services. Moreover, such services are far more commonly found in minority world societies, with very little if anything available in majority world countries, where the family itself is more or less the only port of call for assistance or support.

Here we have chosen two areas, parenting skills services and measures to facilitate the reconciliation of paid work with family responsibilities, to provide illustration.

- **Parenting skills services**. Across Europe as well as in North America, governments have begun to stimulate the development of services to improve the ability of parents to care for their own children (Appleton and Hantrais, 2000). The rationale behind this is that parenting classes can make an important contribution to social integration. It is anticipated that parents who are given more support in preparing for and carrying out their family roles will be more effective in carrying out their commitments to their children. This will in turn reduce the social and economic burden that anti-social, emotionally disturbed and poorly supervised children and young people impose on society (see Box 4.11). This is one example of 'early intervention' that was referred to earlier in the description of Harlem Children's Zone (Box 4.7). Intervening early is a preventive approach that has the potential to deliver considerable cost savings (Aos et al., 2004), the rationale for government involvement in areas that would otherwise be considered private.

Box 4.11   Tackling 'anti-social behaviour'

In 2006, the *Respect Agenda* was launched by the UK government. It aimed to tackle the anti-social behaviour (defined in the Crime and Disorder Act 1998 as acting in 'a manner that caused or was likely to cause harassment, alarm or distress to one or more persons not of the same household as the complainant') of some individuals and families which was deemed to be having a deleterious effect on the quality of life in whole communities. The Agenda's starting point was that a lack of respect for shared values, such as consideration for others and recognition of responsibilities as well as rights lies at the heart of this behaviour. Most individuals learn this respect from their parents and families, but those who do not lack a sense of what is acceptable or unacceptable, and their problematic behaviour often leads to unemployment, serious drug and alcohol, misuse and crime.

Poor parenting skills, weak parent–child relationships and sometimes parental involvement in crime or anti-social behaviour were identified as targets for

(Continued)

(Continued)

policy intervention. Policy focused on delivering a range of services to remedy parenting deficits, including parenting services to help those parents most in need and the establishment of a new National Academy of Parenting Practitioners (NAPP) to train front-line staff.

Parents whose children had engaged in anti-social behaviour were mandated to attend parenting classes such as Triple P ('Positive Parenting Program'®). Developed in Australia, Triple P was sufficiently evidence based (backed by over 25 years of international research) to be paid for by public funds. NAPP's role was to identify existing parenting programmes with proven effectiveness (another example of evidence-basing in policy and practice), to train providers to deliver these programmes, and to conduct research to develop the next generation of parenting services.

In several European countries, intervention happens even earlier, with the teaching of basic parenting skills as part of basic education. In Sweden, all secondary school pupils are taught subjects concerned with children and family life. In Hungary one of the main goals of the society and ethics classes in the seventh grade of elementary school is to prepare children for developing and maintaining interpersonal social relationships.

Finally, family services in some countries, such as the UK, may be almost exclusively focused on improving parent–child relationships, and pay little or no attention to parents' (couple) relationships with each other despite the contribution this makes to the quality of parenting (Cowan and Cowan, 2008). There is, however, a growing body of literature from the USA, Australia and Europe on what is termed 'couple relationship education'. In Australia a network of family relationship centres has been established with government funding, following a series of changes to the family law system in 2006. Policy was developed with the aim of bringing about a cultural shift in the management of parental separation, away from adversarial litigation and towards co-operative parenting. These centres also work with families before separation, with the aim of preventing relationships from breaking down if possible.

?   Why do you think there is more emphasis on improving how parents relate to their children than on relationships between couples? One reason that has been given is that couple relationship education is more culturally acceptable than parenting education – why do you think this is the case and what do you think might make this perception change over time?

Box 4.12 describes one application of relationship education in a Nordic country.

Box 4.12 'Living Well Together' – a government-run relationship education programme

A policy initiative of the Norwegian government has made relationship education available to parents the first year after their first child is born, in the form of a one-day course called 'Living Well Together' (*Godt samliv*). The aim of the programme is to strengthen relationships and prevent divorce. In 2007, 335 of these government-run couple-courses were held all across Norway; over 2,000 couples participated in courses and 58,500 children were born in Norway during that year (Statistics Norway, 2008). Norwegian government documents claim that 'couple relationships are public health', and argue that fewer divorces will have positive effects in society, both on a human and an economic level (e.g. divorce can result in difficulties at work). The most important argument though is that sustainable and stable couple relationships 'are basically concerned with the life situation and growth of children. The welfare of the child is therefore the main reason why the Norwegian state involves itself in people's couple relationships' (Helskog, 2009: 145).

- **Reconciliation of paid work and family responsibilities**. Much has already been said in this chapter about policies and services which enable parents to combine engagement in the labour market with their role as carers for other family members. (Chapter 6 looks in closer detail at how work impinges on families and affects the functions or processes they are able to carry out.) In the Nordic states of Denmark, Sweden, Finland and Norway and in France this has been a policy issue for governments for several decades (in some cases since the 1960s), although there is significant variation in approaches between these countries. It is still not high on the policy agenda of southern European countries such as Spain and Italy, where the expectation is that families will make their own arrangements and little support will be available through government measures.

    Turning to the very different context of many poorer nations, parental engagement in the labour market increasingly involves transnational migration where, in order to reconcile paid work and family responsibilities, children may have to be left behind in the care of the extended family. The term, 'global care chains' has been used to describe the phenomenon of migrants moving from poor to rich worlds specifically to look after other people's children or elderly people while leaving behind those for whom they would normally provide care (Hochschild, 2003a; Lan,

2006). The International Labour Organization (ILO) states that 'Worldwide, today almost every nation is a country of origin, of transit, of destination; many are all three' (Taran and Geronimi, 2003: 8).

Whether countries send, receive or give passage to labour migrants, there are corresponding national and supranational policy implications if governing institutions are to ensure the well-being and protection of migrants and their families. Certain countries (for example, Indonesia, Thailand and the Philippines) have particularly high numbers of citizens working and living abroad. The Philippines sends labour migrants to over 100 countries with more than 10% of its population working or living abroad. The impact of migration can be positive, with economic benefits for the family and the country in general through financial remittances, although the money being sent back may be insufficient to improve significantly the lives of the families left behind.

> ➜ The section in Chapter 6 on migrant domestic workers also discusses this issue, and the impact on relationships within the family is described in Chapter 5.

The 'transnational family' has become accepted in the Philippines, with one or both parents working abroad (Reyes, 2008). Almost three-quarters of migrants are women workers, many of whom work as domestic helpers, nurses, caregivers and entertainers in order to provide for their families.[2] As women more typically fulfil nurturing roles in the Philippine culture, their absence may have more of a social and emotional impact on the children they have been unable to take with them. Although there are no systematic data on the numbers involved, it is estimated that nine million or 27% of the country's total population of children and young people are part of a transnational family (Reyes, 2008). Given the significant contribution of overseas workers to the Philippine economy, the government has provided support mechanisms and policies to assist overseas workers and their families. For example the Overseas Workers' Welfare Administration provides insurance and healthcare benefits, education and training, social services and family welfare assistance, and workers' assistance and on-site services, among others. The Philippine government's medicare programme provides mandatory healthcare (including medical assistance and hospitalization benefits for overseas workers and their dependants). There are also several non-governmental and community

---

2   A concerning number of migrant labourers become targets of sex and other forms of trafficking. Travel and job placements abroad are arranged for people who accompany traffickers based on promises of opportunities unachievable in their native country. However, once they arrive at their destination, they realize they have been deceived about the work they will be expected to do and about the financial arrangements and conditions of their employment. Usually women are forced into the sex trade. They find themselves in coercive or abusive situations from which escape is both difficult and dangerous (Kara, 2009).

organizations in the country that provide services and programmes for migrants and their children.

At a supranational level, the United Nations International Convention on the Protection of the Rights of All Migrant Workers and Members of their Families 'takes into account the fact that migration is often the cause of serious problems for the members of the families of migrant workers, as well as for the workers themselves, in particular because of the scattering of the family' (UN, 1990: 2). In signing up to its 93 Articles, nations bind themselves to uphold a comprehensive range of rights and duties towards migrants and their families, and to provide the Convention's subjects with grounds of appeal against host governments' adverse treatment of them. However, as we stated in the section 'Families and Social Cohesion', many nations with high numbers of child soldiers are signatories to the UNCRC, which requires governments to do everything within their power to prevent children under 15 from being drawn into armed conflict. Implementation of the UN convention to protect migrant workers is similarly patchy and, despite the best intentions of the international community, reflects comments made earlier about the 'muddle' that surrounds the making of policy and the unpredictability of its effects for those it is seeking to assist.

SUMMARY

The material in this chapter has ranged widely across the politics and policies concerned with families and the services delivered, on the ground, to help facilitate beneficial family practices in contexts of change. The intervention of governments in family life varies enormously cross-culturally. The political context (particularly the 'politics of the family') in an individual country or in a group of countries which share a similar outlook may preclude or make possible the development of a particular family policy agenda. Family policy, whether this is limited to explicit policies designed to achieve specific goals regarding families or it includes the more implicit 'family perspective in policy making', can be highly controversial where it is perceived as intervening in a private domain. However, the importance of families is common to all governments not least because of the role they play in building and maintaining social cohesion.

The nature and degree of the many changes families are undergoing, whether it is in patterns of formation and dissolution or due to pressures from globalization, have placed a burden on governments and supranational institutions to develop policies to meet social needs that may previously have been met within and by families. Therefore policies frequently result in the provision of services in response to changes in family practices. Services may also be intended to modify family practices, especially where vulnerable members are at risk of harm.

?   If you could design one family policy what would it be and why?

EXPLORE FURTHER

Becker, S. and Bryman, A. (2004) *Understanding Research for Social Policy and Practice: Themes, Methods and Approaches*. Bristol: Policy Press.

Bogenschneider, K. (2000) 'Has family policy come of age? A decade review of the state of U.S. Family Policy in the 1990s', *Journal of Marriage and the Family*, 62(4): 1136–59.

Edin, K. and Kefalas, M.J. (2005) *Promises I Can Keep: Why Poor Women Put Motherhood Before Marriage*. Los Angeles: University of California Press.

Hudson, J. and Lowe, S. (2009) *Understanding the Policy Process: Analysing Welfare Policy and Practice*. Bristol: Policy Press.

USEFUL WEBSITES

The Centre for Social Justice is an independent thinktank established to seek effective solutions to the poverty that blights parts of Britain by developing policy for local and national governments. By conducting policy research that seeks to gain an accurate picture of poverty in Britain, and its causes and consequences, the centre also aims to put social justice at the heart of British politics. See www.centreforsocialjustice.org.uk.

Another leading British thinktank (based in London and Manchester) is the Institute of Public Policy Research. It describes its work as always 'driven by a belief in the importance of fairness, democracy and sustainability'. It also works in more than 25 countries around the world in which it has pioneered thinktank research and engagement in local communities. See www.ippr.org.

Internationally, the Australian government's website Family Relationships Online (http://familyrelationships.gov.au) has some useful factsheets on maintaining healthy marriages/relationships intended to be of use to policy makers, service providers and family members.

PART III

FAMILIES IN ACTION

5 Relationships and Sexualities

Keywords: marriage, emotions, same-sex relationships, civil partnerships, same sex, breakdown, cohabitation, solo living, friendships, networks, communities, neighbourhoods, sexualization, intimacy

INTRODUCTION

Relationships are at the heart of families, neighbourhoods, societies and even international communities such as the EU and UN. Salient experiences of daily life and key moments in the lifecourse are largely framed and constituted by relational interactions. Undoubtedly some relationships have more influence on, and significance for, people than do others. Those we treat as 'intimate' are important because it is in these relationships we connect at a deep level. What distinguishes one's intimates from those outside this category is that such relationships entail bodily, emotional and/or privileged knowledge of the other person (Jamieson et al., 2006). Sexuality is often, but not always, intrinsic and highly important to intimate partnerships (and also to individuals' identities).

At this point in this book many themes such as marriage and cohabitation, solo living, friendships, social networks and communities have been considered more than once and in various ways. In this chapter we will draw these threads together and discuss the many different partnering arrangements that exist and affect family formation (referred to throughout this book as family structure) within a society as well as across societies around the world. We also revisit the theme of family process by paying attention to what changes and what stays the same in relationships even when family circumstances undergo marked transitions, such as separation, divorce or bereavement.

> ➔ The globalization of working and education patterns, discussed in Chapters 4 and 6, and periods of war, conflict, civil unrest or imprisonment, can also result in parents and partners being apart from their families for long periods if not indefinitely.

We start by looking at procreative relationships, mainly experienced in the context of marriage but increasingly commonly found (in Western societies) in cohabitation or less formalized partnering arrangements, as they are necessary for the formation of any family or wider social group. As we noted in Chapter 1, Goran Therborn (2004) makes the point that without sex at some point in most adult intimate relationships there might be no family. However, this chapter also considers relationships where no sex is involved, such as friendships, and sexual relationships without procreative intention or procreative potential, as is the case in same-sex partnerships or when one or both partners experience fertility problems. Information and communications technology, increasingly used for relational purposes, enables the virtualization of sex where erotic encounters between people (who need not even be on the same continent) are facilitated through the internet but involve no physical contact. Another, darker aspect of globalization is the trafficking of women and children across international borders, fueling the local and regional sex industries. We then move onto the increasing sexualization of societies, which is closely bound up with consumerism and is especially of concern when associated with the commercialization of childhood.

We go beyond what is known as a dyadic approach (namely what goes on at the level of the couple) and consider how two people's relationship with each other has ramifications throughout the wider social networks to which they belong. At the same time, the wider social environment shapes relationships through more or less prescribed rules about who can marry whom and with whom it is acceptable to be friends or associates. It is for this reason that Steve Duck and others recommend taking a culturally contextual approach which recognizes that relationships are networked experiences (Duck, 2007; Boss et al., 2008; Neuliep, 2008).

Throughout the chapter we remain aware, as emphasized in Chapter 1, that a dry and dusty treatment of the subject of relationships does not do justice to the meaning they hold for the individuals concerned. We try to bear in mind that relationships are saturated with emotions: emotions do not just have an impact on social life; they are what social life comprises (Gergen, 1994). Smart emphasizes the absolute centrality of emotions to social and personal life: 'the magical quality of emotions – they can turn everyday acts into interactions laden with meaning' (2007: 60). Many of these everyday acts are examples of what Morgan (1996) refers to as 'family practices' and they take place with people who share our histories and will help shape our futures. Thus the chapter ends with a consideration of the importance of enduring relationships to society, to the continuity of families and to the individuals involved.

➜ Look at Chapter 2, page 59, for an extended discussion of David Morgan's important recognition that contemporary families are defined more by doing family things than by presumptions or assertions of being part of a family. 'Doing family' can involve rituals (such as particular ways of celebrating annual events) and many other activities and thoughts (including shared memories, anticipations and potential plans), with family representing a 'quality' rather than a 'thing'.

LET'S GET TOGETHER: MARRIAGE AND COHABITATION

UNIVERSALITY OF MARRIAGE AND PARTNERING

Across the world, in a more or less socially prescribed way (Fortes, 1983), intimate partnerships are formed between individuals who are usually, but not always, consenting adults of the opposite sex. While marriage is not the only basis on which such partnerships are formed, it is a highly important social institution. The legal, religious or cultural recognition of intimate partnerships that equates with the term 'marriage' is treated by many anthropologists as a cultural universal (Murdock, 1945; Ferraro, 2006) that is, common to all human cultures worldwide. Enormous variation exists within and between societies in terms of how relationships are structured (for example, who is partnered with whom, at what age and upon whose decision) and in terms of the ceremonies at which partners make public statements about their agreement to associate (Coontz, 2005).

Marriage ceremonies are social rituals of great significance, not least because they are 'rites of passage' that mark the point at which individuals and their families become joined together with the wide range of social and legal obligations this entails. Marriage is also a common marker of having entered adulthood (Mansfield and Collard, 1988) and brings with it certain responsibilities. Particularly young couples can find these hard to bear, especially without extended family or other social support, to the point that the relationship may become unsustainable (Bumpass et al., 1991).

Signs that people subsequently 'belong together' as a couple are often used, such as rings or other adornments. Sometimes the ceremony is followed by a period where the couple leaves their usual social setting and spends time together (on what is referred to in many Western cultures as a 'honeymoon'). This period of time enables them to carry out a role transition from single to married and can serve a social reorganization function as they leave those who knew them as 'singles' and return as a socially recognized couple (Hagestad and Smyer, 1982).

DEFINITION OF PARTNERING – HOW DO PEOPLE PARTNER?

David Cheal (2002) describes how the most significant family events are changes in family composition or structure, and marriage and partnering are very important to family formation. 'Getting together' means that individuals each join a new family, they join their two families together and, especially when it involves setting up a new home, they start a new family unit.

How do people get together in a way that leads to this significant social rearrangement? Firstly, it is noteworthy that human societies have unprecedented within-species diversity compared with the fairly defined mating systems of other animal species (Low, 2005). This diversity produces the wide range of family forms described in earlier chapters: mother and child families (and father and child families); monogamous families (where each partner is married to one other person) living with either the husband's or the wife's parents, other relatives or in a new location (this is known as neo-local residence); polygynous families in which one man marries more than one woman, sisters or non-sisters (who may have been forcibly captured from other groups) and in which co-wives live together or apart; and polyandrous families where one woman marries more than one man and, often, brothers share one woman. Some women are bought by their husband's families, whereas in other societies their families pay future husbands a dowry.

Lest we should think that many of these forms of partnership are very rare in comparison with the monogamous norm found in Western or minority world societies, it is instructive that 90% of societies listed in Murdock's (1981) *Atlas of World Cultures* are polygynous (including many African, Islamic and South-East Asian societies). Low (2005) notes that although a large proportion of married people alive today are monogamously married, that is because there are a few very large socially monogamous societies, such as those in North America, much of South America, and across Europe.

Similarly, notwithstanding the comments made earlier about the importance of considering the emotional content of relationships, we should be aware that it is a Western assumption that relationships result exclusively from emotions and that 'falling in love' is the usual basis on which long-term pair bonds are formed. Steve Duck has said that 'culture constrains expressions of biologically-based desire' (2007: 1) and that societal and sociological forces impose practical constraints on our ability to act on emotions. When we consider which people form intimate relationships it is obvious that our social, geographical and even political environments shape our relationships by influencing the kinds of people we meet and by restricting or facilitating our ability to form a long-term relationship with them. For example, under the apartheid regime in South Africa, until 1991 people of different colours led segregated lives under laws forbidding interracial marriage.

Allan and Crow (2001) point out that there is a degree of homogeneity in the love market with people falling in love predominantly with those who are socially equivalent and therefore likely to be acceptable to others in their social networks. There thus tends to be a lack of social mobility involved in the pair bonding process, notwithstanding that the primary traditional means to achieve upward mobility for women has been hypergamy, marrying men higher in socioeconomic status (Buss and Barnes, 1986). As evidence of this predictability, Allan and Crow (2001) cite the *modus operandi* of computer dating agencies which match people according to a range of submitted characteristics. However, it is instructive that 'speed dating', which enables people to meet a very wide range of people in one evening, each one for a short time only, is becoming increasingly popular. Although speed dating could facilitate far greater variation in *temporary* pairing, this is very different from couples forming lasting bonds.

? Think about the established couples you know, both in your generation and also in your parents' generation. In which generation is the degree of partners' homogeneity greater or is there very little difference?

Furthermore, sexuality, a key aspect of intimate partnerships with great potential to influence social structure (for example, through unintended pregnancy), is often shaped and controlled by society. In most countries marriage is arranged by families rather than by the bride and groom (Bernardes, 1997), reflecting the important role it continues to play, as an institution, in ordering social relations and ensuring material welfare. Yet in many parts of Asia this practice has evolved into negotiated marriage, where prospective couples are brought together for 'arranged meetings', thus introducing an element of choice and a decrease in parental control (Cheal, 2002). Romantic love does exist in such cultures, as is evident from the output of the Bollywood film industry, but its role and importance in determining who marries who is different. The Western emphasis on individual preference in marriage contrasts with the way other cultures look at the benefit of a match accruing to the family overall (Gaines and Ickes, 2000) and has its disadvantages as Box 5.1 points out.

Box 5.1   A sardonic consideration of the drawbacks of the 'love marriage'

In the preface to his play *Getting Married*, first performed in 1908, George Bernard Shaw described how unwise it is for people in love to marry, because the result is that when 'two people are under the influence of the most violent, most insane, most delusive, and most transient of passions they are required to swear that they will remain in that excited, abnormal and exhausting condition continuously until death do them part' (2007: 29).

DIVERSITY IN PARTNERING ARRANGEMENTS

While marriage remains the usual prerequisite for family formation and procreation across the world, global trends indicate an increase in premarital sex and earlier entry into sexual activities. At the same time, the number of females marrying before the age of 18 has declined almost everywhere, including in Islamic societies where early marriage has a strong cultural basis and is associated with parental control (Cheal, 2002). In Jordan, Egypt, Indonesia and Malaysia the average age at marriage rose sharply in the second half of the twentieth century. Cheal (2002) points out that a major factor in this shift is the greater prevalence and longer duration of female education. In general, parents are now more likely to want their daughters to be educated not least because this helps them to marry more educated and upwardly mobile men.

Other trends include a decreased emphasis on bride wealth (where the groom's family makes a payment to the bride's family), dowry (where the bride brings money and other property from her family with her) and marriages where partners are chosen to a greater or lesser extent by parents ('arranged' marriage), movement towards a greater number of romantic or love marriages, e.g. in Turkey and Japan (Roopnarine and Gielen, 2005), and a partial replacement of polygyny by concubinage (e.g. in parts of South Africa). Whereas the women involved in polygynous unions all have legal and social status as wives, concubines in a durable and long-term partnership with a married man do not. This difference in status usually implies a lack of automatic inheritance rights for children of the union and a precarious economic position in society for such women, whose claim to their partners' material assistance is far more open to contest.

? We have talked about the importance of not looking at other family structures through our own lens of experience. It might be assumed that polygyny (men having more than one wife) is always disadvantageous to women. Under what circumstances might this practice increase a woman's ability to survive and prosper?

Despite these shifts, feminists still tend to emphasize that many aspects of marriage place men at a distinct advantage. In her famous analysis titled *The Future of Marriage* first published in 1972, sociologist Jesse Bernard argued that in every marriage there are in reality two distinct and unequal marriages, 'his' and 'hers', that each reflect rather different experiences, expectations and outcomes (Bernard, 1982).

This analysis of marriage is the foundation for much subsequent feminist work on the extent to which the institution is the socially approved place for the ongoing domination of women by men. However, Kathy Davis (1991) cautions against the tendency in feminist thought to treat women as cultural dopes and argues that we cannot conclude that family and marital relationships are automatically disempowering for women and empowering for men. This does not mean that marriage is experienced in the same way by men and women, and that partners do not make different emotional investments in marriage. Box 5.2 discusses more recent theorizing around gender differences in relationship formation.

Box 5.2   Men, women and commitment theory

Research suggests that the processes men and women go through to arrive at the point of becoming committed to each other may be different. It has been hypothesized that men tend to commit as a result of making a decision whereas women tend to commit through attachment processes (Stanley, 2002, 2010).

A team of psychologists at Denver University has been looking at how commitment-forming behaviour in relationships is triggered differentially in partners in heterosexual relationships. Their findings have led them to theorize that attachment-forming processes (such as sharing living space and performing/receiving domestic services such as meal preparation) typically engender feelings of commitment in women, whereas men's level of commitment tends to remain unchanged until they make a conscious decision to become committed. One implication of what is becoming known as 'commitment theory' is that men and women in relationships may each perceive their level of commitment very differently but be unaware of the lack of congruence between their own and their partner's expectations.

Studies of marriage and other relationships tend to separate out what is *endogenous* to, or inside a relationship (the emotional factors such as feelings, communication style and the relative power of each partner), from what is *exogenous* or outside the couple themselves, most notably the social norms that act as a guide to what is acceptable and desirable within a relationship. Within each society there is a dominant ideology of what it means to be a couple, usually reinforced by media representations.

➔ Think about endogenous and exogenous aspects of the couple relationships you are aware of or even a part of. To what extent are the internal dynamics of a relationship affected by external factors?

This ideology is comprised of a set of cultural stereotypes about, for example, the 'right' average age of marriage, the relative worth of arranged marriages, monogamy and polygamy, and perhaps most significant for many Western societies, the importance of role equality. Georg Simmel emphasized that the conduct of relationships will ultimately be judged not by partners alone but also by social communities (Simmel, 1950). The extent to which marriages are satisfactory to partners is thus somewhat dependent on social norms and not just on how well they communicate with each other, how much they have in common and how egalitarian the relationship is. However, these aspects of marriage and intimate relationships are considered to be very important in many Western societies, although this has not always been the case, as Box 5.3 makes clear.

Box 5.3   Transitions in the meaning of marriage

The sociologist Andrew Cherlin (2004) argues that marriage has undergone a process of *deinstitutionalization* – a weakening of the social norms that define the partners' behaviour – over the past few decades. This is evident in the increasing number and complexity of cohabiting unions and the emergence of same-sex marriage. Two transitions in the meaning of marriage that occurred in many Western societies during the twentieth century have created the social context for deinstitutionalization.

The first transition, noted by Ernest Burgess, was from institutional marriage to companionate marriage (Burgess and Locke, 1945). Social changes that took place in the wake of the Second World War placed more emphasis on the emotional satisfaction of the spouses – being each other's companions, friends and lovers – for marital success and less on the importance of marriage as a social institution than in the previous era.

> The second transition was to the individualized marriage in which the emphasis on personal choice and self-development expanded. Although the practical importance of marriage has declined, its symbolic significance has remained high and may even have increased. It has become a marker of prestige and personal achievement.

In these societies sociologists describe how contemporary ideals of intimacy particularly emphasize the need for partners to relate as complete equals if they are to know each other fully. To relate as equals is achieved by being completely open with each other, in a process known as disclosure. It is argued that disclosure has become the central goal of the relationship (Giddens, 1992) but, as Jamieson points out, this seems to be 'a near impossibility for domestic partnerships and parent–child relationships that are necessarily embroiled in financial and material matters over and above the relationship' (1999: 490). In other words, relationships do not exist purely for themselves but are the context in which much care for others and other more or less mundane activity take place, the demands of which make complete equality and disclosure very difficult to achieve. Many marriages that begin with a socially approved ideology of equality find the reality dissipates, particularly when children are on the scene and one of the partners (usually but not always the woman) takes on the lion's share of domestic responsibilities including the organization of childcare (Brannen and Moss, 1992). Box 5.4 describes how the overall picture is relatively nuanced in the minority world and varies according to social background and other characteristics.

➡ Women's ongoing responsibility for the domestic sphere in many majority world contexts is discussed in more depth in Chapter 6.

Box 5.4 'Changing differences'

There has been a meaningful shift over the past 40 years in the domestic division of labour across the countries of western Europe and North America, with men contributing more both to childcare and to housework (Sullivan, 2010). Differences in patterns of domestic engagement exist between subgroups of the population (for example between those who are employed/unemployed;

(Continued)

(Continued)

better educated/less well educated; cohabiting/married; Black/White, etc.), but as these have not remained static and vary according to task, it is useful to think of them as 'changing differences' (Sullivan, 2010). Since the 1970s there has been an increase from a previously low baseline in the time spent in housework by men with lower levels of educational attainment, so that they now more closely resemble those who have above secondary level education. Over the same period, men with higher levels of educational attainment have come to contribute a substantial amount more to childcare than men with lower educational attainment.

Sociologists tend to agree that there has been a significant shift in the meaning that people attach to their relationships and therefore in the basis on which they make decisions about whether or not to continue with them, as we discuss in the next section on relationship breakdown. Whereas previously aspects of social commitment were emphasized in shared understandings of marriage, in an ideological climate that emphasizes the role of personal relationships as a principal route to self-fulfilment, there has been a marked shift towards focusing on the continuing quality of the relationship (Giddens, 1992; Jamieson, 1999). This undermines the belief not only that marriage is a lifelong commitment but also that it is necessary to marry at all. Cohabitation and other ways of organizing relationships such as 'living apart together' (see next section), are socially acceptable but not always legally recognized. This is a trend in societies which emphasizes the importance of love and self-fulfilment, to the extent that these are increasingly regarded as legitimate alternatives to marriage, a theme expanded on in Box 5.5.

Box 5.5   What is new about contemporary partnering patterns?

It is the comparable legitimacy of other partnership forms to marriage in many societies that social historians such as Stephanie Coontz point to when attempting to sum up what is genuinely different about family life in the early twenty-first century: '[W]hen it comes to any particular practice or variation on marriage, there is really nothing new under the sun. But when we look at the larger picture, it is clear that the social role and mutual relationship of marriage, divorce, and singlehood in the contemporary world is qualitatively different from anything to be found in the past. Almost any separate way of organizing family life has been tried by some society at some point in time. But the coexistence in one society of so many alternative ways of doing all of these different things – and the comparative legitimacy accorded to many of them – has never been seen before' (Coontz, 2004: 974).

COHABITATION

It is difficult to collect accurate statistics about cohabitation because entry and exit into it are less clearly marked than is the case with marriage and divorce (see Box 5.6). A further complicating factor is that cohabitation is far from being a single type of relationship or arrangement (the continuum of cohabiting relationships is described in Box 5.7). Indeed it allows couples some freedom to choose how their relationship is constructed, and the extent to which the act of setting up home together expresses a couple's marriage-like commitment to each other is variable. Allan and Crow (2001) argue that while cohabitation does make a statement about commitment, at the same time living together retains important elements of independence for many.

Box 5.6   How many people are cohabiting?

OECD statistics indicate that more than 10% of couples are cohabiting in Denmark, Estonia, Finland, France, Luxembourg and Norway. In all OECD countries, cohabitation is more frequent among adults aged from 20 to 34 years (OECD, 2010). In non-Western and less industrialized nations (terms used by the OECD to refer to the majority world), and particularly where religion has more control over family formation, it is common for cohabitation to be stigmatized and in some countries to be illegal (Tyyska, 2000), to be severely discouraged and, thus, to occur far more rarely (Pastorino and Doyle-Portillo, 2008).

Although many countries have granted legal rights to cohabitees where the relationship has lasted a reasonable length of time, part of cohabitation's attraction is that it is not formal or legal in the same way that marriage is. It does not usually represent a promise that the tie will last for ever, even if the couple embark upon it with this intention. Many see it as a trial marriage where an irreversible decision has not yet been made. Yet in reality, cohabitation still creates expectations and obligations and co-ownership of possessions that can make it increasingly more difficult to break away from the cohabiting relationship as it becomes more established (Kiernan and Estaugh, 1993). Box 5.7 describes how families structured by cohabitation can vary enormously in terms of the processes internal to these relationships.

Box 5.7   Cohabitation and commitment

In a study of unmarried parents, Smart and Stevens (2000) identified a continuum of commitment ranging from mutual to contingent. Mutual commitment is where there is some agreement on what is expected of the relationship and people have a long-term perspective. Contingent commitment characterizes a relationship maintained out of expediency; issues are not resolved but a couple stays together as long as the arrangement is working reasonably well or if it is necessitated by some external constraint like shared financial responsibility.

It is at the far end of the mutual commitment range that these relationships more closely resemble marriage although, as stated earlier, partners' commitments to each other are not necessarily accompanied by a legal recognition of the relationship.

⟵——————————————————————————⟶

Contingent commitment   Mutual commitment

In the same way that co-residence does not always involve marriage, marriage does not always involve co-residence, illustrating again the difference between structure and process. We look later in the chapter at the phenomenon of 'living apart together' which has begun to attract researchers' attention, but there have always been married couples in different societies living separately, often for long periods of time. It is important to recognize the extent to which people freely *choose* to live in this way. In the majority world it is often the case that one partner is compelled by economic circumstance to migrate to find employment to enable their family to survive. Whether it is Egyptian men moving to oil fields, Caribbean men to pick fruit in the USA, rural fathers to cities and towns in India, or Filipino mothers to perform care work in other countries, this phenomenon is likely to increase in the global workplace. Spouses living apart, during the work week or for longer, in commuter relationships have also become more commonplace in minority world countries but they are typically less compelled by survival needs and more by a desire to maximize their career and earning potential.

SAME-SEX COUPLES AND FAMILIES

Just as the detachment of sex, co-residence and parenting from marriage is becoming increasingly common in some but not all societies, so too is the acceptance of sexual practices and identities other than what was previously seen as the heterosexual norm.

The heterosexual character of marriage has a high symbolic element which polarizes opinion and generates impassioned debate between those wishing to retain it as an essential feature and those wishing to remove it. Despite such intense controversy, many countries now have legal provisions for same-sex couples to register their partnerships.

Thereafter they are subject to the same or similar rights and responsibilities as heterosexual married couples. Countries that have taken this approach include the UK, Denmark, New Zealand, Slovenia and some parts of the USA and Australia. Other countries have gone further, often after a period of allowing registered partnerships, and have introduced full-fledged gay marriage, although Box 5.8 illuminates reasons for remaining opposition in these countries.

In the Netherlands, registered partnerships (*geregistreerd partnerschap*) were introduced in law on 1 January 1998. Although intended for same-sex couples as an alternative to marriage, registered partnerships can also be entered into by opposite-sex couples. However, a law came into effect in April 2001 allowing 'marriage to be contracted by two people of different or the same sex', which made the Netherlands the first country to recognize same-sex marriage. Other jurisdictions that have since passed similar laws include Norway, Canada, Iceland, Spain and South Africa, the only African nation to give same-sex partnerships legal recognition. At the time of writing Nigeria and Uganda, in contrast, have tabled laws to oppose same-sex marriage and other African nations such as Kenya, and for example some states in America, have punitive laws against homosexual acts. This was the case in many parts of the minority world until recent times.

Box 5.8   Opposition to same-sex marriage

In many countries where legislation is being introduced for same-sex partnerships and particularly same-sex marriage, there are a range of voices on both sides of the debate. Although Reidel (2008) points out that in Canada nearly all of the active opponents of legalization claimed to speak for a particular religious or cultural constituency, arguments were often couched in terms of concern for the rights of children to know their biological parents and be brought up by them (see Somerville, 2004).

The claim is that a key aspect of marriage is its procreative potential and that marriage established the societal norm that in entering it a man and a woman take on shared obligations to look after children born from their genetic material. Although assisted reproduction enables gay couples to have children, their relationship can never be procreative. Thus, they argue, enabling same-sex couples to marry changes the nature of a social institution which enshrines the importance to children of being raised by both biological parents. While the diverse make-up of families in many countries means that many children are not being raised in such a context (through parental death, separation or absence for economic or political reasons), they argue against eroding still further the social norm which tends to produce the best outcome for children.

(Continued)

(Continued)

The gay and lesbian community is not unanimous in calling for legal recognition for their relationships, but for almost entirely different reasons (Cheal, 2002). They are concerned that it might destroy the greater inherent flexibility and equality they perceive as characterizing their relationships, and want to avoid any association with the institution of marriage which they consider to be flawed, not least because it implies a 'heteronormativity' which they find inappropriate. In other words, they do not subscribe to many of the social norms bound up with marriage, including a heterosexual basis for relationships and family life, partly as a reaction to the homophobia-related violence and hostility, whether physical or verbal (Mason, 2002), to which many have been subjected.

Many embrace instead the notion of 'families of choice'. Weeks et al. describe how 'many non-heterosexuals are experimenting with ways of living that challenge all the assumptions of traditional heterosexual family life. Friendships – including those with ex-lovers – are being celebrated and held in esteem comparable with that of kin in traditional families' (2001: 98).

Finally, it is important to acknowledge that in the absence of legal provisions for civil partnership or same-sex marriage, or as an alternative once these have been introduced, many same-sex couples create their own commitment ceremonies. These are often bespoke and highly personalized rituals but Carol Smart emphasizes the social dimension, that these are also 'relational events set within networks of friends and family' (2007: 77). Smart's research identified three slightly different reasons that same-sex couples give for the decision to go through some kind of ceremony (although these sometimes overlapped in people's accounts). The commitment was often seen as a promise for the future, an affirmation of a shared past, or a way of shoring up a potentially fragile relationship (Smart, 2007).

➜ See Chapter 1 and the section 'Defining Families 1: Common Characteristics' for a discussion of the important place of memories and rituals in family life and the way they are often adapted to create markers of difference between families to build a distinctive identity.

CHILDREN RAISED BY SAME-SEX COUPLES

The success of what Silverstein and Auerbach (2005) refer to as the gay civil rights movement has been a marked increase in lesbians, gay men and bisexual and transgender individuals forming families: men and women living an openly gay lifestyle forming households which often involve children. (The acronym LGBT is often used to refer to lesbian, gay, bisexual and transgender individuals as a group, although this is not unanimously accepted among the populations so designated.) Previously many gay women and men who were keen to have children would have done so in a heterosexual union and would have more or less concealed their gay identity from others if not themselves. It was much rarer for those openly living in a same-sex relationship to bring up children together.

As legislation changes in many countries, gay men are now increasingly able to adopt children or procreate with the assistance of a surrogate mother or a lesbian or heterosexual woman. Asssited Reproduction Technology (ART) also enables lesbian couples to have children together. Precise figures on the prevalence of these families are hard to obtain as many are reluctant to disclose their lifestyle because of ongoing stigma. Certainly statistics on the last census in the UK in 2001 found that only 0.3% of all couples live together as same-sex couples. At the same point in the USA, Patterson and Friel (2000) estimated a range of between 800,000 and seven million LGBT parents raising 1.6 and 14 million children. Statistics Netherlands reported that the number of same-sex couples has risen in recent years but couples registered form less than 1.5% of all known relationships (Steenhof and Harmsen, 2002).

The diversity found among many heterosexually based families is also found in the living arrangements of LGBT couples and their children. From their research Silverstein and Auerbach (2005) describe families where the gay father lived next door to the lesbian mothers of children who had rooms in the homes of both parents. Other gay and lesbian individuals decide to parent alone from the outset or after separating from a previous partner. Another option is to move in with a new partner and form an LGBT step-family.

MOVING APART: BREAKDOWN AND DIVORCE

As we said earlier, the most important family events are changes in family composition, entries but also exits of members through death, estrangement and the breakdown of couples' relationships. The last category is the focus of this section. Divorce rates increased substantially in most minority world societies between the 1960s and the end of the 1980s (Cheal, 2002) while other countries have experienced a later rise. In China the divorce rate rose rapidly from less than 5% of marriages in 1980 to 13% in 1997, although it was much higher in major cities such as Beijing and Shanghai, reaching 25% (Chen and He, 2005). The upward trend has continued with year on year increases; for example, 1.71 million couples divorced in 2009, up 10.3% from the previous year (Ministry of Civil Affairs, 2009). Similarly, Korea's divorce rate nearly quintupled between 1980 and 2004, from 0.6 per thousand of the population to 2.9 (OECD, 2009a). Despite a very low national divorce rate in India (Laungani, 2005) large cities are seeing a rise in divorce. Court statistics show that for every five marriages contracted in Mumbai between 2002 and 2007, two applications for divorce were filed (*Times of India*, 2008).

> **?** Why do you think the divorce rate in rapidly industrializing countries such as India and China is rising so fast? What challenges will this present to the governments of these countries and where would the difficulties lie in trying to address these social trends?

Higher divorce rates often mean the formation of more single-parent families, with the policy implications for governments described in Chapter 4. Given the greater acceptability of cohabitation in the minority world and the tendency for cohabiting relationships to be less stable, it is important to be aware of the breakdown of these less formalized relationships (Kiernan, 2003). Silverstein and Auerbach (2005) point out that in high divorce societies, separating from a partner is rarely an isolated event, with, they say, about 50% of (heterosexual) couples now embarking on a journey of serial coupling/uncoupling that often extends over the lifecourse. Cheal (2002) concurs that serial relationships are increasingly the norm and that it is now less useful to think in terms of a 'typical family lifecycle' than of the highly variable sequence of relationships and family transitions that people go through.

WHY DO RELATIONSHIPS BREAK DOWN?

Families have always been subject to the shock of one partner or parent leaving, although historically this was more likely to be due to early death, frequently in childbirth (Thane, 2010). However, the international increase in the prevalence of divorce and separation has excited much sociological interest (González and Viitanen, 2009) and although, to paraphrase the opening line of Tolstoy's novel *Anna Karenina*, every unhappy couple is unhappy in their own way, researchers have identified some common causes of relationship breakdown.

While violence and abuse between intimate partners are not at all new, in many societies across the world (but by no means all) it is becoming increasingly acceptable to leave a relationship where these destructive practices occur. This is not always an easy step to take, not least because intimacy can still exist in an abusive relationship and children are frequently involved. Leaving a partner often means that any children will lose contact with one of the parents (in some cultures mothers may only be able to leave, for their own safety, if their children remain with an abusive husband or his family). Finally, economic survival is usually far harder to achieve on one's own.

Relationships in many countries are also under significant pressure from the high expectations that now come with marriage and intimate partnerships. Couples part on the grounds of incompatibility, disagreement over roles, breach of trust (particularly in cases of infidelity) and inability to communicate well with each other. Many relationships that begin with the expectation that they will last for life can founder when the quality of the relationship is perceived to have diminished. The transition to parenthood, for example, is a time when relationship quality can fall markedly, particularly if there is inadequate support from extended family and wider social networks (Cowan and Cowan, 1995, 2008).

Allan and Crow state that 'Changes in the emotionality of the love tie can be experienced as indicative of its "failure" and as grounds for terminating the relationship' (2001: 62). Yet it is important to bear in mind, as we said in the last section, that this emphasis on the emotional content of marriage (in particular) for the individuals concerned, over and above its social functions, is fairly new in historical terms and still cannot be taken for granted in some societies. Women's earning power also makes it somewhat easier for them to leave relationships they find unsatisfying or abusive (Becker, 1993).

Naito and Gielen (2005) describe a shift in Japan since 1960 from the 'traditional' type of divorce that occurred when a wife could not adapt to living with her husband's extended family, to the 'modern' type of divorce that is typically due to partners' incompatible expectations of each other and their relationship. Partners now expect greater equality within marriage to the extent that women in particular are now more willing to terminate the relationship if, for example, they have tried and failed to achieve an equitable sharing of household tasks (Silverstein and Auerbach, 2005).

Exclusivity has always been important in intimate relationships not least because marriage 'ordered' society but also because of the monogamous ideal adhered to in many contexts (even in polygamous societies, socially acceptable sexual relations are usually restricted to other wives and husbands). Contemporary Western expectations that couples will be completely open with each other are perhaps most devastatingly confounded when illicit sexual relations take place and affairs are discovered; research from the USA has found that infidelity was the most commonly cited cause of divorce (Amato and Previti, 2003).

Good communication between couples is valued and considered necessary to resolve interpersonal differences or overcome difficulties external to the relationship which can put intense pressure on it. These include having and bringing up children (and becoming step-parents), financial crises, redundancy, illness and disability, death and retirement. These ubiquitous strains, and the high social and emotional costs associated with relationship breakdown, have led some to conclude that it would be sensible for societies to engage in widespread preparation of members for intimate relationships (Stanley et al., 2006). Educational programmes designed to generate reasonable expectations and to modify or even eliminate unrealistic expectations for love, sexuality and personal fulfilment are suggested by Bernardes (1997). Although these now exist in many countries (Benson and Callan, 2009) take-up and cultural acceptance remain low.

? Given that lifelong learning and continuous professional development are valued pursuits in many minority world societies, why do you think couples who want their relationships to succeed would be reluctant to undertake 'relationship education'?

WHAT CHANGES AFTER DIVORCE AND WHAT STAYS THE SAME?

Although divorce and separation bring about significant changes in family composition, researchers are increasingly drawing attention to what stays the same in the wake of relationship breakdown. Obligations, even to former in-laws, can continue beyond divorce despite the absence of formal links and the lack of a conventional kinship terminology with which people can describe one another (Cheal, 2002). Finch and Mason (1993) explain that the history of interpersonal relationships (how well people 'got on' and what they went through together) is key to understanding why some people sustain close and supportive relationships after divorce while others cut off contact completely. However, biological ties of descent take priority and obligations remain, for example, between grandparents and grandchildren and particularly between parents and children.

Social norms, supported by legislation, are shifting away from treating a complete split between divorced partners as being in the best interests of any children involved, and are moving towards an expectation that parental relationships will continue, albeit in a different form. In what has been termed the 'durability model' of post-divorce family life, divorce does not necessarily bring an end to the family (Thompson and Amato, 1999) and the loss of a wide range of relationships. Others have described the existence of 'post-marital marriage' (Beck and Beck-Gernsheim, 1995: 145) and the need for former partners to be able to communicate and work together even after separation in order to create the most congenial environment for their children.

Thus, policy makers in various countries, such as Australia, have developed measures to assist parents going through divorce and separation to help them build relational skills that will enable them to co-parent with their ex-partner (Parkinson, 2006), as was described in Chapter 4. The development of such measures always requires mediating between different and often sharply contested interests. Single-parent organizations, largely but not exclusively representing mothers, tend to be concerned with securing adequate child maintenance (financial support from ex-partners) and guarantees of safety in any post-separation contact arrangements (where there has been any history of domestic abuse). Fathers' rights organizations focus on whether post-separation arrangements promote parents' ability to maintain a sufficient level of contact to maintain a relationship with their children.

?   Think about the relationship 'splits' you are aware of that have involved children. What kinds of arrangements have been made to enable both parents to spend time with their children? How have fathers' and mothers' housing provision affected decisions made about how many nights are spent under each parents' roof? What other factors have been taken into account?

BEING TOGETHER AND LIVING APART: SOLO LIVING, FRIENDSHIPS AND SOCIAL NETWORKS

Just as one's family is larger than the nuclear and co-resident set of marital/couple, parent–child and sibling relationships, we also have a variety of meaningful relationships which go beyond those with the people with whom we live and who are in our extended family. Most if not all of these relationships are non-sexual and would not be characterized as intimate, but they are an important part of what Pahl and Spencer (2003) refer to as one's personal community, the set of active and significant ties which are most important to people even if they are geographically distant. This set of ties includes family and friends, and it also includes one or more and usually several social networks. This section begins with a look at how living on one's own does not preclude intimate relationships (described in Box 5.9) or strong connections with family, followed by a consideration of what role friendship plays in personal communities, whether that role is markedly different from family relationships, and how important both are to social networks.

Box 5.9   What is intimacy?

Intimacy is a relative term concerned with the closeness we feel to someone, a process 'by which a couple – in expression of thought, emotion or behaviour – attempts to move towards more complete communication on all levels' (Zinn and Eitzen, 1990: 221). Bernardes (1997) explains that while many personal relationships lack a sexual base and many sexual relationships lack a personal dimension, sexuality is often key to an intimate partnership.

See Chapter 2 for a discussion of contemporary voices on intimacy, and the ways in which gender, sexuality and intimate relationships are connected with 'reflexivity': in which we observe and reflect upon our social world and ultimately reshape it in the process (Jamieson, 1998).

'COUPLENESS' OUTSIDE OF COHABITATION

Sexual relations are not restricted to those we live with (whether married or cohabiting) although the legitimacy of extramarital intercourse varies between societies. In many societies, sex is now often an accepted part of dating relationships in which partners may or may not be on a journey towards greater commitment and/or setting up home together. Sociologists of personal life are increasingly aware that not living with a partner does not necessarily mean not having a partner – established couples are not always co-resident (Roseneil, 2006). The term living apart together, or LAT, has been introduced to describe this relationship type. Numbers of those in LAT relationships are significant in some countries; LAT is generally viewed as monogamous in nature and an arrangement that is more than a temporary, fleeting, or casual relationship (Haskey, 2005: 36).

A UK National Statistics study of non-residential relationships (Haskey, 2005) found that roughly the number of people in LAT partnerships is the same as those cohabiting. Numbers may be rising, for example in Sweden; data suggest the prevalence of LAT relationships among those aged 18–74 who were neither married nor cohabiting increased from 6% in 1993 to 14% in 2001 (Levin, 2004).

People live apart together for a variety of reasons. The structure of state benefits can be a disincentive to living with a partner (Draper, 2009). Levin (2004) found that some are more or less forced to live separately by travel demands placed on them by their careers, while others prefer to do so because they are caring for children from a previous relationship or for elderly parents. Older people are often concerned they will jeopardize their children's inheritance by moving in with a partner. Some have previously cohabited and then decided to live separately, but maintain their relationship. Roseneil's research (2006) also identified an 'undecidedly apart' category which contained couples whose attitudes to their relationships were much more contingent, unsettled and insecure. 'Moving in' entailed a commitment they were not yet ready or willing to make. While sociologists are treating LAT as a fairly recent phenomenon, 'visiting' relationships have been very common among for example, young, low-income African Caribbean people for 150 years (Silverstein and Auerbach, 2005), with most sexual relationships and childbearing taking place outside of a cohabiting relationship until people are in their late 30s or significantly older.

> **?** Think about the 'living apart together' relationships you are aware of – what reasons are you aware of for people maintaining separate households?

WHY ELSE DO PEOPLE LIVE ALONE?

Since the early 1970s a new and significant trend away from family households and towards solo households has been identified across Europe (Hall et al., 1997). Although solo living tends to be seen as 'normal' only at certain stages of life and there remain strong social expectations that people will and possibly should partner 'before too long' (Bernardes, 1997), the reality in some societies is a growing number of people living alone at *all* ages of adulthood (Jamieson, 2010a). Forty years ago, in the UK, the majority of people living alone were over retirement age and female (women are more likely to be widowed than men). Since then, the number of working-age people living alone has grown to match the number among pensioners, and the number of men living alone has grown more rapidly than the number of women. Under the age of 55, more men than women live on their own (Office for National Statistics, 2009a). Europe-wide, young people show an increasing propensity to live alone, the numbers of those divorcing or never marrying is rising and, with the 'greying' of the population, the proportion of elderly people is rising. While it is rare in some countries for elderly people to live with their adult children, it is more common in others. One example is Russia, where there are acute housing shortages, and where three-generation households are formed out of necessity (Rimashevskaya et al., 1999).

> → Topic 1: The Impact of Welfare Regimes on Families, Chapter 1, looks in more detail at living conditions in the Russian Federation since changes took place in the political regime between 1989 and 1991.

Jamieson (2010a) makes the important observation that while people living alone may not be families, most have families and their engagement with their family is of great importance. When adults who live alone were asked in a British study about what recent events they personally regarded as important, they were almost as likely to mention other family members as were those living in married households (Cheal, 2002). Similarly, d'Abbs' (1991) Australian research on who people wanted to receive help from when they became incapable of coping on their own revealed a strong preference for family-based care.

> **?** Think about who you would go to for help, in what circumstances and in what order. How often do family members feature or are friends more prevalent?

BEYOND THE FAMILY – FRIENDSHIPS

We have already noted the variety of people's meaningful relationships that go beyond the boundaries of the family, but these boundaries are in fact highly permeable. In Chapter 1 we described the importance of 'fictive kin' – godparents and other unrelated 'uncles' and 'aunts' – particularly for children, but gerontologists note that professional carers act as pseudo-kin for the very elderly (Pahl and Spencer, 2003).

However, we also value highly our 'friend-like' relationships because of the ways they differ from those we have with family, particularly the extent to which they are chosen by us, rather than given. The French poet, Jacques Delille (1738–1813) said 'Our relatives are ours by chance, but choice makes our friends'. It is important to acknowledge the range and diversity of friend-like relationships. Some are simple, based on just one main type of interaction, such as the infrequent exchange of neighbourly favours, whereas others are more complex and multifaceted, involving emotional support and the exchange of personal confidences as well as shared interests and companionship.

Sometimes we refer to close friends as being 'like family', where the relationship has been of long duration, lasting through many ups and downs and proving its durability and absolute reliability. For example, we might say, 'He was like a brother to me'. However, family relationships which grow close and highly important to individuals may also more closely resemble friendships as there is an element of a soulmate having been *chosen*. For example, a mother-in-law may, after several years, begin to be seen as more of a friend and a confidante by her daughter-in-law, but not because that is her ascribed role in the family. On the contrary, relationships with in-laws can be very strained (Apter, 2009).

These kinds of practices challenge any easy categorization of relationships with friends as being chosen and those with family as being given – in fact some friendships can begin to be taken for granted in the way that is usually more common with family relationships, making them feel fixed and given. This is significant because some sociologists emphasize the growth of what they call 'families of choice' especially among many non-heterosexuals, which is seen as a shift away from the importance of given family relationships in favour of freely chosen ones (Weeks et al., 2001). Yet this blurring of the edges between friends and family that has always taken place suggests this is less of an innovation than is claimed.

Further, Roseneil (2005) cautions that using the term 'families of choice' to describe the friendship networks which characterize lesbian and gay communities can detract from an understanding of what is distinctive, *extra*-familial and radically 'counter-heteronormative' about many of these relationships.

SOCIAL NETWORKS

All of our relationships function in social networks, sets of people to whom we are connected directly or indirectly in various ways. As well as friends and family, we all interact with an enormous variety of people for very different reasons and thus it is more helpful to think about types of personal networks rather than a single social network (Dragon and Duck, 2005). Milardo (1992) has identified four types of personal networks: one's *significant others*, usually parents, close friends and kin; *exchange networks*, those who provide material or other support; *interactive networks*, those with whom interactions typically occur (such as work colleagues we greet in the corridor or people we acknowledge in the village); and *global networks*, all the people we know, some of whom we very rarely if ever see. Those who have access to social networking sites, email, texting and other forms of more or less instant communication, are likely to have a global network running into thousands of individuals. (Without taking the communication possibilities of the Internet into account, Milardo estimated a global network size of 1,700 individuals +/– 400 for North Americans and one of 570 +/– 460 for adults in Mexico City.)

> **?**   Think about your own personal networks. Do you think Milardo's typology is comprehensive or are there people you know who do not seem to fit into any of these types?

COMMUNITIES AND NEIGHBOURHOODS

We have noted that relationships function within social networks and personal communities. They are also *spatially* embedded in physical communities and neighbourhoods (see Box 5.10 for a discussion of how these overlapping phrases tend to be used). Many of our active and significant ties are with people who are geographically distant, yet electronic means of communication (also known as 'relational technology') make these increasingly possible to sustain. Relationships with those who live in close proximity to us and our immediate family, but who are outside our kin and friendship networks, are also impor-tant. Morgan (1996) describes these as 'relationships beyond the household', and these are evident when we see people talking at street corners, outside their front doors, at the bus stop or at the bazaar. These interactions may be brief, fleeting and isolated events (one may talk to a particular neighbour very rarely or even just once), but being able to have them is a significant part of feeling that one 'belongs' to a locale.

Box 5.10 Can the terms 'community' and 'neighbourhood' be used interchangeably?

Although the term 'community' is often applied to a group of people who hold something important in common (for example, we talk about the political com-munity, the student community or the social work community) this term can also refer to people living in a common location who interact on a frequent if not daily basis. Thus there is much overlap between the notions of community and neigh-bourhood, but it is far more common for the latter to be restricted to the imme-diate environment, surroundings or district where people live. Hilder (2005: 118) states that 'Neighbourhood means living together in a particular place, its vital foundations are proximity and commonality'. However, he also reminds us that nations live in neighbourhoods too, so the term has application across a broad range of scale.

Although we have very different expectations about what we can receive from those in our community (usually it is far less in comparison with family members), research shows that such weak ties are becoming increasingly important in neighbourhoods, helping to provide a feeling of home, security and practical as well as social support (Henning and Lieberg, 1996). One of the reasons we can feel lonely when we move house is because it takes a while before we begin to recognize people we pass on the street. The length of time it can take before neighbours begin to treat newcomers as if they are part of the community can vary greatly from one society to another, with sig-nificant within-country variation. Given how long it can take to integrate, and the transitional insecurity we can feel, we do not readily give up that sense of attachment to a neighbourhood; UK data recently suggested that two-thirds of house moves are within a five-mile radius (Future Foundation, 2003).

THE EFFECTS OF NEIGHBOURHOODS AND COMMUNITIES ON FAMILIES

From the outset of this chapter we started with a focus on the family and then worked our way into the wider community. Yet historically, certainly in British sociology, the study of family relationships tended to be woven into studies of communities as a whole. Morgan (1996) draws out the merits of this close identification of family and community, not least that it encourages thinking about family relationships in a wider context of overlapping ties of family, kindred, friends and neighbours. It also helps to identify continuities between work and non-work, home and the workplace, and the public and private parts of life. Earlier chapters of this book have emphasized the importance, when thinking about family, of going beyond a narrow focus on a limited range of marital and parental relationships.

The social and geographical environment matters greatly, in designing social policy, when trying to understand what helps families 'produce' satisfactory outcomes for all members but especially for children. Neighbourhood effects can significantly influence how families function, with some areas experiencing a particular concentration of inter-linked disadvantages that make life very different from that experienced just a few streets away. Slums in Nairobi and Bangalore exist in close proximity to far wealthier areas. It is not at all unusual for sharply contrasting neighbourhoods with significant inequalities in infant mortality and life expectancy to exist cheek by jowl with one another.

While resident families strongly influence the character of a neighbourhood, effects of the latter make it hard to break out of cycles of disadvantage. US policy researcher Ooms describes how 'Low-income families, especially those who reside in poverty neighbourhoods, are daily exposed to a variety of experiences that place extraordinary stress on the couple and family relationships ... they have the frustrations of living in substandard housing in poorly serviced neighbourhoods, without adequate transportation and they and their children are continually in fear of crime and violence ... In addition black and other minority individuals are constantly exposed in the workplace or on the streets to incidents of racism and discrimination' (2002: 88). Finally, the pervasive and corrosive effects of violent locality-based gang culture have led researchers to conclude that it is far better for young people's life chances to come from a troubled family in a good neighbourhood than to be in a good family in a troubled neighbourhood (Newcastle City Council, 2009).

> ➡ Think about the neighbourhood you grew up in. Compared with the influence of your parents, how much did the people and place itself shape your attitudes, and, for example, make it easier or harder to pursue education?

SEXUALIZED SOCIETIES

Earlier in the chapter we described how expectations shape relationships and affect our likelihood of remaining in them. They are also significantly affected by pervasive cultural influences such as what has been termed 'the sexualization of society'. Anthony Giddens (1992) describes how the separation of sexuality from reproduction (and of reproduction from sexuality through the development of ARTs such as *in vitro* fertilization) has made sex a vehicle for self-expression and self-actualization. Moreover, the development of what he refers to as 'plastic sexuality' has encouraged very real changes in the social order because sex has been transformed into a commercial commodity, a means to sell goods (Weeks, 1991).

The media (television, music videos, music lyrics, movies, magazines, sports media, video games, the Internet, and advertising) creation of an erotic environment in which all kinds of 'possibilities' are portrayed, generates expectations surrounding sexual activity that can be unrealistic and detrimental to relationships (Bernardes, 1997). For example, media images emphasize a narrow (and virtually unobtainable) standard of physical beauty which places exacting demands on men and women, and particularly on young people. American Psychological Association research has linked exposure to sexualized female ideals with lower self-esteem, negative mood and depressive symptoms among adolescent girls and women (American Psychological Association, 2009). Schooler and Ward (2006) describe how exposure to narrow ideals of female sexual attractiveness may make it difficult for some men to find an 'acceptable' partner or fully enjoy intimacy with a female partner.

There is concern in many industrial societies about the effects on children of being exposed from an early age to the prevalence of sexual images in the media. If sex is everywhere and used to sell anything and everything, and casual, short-term and unfaithful relationships are prevalent on films and television (e.g. in 'soap operas'), this subverts expectations that long-term relationships are possible or even desirable. Where sex is treated as an automatic part of relationships this can reduce (particularly) young women's sense of agency or being in control of their own sexuality.

ENDURING RELATIONSHIPS: GENERATING HISTORIES

➔ Across Chapter 1 we highlight the importance of memories in defining families. Recap what is said on page 24 about how memories generate shared history.

This chapter has outlined many of the pressures relationships are under such as interpersonal difficulties, unrealistic expectations, poverty, poor housing, demanding employment requirements (including the need to migrate very long distances to generate an income) and family 'shocks' such as bereavement or financial crisis. Yet in spite of often very significant challenges, many families do keep in close contact and a surprising number of couples stay together throughout the lifecourse. Given the amount of family-based and particularly spousal care that takes place in most if not all societies, this has important social policy implications.

Although in many societies strong familial obligations dictate that care and contact will be ongoing regardless of the quality of relationships, where such obligations are less defined, for example in the USA and Britain, the wider family connections people maintain in later life depend in part on the history of those relationships in earlier life phases (Finch and Mason, 1993). Schneider (1968) described the 'diffuse, enduring solidarity' that particularly characterizes parent–child relationships later in life; few children and parents lose contact completely with each other, but there are no set rules to interactions, and reciprocity is not the dominant consideration. 'Each relationship has its own logic, with that logic being structured over time by the different configurations of interest and commitments both sides have. One way is to think of each relationship having its own "trajectory" with its future patterning depending in part on the "route" it has taken earlier' (Allan and Crow, 2001: 182).

In the main, ongoing interaction and sharing of lives with family members can provide a major source of continuity in individuals' evolving life stories (Coleman et al., 1999; Morgan, 1996). Being a family means, in part, sharing memories of past events and transitions, though this may not be done harmoniously or in complete agreement. Many families bemoan the fact that they only get together for weddings and funerals, yet assembling together to mark these important milestones and to witness 'rites of passage' builds on the foundation of a jointly maintained and completely unique 'history'. Thus, by doing this 'memory work', families constitute or reconstitute themselves (Morgan, 1996). Cheal (2002) refers to 'voices off stage' in a family, and those with whom people interact in family contexts, through memory work, are not just those people who are physically present in time and place but are also people who are physically distant or even dead.

> ➜ In Chapter 1 we saw how memories, along with values, spaces and places, are an important part of what defines families.

Informal monitoring of family pasts and memories can take on a more formal character in many societies, with a growing interest in genealogies, personal family histories (the details of forebears, not just their names in a family tree, however far back that might stretch) and popular television programmes that go back into the ancestry of current celebrities. Australia, with its roots in a displaced indigenous population and shiploads of transported convicts, has in particular seen the growth of a 'massive industry' of genealogy (Curthoys, 1993). Morgan (1996) suggests that in societies where this is common, it reflects in part the multiple discontinuities brought about by migration, war, divorce and separation, which may compel people to seek out some sense of having the past somehow under their control.

ENDURING INTIMACY

Given the number of partnerships that do not last, long-lasting couple relationships cannot be taken for granted although they are somewhat under-researched (Gutteridge, 2003). The psychologist Janet Reibstein reports from her interviews with 200 couples (from the

USA and the UK) who had been together for more than nine years, and some for over half a century, that 'being in a marriage-like partnership … is the central, transformational and ever-replenishing relationship of their lives' (2006:3). Although stories differed greatly she noted that 'every individual love story today pivots around the same conundrums: the tension between individual freedom and commitment, the task of regenerating mutual interest and desire in the teeth of predictability and routine, the need for security and stability against the push for novelty and the sheer difficulty of the economy of time and energy for each other within two complex lives. All these over increasingly long lives' (Reibstein, 2006: 7).

While there is no doubt that there are many couples across the world remaining together throughout the lifecourse because of the dictates of finance, social custom or because one partner is fearful of leaving, Carol Smart's (2007) plea that we remember the emotionality of relationships is worth recalling at this point. The meanings people attach to getting together and staying together are vital to our wider understanding of why families matter so much to people and just how deep-seated familial relationships are for each new generation.

SUMMARY

This chapter, which draws on preceding material, particularly in Chapters 1, 2 and 4, underlines the extent to which relationships, 'saturated with emotions, feelings and affect' (Smart, 2007: 53), are of substantial importance not only to individuals but also to society itself. This is strikingly evident at the level of popular culture virtually everywhere. Whether in tribal mythology, soap operas or obsession with the 'wives and girl-friends' ('WAGs') of famous sportsmen, there is a strong folk tradition around relationships that explores issues of love, passion, duty, honour, shame, property inheritance, incest, wealth, (im)propriety and racial purity (Bernardes 1997). This acknowledges that emotional, or a more prosaic, but socially acknowledged, commitment to a partner sends ripples throughout the larger network to which couples belong. These media also convey culturally recognized standards for the internal organization of relationships, such as guidelines for who should do domestic and other tasks within a marriage and what equates to good relationship conduct.

Societal and sociological forces influence how we *see* relationships and the goals of relationships are not universally the same. When couples get together the Western emphasis on individual preference and falling in love contrasts with other cultures that look at the good accruing to families overall and ask whether or not this is a good match for them as well as for the individuals concerned. Treating wider relationships as ends in themselves, vehicles for achieving personal growth and emotional closeness, will also be far more prevalent in societies where physical, social and political survival is not at stake. In subsistence tribes, such as the Himba of north-western Namibia, people will, to a much greater extent, depend on their ties to search collectively for food, and it is not unreasonable to suggest that 'liking one another' will be a lower priority. Such broadbrush cultural differences must not, however, distract from the significant variation that also exists *within* societies, social networks and individuals' lives in terms of what drives the formation and maintenance of all types of relationships (or, returning to our themes, what determines the structure of families and the internal processes keeping them together). The common longing for deep, lasting and exclusive emotional bonding we described at the end of Chapter 1 is often thwarted. Families can encounter a range of pressures including interpersonal difficulties, geographical distance or other pressures rooted in economic issues.

EXPLORE FURTHER

Coontz, S. (2005) *Marriage, a History: From Obedience to Intimacy, or How Love Conquered Marriage*. New York: Viking.

Cowan, C.P. and Cowan, P.A. (1992) *When Partners Become Parents: The Big Life Change For Couples*. New York: Basic Books. Republished by Lawrence Erlbaum Associates, Fall, 1999.

Duck, S. (2007) *Human Relationships*, 4th edn. Thousand Oaks, CA: Sage.

Finch, J. and Mason, J. (1993) *Negotiating Family Responsibilities*. London: Routledge.

Jamieson, L. (1999) 'Intimacy transformed? A critical look at the "pure relationship"', *Sociology*, 33(3): 477–94.

Smart, C. (2007) *Personal Life: New Directions in Sociological Thinking*. Cambridge: Polity Press.

USEFUL WEBSITES

Professor Scott Stanley from Denver University Psychology Department, moderates and is the main contributor to The Sliding vs Deciding™ blog about relationships, especially about marriage and romantic relationships. Most of the entries contain small, research-based insights about how relationships develop, or about what makes or breaks relationships over time. See www.slidingvsdeciding.blogspot.com/

For more publications that focus on how couple relationships interact with parenting in family systems, see Professor Philip Cowan's University of Berkeley profile at http://psychology.berkeley.edu/faculty/profiles/pcowan.html

The Australian Family Relationships Clearinghouse website has several sections looking at research on different types of couples and how relationships are formed. See www.aifs.gov.au/afrc/

6

Families and Work

Keywords: paid work, unpaid work, domestic labour, poverty, gender, policy, transnational migration

INTRODUCTION

Work infuses our life whether that work is paid or unpaid, undertaken in the home or in other locations. Work, in all its varied forms is critical to the goal of securing a level of sustenance for families and the possibility of anticipating and planning for family futures. Flexible working hours and work undertaken outside the office aided by mobile communication and other technologies are among the changes that offer challenges and opportunities for family members to negotiate when managing home and work life. Families and individuals gain identity, status and focus, security, and a future through paid work (Hurst, 2004). Paid work cannot be undertaken without the unpaid tasks of, for example, cooking and cleaning. The daily activities undertaken in and around families involve work whether this is paid, unpaid or a combination of these.

Work can be defined as physical or mental activity and effort to produce or accomplish something (de Botton, 2010). The process and outcomes of work can vary from purchasing food and producing a meal, to completing a report on the sales of fruit and vegetables for your departmental manager. The former is generally unpaid and takes place in a domestic context while the latter is paid and conducted in a workplace. The boundaries between these types of work are increasingly blurred, especially for those with the main domestic responsibilities, unless these are genuinely evenly shared (Edgell, 2006). Money and resources, generated by paid work, underpin these tasks and allow us to purchase food. It is not unusual for a worker, often but by no means always a female, to take time during a lunch break or on the way home to decide on the food to buy and the meal to produce.

> **?** Think about the work you have undertaken in the last 24 hours. Make a note of some of the tasks. How much was paid or unpaid? Do you link the paid and unpaid tasks in any way?

DEFINING AND EXPLAINING WORK

For the purposes of this book we define paid work as all forms of labour which receive payment in cash or benefit in kind in lieu of pay. Central to this definition is the labour market and how people sell and develop their labour power through education, training and participation in paid work (Ransome, 1999). The factors of social class, gender, ethnicity and age continue to determine many dimensions of a person's job, rate of pay and benefits, future opportunities, and amount and nature of unpaid work (Hurst, 2004). As Grint (2005) reminds us, while work is activity based, whether we consider we are in a job or career locates individuals and their families. A career presupposes that an individual has secured qualifications, can identify a 'career path' and, as a consequence, a level of status in working life which increases their social standing more generally. To be in a job suggests paid work is the main method of gaining a level of income for day-to-day and longer-term sustainability of the person and their family.

On occasions people may talk of a dead end job, referring to the low pay or relative insecurity of the paid work they are engaged in. By contrast, gaining entry to a profession or occupation may take years of education, training and working through stages of practice to gain experience; for example, a doctor who decides to specialize or a lawyer who trains for a specific topic such as criminal or corporate law. As a student they may have engaged in dead end jobs in a bar or supermarket. Now in a professional occupation their futures are more secure than those of many others. The benefits of an occupational pension and access to other workplace policies and services (such as flexible working and health and social benefits) add to the sense of belonging to an occupational group. The skills and experiences that can develop in professional occupations are recognized in the world of paid work and enhance social standing of the individual and their families through association.

?   List three occupations and three jobs. What distinguishes the jobs from the occupations? Which are associated with a career and why?

UNDEREMPLOYMENT AND UNEMPLOYMENT

People may experience underemployment at particular points in their lives. For example, an accountant, returning to work following maternity leave, may accept an administrative job to rejoin the labour market. This decision may be a compromise so as to work in more flexible ways, including part-time working, or to be located close to home and domestic tasks. In times of economic change and recession various groups of workers may find themselves underemployed, and students in higher education, working part-time during their degree course, are also unlikely to be in jobs that are relevant to their qualifications or aspirations. Groups of workers with less secure positions in labour markets are over-represented in this category of underemployment for a range of factors that are often related to the opportunities available and to the management of paid and unpaid work (Hakim, 2000; Crompton, 2006; Edgell, 2006).

Unemployment can have severe consequences for families, especially in societies which have no or limited access to welfare benefits linked to unemployment (Spicker, 2000; Leeder, 2004; Cusworth, 2009). Further, certain groups and social categories are over-represented among the unemployed, particularly during periods of economic downturn; younger and older people, and those in lower skilled or sectors of work superseded by technological change (Edgell, 2006). A recent report published by the UK Equality and Human Rights Commission (2010) demonstrates how groups affected by periods of technological change and economic downturn vary. The report concluded that in 2009 it was young people, those living in deprived areas and men who suffered the biggest rises in unemployment. However, the commission predicted that in the following one to two years this situation would change as cuts in the public sector take effect. Women, disabled, black and ethnic minority groups who are over-represented in public sector and low paid jobs, will be hit hard, especially those on temporary or fixed-term contracts (Trades Union Congress, 2009).

> **?**   Unemployment can be defined as being out of formal paid work. Each month governments calculate the numbers of people defined as unemployed. These calculated figures are reported in the media. Unemployment statistics are viewed as an indicator of social cohesion and the source of some concern. Why are governments and societies so concerned about unemployment? And why does unemployment among the young, ethnic groups or disabled people raise particular concerns?

Unemployment in any family dents the ability to maintain household standards of living. It also challenges core identity, given the prominence of paid work to social standing and well-being. For some who are unemployed the associated stigma may be a factor in substance misuse, self-harm and suicide, such is the powerful force of paid work in identity formation and survival (Layard et al., 2005). Letkemann (2002) has drawn attention to the ways in which some male workers in Tokyo attempt to conceal unemployment by continuing to leave for and return from 'work' at the usual times of day. To be without a ready source of money in cash-based economies is extremely difficult. However, being unemployed does not necessarily preclude involvement in paid work. Casual labour in the informal economy allows people to be paid 'cash in hand' (Grint, 2005).

BOUNDARIES: PAID AND UNPAID WORK

Unpaid work includes all domestic labour. Many aspects of unpaid work may, however, also constitute paid work, for example, child minding, washing, ironing and cleaning. It is no coincidence that these tasks, whether paid or unpaid, are often deemed to be feminine skills, undertaken by women. While valued by those in receipt of the activities, such work often fails to receive the status or pay that might be expected (see Office for National Statistics, 2009b). This form of work is discussed in more detail in later sections of this chapter.

> **?**   In Chapter 1 we noted that roles in families can be determined by gender and assumptions are made about who does what. A 2007 survey of housework in Europe found a 53% female–male difference. In Greece this was 75% and in Denmark 21% (Voicu et al., 2007). Why are men doing more housework in Denmark than Greece? What are the implications for paid work of both women and men?
>
> These trends have broader implications as caring and people skills and tasks are disproportionately undertaken by women in both unpaid and paid labour. List some jobs or occupations based on caring skills.

Some employers seek to blur the boundaries between paid and unpaid work through the creation of residential communities close to the place of work. For example, in previous centuries, the religious community of Quakers combined work and non-work through 'religious missions and commercial travelling' (Davidoff and Hall, 1987: 216). Other examples in the UK include the Bourneville village created by the Cadbury family in the late nineteenth century, and Port Sunlight created by the Lever brothers around the factory producing Sunlight soap. In Brazil, Henry Ford created Fordlandia, a prefabricated town in and beside the raw materials for a rubber plant. Housing, health-care and education were provided in return for workers adopting a strict moral code. Unions were not allowed and life was highly regulated. After a decade Fordlandia began to collapse as managers sent from the USA came into conflict with the workers, and isolation and disease led to mutiny (Grandin, 2010).

Contemporary examples would include the Amish communities in the USA, which value rural life, manual labour and family relationships. Remaining outside mainstream society, the Amish trade in crafts and crops, drawing upon science and technologies to the degree that they feel it is consistent with their religious beliefs and way of life (Kraybill, 2003). More liberal strands in the Amish community allow electricity and running water for example. In more conservative communities special permission is required to use motorized transport. Other examples include corporations and companies that provide benefits for families (childcare, health insurance, advice services, clubs and social activities) that encourage commitment and loyalty to the goals of the employer. These benefits and practices may also be cited as components of a firm's wider role in societies and their corporate social responsibility (Banjee, 2007).

THE GLOBAL CONTEXT

As noted above we cannot always distinguish clearly between work and non-work, or between paid or unpaid work. When we talk of work there is usually a presumption of physically travelling to a specific location, to participate in organized activities for which payment is received. Changing communication technologies have blurred boundaries as access to phones, email and other forms of social media is readily available for some workers. Physical features and linguistic descriptions of work are, as Grint (2005: 11) notes, always changing and reflect broader contexts of societies and families.[3] Further, individuals may do paid work at home, commonly termed homework, as employees or on a self-employed basis. As Edgell comments, 'working at home was the norm prior to the rise of industrial capitalism' (2006: 136), and this continues to be the case in many parts of the world. In industrial and post-industrial societies working at home illuminates extremes in working experiences. These range from low-paid service work, for example, sewing, knitting, and putting leaflets into envelopes, to higher paid professional work such as engineering or management consultants using technology to facilitate

---

3   While we note the value of volunteering to families, and of family members' participation in charitable activities, in this chapter we focus on the family management of paid and unpaid work.

work across localities and sectors. In sum, engagement in paid work has come to dominate the lives of most families across the world. Education, training and welfare systems underpin and promote this goal as individuals pursue work, jobs or careers. Pay, and the taxes drawn from this by governments, allows for both day-to-day survival and, in the longer term, entitlement to welfare benefits that may also accrue to workers and their dependants.

> **?** Bear in mind some welfare benefits can be a set of discrete payments intended to match a person's or family's needs and circumstances, for example tax credits. Can you think of any welfare benefits associated with paid work?

Regardless of strategies and programmes to address global inequalities, governments face a future in which the size and age of populations matter as never before. In minority world countries with ageing populations, the dependency ratio, that is, the proportion of people of working age in the population compared with those unable to work (largely children and retired people), has become important. The sex ratio, the relative numbers of men and women in the adult population, is a global concern but for varying reasons. In the majority world, a preference for boys driven by certain belief and familial systems has led to populations with significantly fewer women than men, with resultant problems for relationship and family formation, for example, in parts of China, India and eastern Europe.

Across the centuries women have participated in various forms of paid work, although the level of involvement has varied. In the minority world the increased participation of women in paid work, combined with the formation of families, has reduced the number of women available to act as caregivers, especially for older relatives. As Finch comments, the tendency to form a family has longer-term implications for how families manage work and care as 'there are cultural rules' (1989: 103), and these give prominence to the family grouping that produced children over other members, friends and neighbours. Of course, in some groups and societies there are strong claims to care for parents, as demonstrated in Chapter 1, when we discussed family formation in some Asian countries. Nevertheless, the push–pull between wider kinship groups and immediate family has become more complex with the dominant prioritization of work in a global capitalist economy (Edgell, 2006).

SURVIVAL AND LONGEVITY: THE CHALLENGE TO WORK

One notable development in the twenty-first century is the diverging composition of the populations in the majority world (defined as most of the global population and landmass) and the statistically minority world of more affluent societies. Increased longevity in the minority world is a success story that has brought with it a range of challenges for work and care. Those aged 60 and over outnumber the 12–24 years age group in many countries. Most future growth in the world's population will occur in less developed countries of the majority world, where the population is increasing more than five times as fast as that in the minority world. The increased survival of children into adulthood in the majority world is another success story which also presents problems for governments and economies. Nearly half the world's population is aged under 25 years. This equates to about three billion, of which 85% live in the majority world (see http://www.millennium-project.org/millennium/demographics-regional.html).

With economic development comes the movement of people, often from rural to urban areas. The world's urban population is expected to grow by 1.8% a year between 2000 and 2030, almost twice as fast as global population growth. In the twenty-first century the majority of the world's population live in urban conurbations and the number living in these locations will rise to five billion people by 2030 (Rosenberg and Bloom, 2004). The creation of jobs and life chances for young people in the majority world is imperative if poverty is to be tackled and social unrest avoided. Even with falling birth rates, the increased number of women of childbearing age and a decline in death rates will result in population growth to over nine billion by 2050. These trends not only illustrate the impact of developments in medicine and economics but also highlight global inequalities. Improved provision of treatment of infectious diseases, clean water, sanitation and enhanced nutrition, and the growth in the standard of living underpin increased longevity in the minority world. The depth of poverty, social and civil unrest, limited treatment of infectious diseases including HIV/AIDS, and conflict and wars are factors in the unequal life chances between the majority and minority worlds.

Increased provision of paid work, and improved terms and conditions for workers, is central to a number of global programmes. These include the UN Millennium Development Goals with targets set for 2015 to halve extreme poverty, halt the spread of HIV/AIDS and provide universal primary education. The ILO Campaign for Decent Work is a parallel initiative, and both have galvanized global efforts to meet the needs of the poorest communities and workers. The IMF monitors economic developments, providing advice and loans to support economic development and to alleviate financial crises, while the World Bank has a specific focus on fighting poverty through a range of measures, many of which involve the generation of jobs. The attainment and maintenance of paid work is a fundamental premise in these global activities.

DECENT WORK AND RURAL EMPLOYMENT

Given the importance of all forms of work to human flourishing and survival, the nature and rights of workers has come centre stage. A powerful global campaign has evolved with an agenda established and promoted by the ILO (see www.ilo.org). Established in 1999, the Campaign For Decent Work has been endorsed by the international community. A notable range of activities have ensued, led by organizations ranging from the UN and the EU to NGOs, for example, the European NGO Confederation for Relief and Development.

The ending of poverty and hunger, often achieved through 'decent work', is one of the eight UN Millennium Development Goals. Decent work has generally been accepted to mean work carried out in reasonable conditions and for which a sufficient benefit or advantage is received. The full definition refers to 'productive work for women and men in conditions of freedom, equity, security and human dignity' (ILO, 2011). Decent work offers opportunities for a fair income and to generate productive outputs. Further, it should provide security in the workplace and social protection for workers and their families; it should also offer better prospects for personal development and encourage social integration. Within this context people should have the freedom to express their concerns, to organize and to participate in decisions that affect their lives. Decent work guarantees equal opportunities and equal treatment for all.

This is a broad concept and many aspects of this are open to debate. For example, what is 'decent'? This is an ambiguous word. Other terms might also be contested and defined in differing ways between continents, countries, industrial sectors, and family practices; 'a fair income'; 'security' or 'freedom to express concerns'. The ILO agenda and campaign is a worldwide one which is part of an overarching programme that seeks standardization of human rights. Many governments are determined to create public policies for social protection and development, and international communities are grappling with global interdependencies. However, can concepts such as decent work provide a legal basis for minimum work conditions? (See also Box 6.1.)

Across the world the rural labour market and employment numbers are growing. This may seem counterintuitive but it reminds many of us that the minority world perception is just that; a narrowly drawn interpretation of the 'world of work'. The Overseas Development Institute (ODI) and ILO estimate there are 1,100 million people in the agricultural labour force with farm workers forming the largest group at 450 million. While the majority is self-employed, working on their own, generally very small farms, hired farm work is also critical to the lives of many millions and their families. Hired farm work is often temporary and seasonal, with workers combining two or three types of work: fruit picking, harvesting, planting, casual work in tourism or local services. These patterns are prevalent across large parts of Africa, Asia and the Americas. They can exist alongside urban forms of work, as can be seen in the USA, where transnational migrants, illegal migrant workers and poorly paid local workers labour in rural localities close to major urban conurbations.

Low pay and poor conditions seem to be synonymous with rural work. A lot of effort, often physically exhausting and taxing, goes into rural labour. Pay can be so low as to make it impossible to live without a second job or the combined income across the household and family members. The work can be hazardous too, with chemicals and machinery causing injury. In 2003 the ILO estimated that three to four million people are affected by pesticides every year with 40,000 deaths resulting. Accidents are not uncommon, nor are chronic illnesses and longer-term ill health. Inequalities are created and reinforced. Farm work is the largest employment sector for child labour. Women are often paid less; many experience gender discrimination and some, sexual and physical abuse.

Rural people may migrate to urban areas to seek work opportunities that can pay better, are potentially less hazardous and may be more secure. Of course this is a gamble and many migrants are disappointed, experiencing workplace hazards, abuse, violence and isolation. Some try to combine farm and off-farm/urban activities, with families trying to maintain farming and local forms of work such as trading, along with income from members working in urban localities.

Box 6.1   Is 'decent work' possible?

How do international organizations, governments and communities address the complex issues of poverty, migration and exploitation evident in many aspects of farm work? The Overseas Development Institute (ODI) proposed a four-pronged strategy:

1. Demand for labour: improve rural opportunities and rural employment by stimulating the growth of private enterprise. Reducing the cost of establishing enterprises, linking small businesses to address unmet social needs and the provision of public work projects are proposed as the key elements of a programme for improvement.

2. Supply of labour: education and training could improve the quality of labour and the potential for small business start-ups. Cash transfers to encourage schooling, apprenticeship schemes and training for adults can be effective. There are some famous examples, including the Grameen Foundation, which helps the world's poorest, especially women, to improve their lives through access to microfinance and technology. In 2006, the founder Muhammad Yunus won the Nobel Peace Prize and today it is estimated that the Grameen Foundation provides services and support for seven million people worldwide.

3. Facilitate positive migration: illegal migrants risk their lives, often leaving their country of birth in search of economic improvement that can prove illusive. Yet within countries there are often opportunities in other regions. For example, the Chinese and Indian governments have relaxed the regulations imposed on internal migration to encourage family groups to move and thus enhance the potential for familial relationships to be maintained.

4. Direct intervention: governments can set minimum wage levels and/or influence pay settlements, as well as recognizing trade unions and collective voices. Ensuring there are regulations in force, and that these are monitored, can help in addressing child labour and the economic, physical and sexual abuse of workers that can happen.

A major target of the UN Millennium Development Goals is to reduce by half the proportion of the population living on less than a dollar a day by 2015. Achieving this goal now seems unlikely. Rural employment is bound up with this challenge and with the need for better and more work in rural localities.

RELATIONSHIPS AND RESOURCES

Relationships and ties in families are increasingly mobile and fluid. Examples of mobility and change include the steep rise in divorce and cohabitation, discussed in depth in Chapter 5, resulting in relationship formation and re-formation. Fifty years ago, divorce and cohabitation in many European countries was exceptional and carried with it social sanction and stigma, especially for children involved. In the case of divorce, the economic implications were notable with many single parents and ex-partners experiencing a notable decline in income and status. In this coming decade almost 50% of marriages will end in divorce over much of Europe, and in the UK around a third of first marriages will end in divorce. Further, as we noted in Chapter 5, figures on cohabiting couples are difficult to assess as there is no legal requirement for registration. Whereas marriage might once have generated a route plan for adult life, now relationships are made and unmade without much comment, despite attempts by politicians and policy makers to promote marriage and longer-term cohabitation. It is therefore notable that despite the pace of change in the nature of families, these very relationships and ties are more crucial to people's emotional development and stability than before.

> ➜ In Chapter 5 we noted how families are formed, dissolved and re-formed through marriage or cohabitation, divorce or separation and re-marriage or cohabitation. Some commentators suggest that in the minority world we now live in a time of serial monogamy. What are the implications of this for families and work?

In a world where people are striving to compete and achieve security in the labour market and experience increasing anonymity and stress, the family offers a location in which they can forge identity, achieve trust, and share emotions and resources. So while there is no recipe for success in family life, surveys illustrate how most of us prize involvement in families as a response to the trials and tribulations of contemporary working life. Exploring the relationship between home and work, Hochschild (1997) asserted that many of us become well versed in managing tensions and conflict in the workplace, developing a social world in which we feel comfortable. At home, however, tensions may not be so easily managed and the home is not a relaxing, comfortable place for many people to be. The workplace can offer sanctuary and calm from familial pressures.

The lifestyles and plans of couples and families are increasingly diverse, with Kellerhals (2010: 198) noting the evolution of 'bespoke' conjugality in which couples can create a lifestyle with a greater degree of freedom than before. Thus the once common process of forming and living in a family through engagement, marriage, role differentiation, procreation and employment, has given way to a range of possibilities. These include cohabitation, LAT, involvement with friends and neighbours to support childrearing, working away from the home, working at home, and starting out on new phases of working life in one's mid or later years.

ACQUIRING AND ALLOCATING RESOURCES

In all lifestyle choices and partnership ties, the acquisition and maintenance of resources, in particular, money, is imperative. Much of this is attained through wages and salaries; payment for work gained through the labour market. Being able to generate and allocate resources allows families to make choices about lifestyle and to negotiate roles and obligations. Negotiation, however, can lead to a sense of frustration and disillusionment and sometimes result in abuse and violence.

> ➜ See Chapter 5 for an in-depth discussion of families, relationships and violence.

A major risk is no work, resulting in a lack of resources which prevents families from achieving their goals. This may be converted into feelings of guilt, frustration and dissatisfaction. There are times when all families grapple with tensions around money.

Men and women, young and old, sometimes have diverging workload types and interests, as well as differing voices and rights in familial resource allocation. Differences in power, roles and responsibilities are implicated in the ways families offer support to address the needs of the vulnerable. The potential for family support, whether in cash or kind, can be romanticized and is often assumed to be available.

> ➜ In Chapter 4 we discussed the relationship between welfare policies and families. Look again at Chapter 4 and consider why families and work receive a lot of attention by governments and policy makers.

Support depends on the sacrifice of some members in the aid of others. Support for immediate family and kin comes from necessity rather than offered on a regular and formal basis. Increased participation in paid work, the mobility of family members across regions and countries, and existing patterns of paid and unpaid work are all factors implicated in how and when support is available and to whom. Where and when governments can offer support, Finch asserts, people are 'actually more willing, not less willing, to give their relatives some assistance' (1989: 90). A major concern for families and governments is how to articulate and manage varied types of work and familial needs (Marsh and Brennan, 2008).

GENDER AND RESOURCES

Changes in gender roles are slow and explanations for this include the practices in families that men and women undertake, many of which reflect gendered ideas and roles. Public policies, workplaces and institutions such as education and health, form a structural context that often presupposes and promotes gendered roles. Some such as education and health, for example, require unpaid labour among family members in numerous ways, such as getting children to and from school, and the home-based nursing care given to promote recovery after an operation.

Underpinning these two examples are the practices of power in families. The power of economics, or the power of the wage or salary, remains supreme in most households, with those who earn most expected to undertake less domestic labour than others. While there is notable change in higher earning households, often an adult male earns more than his partner and thus the power of pay creates and reinforces gender roles in most families. This, when combined with gender norms evident in all societies, and illuminated in the policies and practices of a range of institutions and workplaces, accounts for the slow pace of change. The study of the gendered nature of unpaid work has identified the dual burden or second shift in which women undertake both paid and unpaid work, thus working more hours than any other member of the household (Hochschild, 1997). Some have asserted this is a stalled revolution or lagged adaptation (Pahl and Wallace, 1985; Gershuny, 2000), while the more optimistic argue change is taking place, and while not as fast as many would like, this is meaningful change (Sullivan, 2006). Women in better paid and professional occupations appear to have relational skills to negotiate change, and men in more secure professional jobs appear more willing to adapt.

UNPAID WORK

Earlier we defined unpaid work to include domestic labour and the many physical and emotional tasks that range from cooking a meal for family members to comforting a partner after a hard day at work. The tasks and skills associated with domestic labour are highly valued by those in receipt of them. However, this work does not achieve the status or reward similar to paid work. We also noted how a disproportionate amount of unpaid work continues to be undertaken by women, despite an increase in the contribution of men (Oakley, 1974; Bowlby et al., 2010). The terms housework or domestic work do not specify a gender, but as we identified at the outset of this book in Chapter 1 much of this work is undertaken by women. These terms conceal the gendered nature of unpaid work and how the paid work women engage in reflects these tasks in their dominance in caring, service and education jobs (Sassen, 2000; Hochschild, 2003b; Crompton, 2006).

Domestic work encompasses a wide range of tasks and skills, which, as Edgell notes, comprises:

unskilled manual work (e.g., cleaning), relatively skilled manual work (e.g., cooking), emotional work (e.g., child-care), service work (e.g. shopping and driving children to school), and a variety of non-manual work activities that put a premium on administrative and social skills (e.g., organizing work tasks and managing people). (2006: 159)

This work involves a vast array of tasks which require numerous skills learnt and developed over time, starting during childhood. Tasks are rotated sometimes by choice and at other times through necessity. Sometimes they are allocated to others or negotiated among family members.

> ➜ Look at Chapter 2, Box 2.2, page 59, for a discussion of how family strategies are negotiated and deployed among members. Think about your family. Can you identity a family strategy for food and eating, weekends or saving for holidays or festivals?

> ➜ Also in Chapter 2, look again at what we say about how family practices are made evident in displays, such as large ritualized gatherings in Box 2.5, page 67.

One family member, however, is generally charged with the main responsibility for specific sets of tasks; for example, child and other care work, food shopping and preparation, painting and decorating, and car maintenance.

There are a number of studies that have considered the time spent on domestic labour and the content of this (Oakley, 1974; Vanek, 1974; Bittiman et al., 2004; Sullivan, 2006). In most societies women, especially mothers, typically undertake more of this work than do other family members. Hours spent on domestic work are at least the equivalent to, or more than, a full-time job. In the 1920s in the USA this was estimated at 52 hours per week and in the 1960s, 55 hours per week. While hours in paid work have declined for most in the minority world to 35–40 hours per week, domestic labour has not gone down substantially despite technological developments. These developments have reduced the level of physical labour but pushed up standards of household maintenance. Jobs that may have been undertaken by men such as washing dishes have been replaced by a dishwasher (Windebank, 2001; Silva, 2010).

GENDER ROLES AND UNPAID WORK

Change in gender roles is evident in the studies of Gershuny (2000) and of Sullivan (2006) which demonstrate that men are in fact undertaking more domestic labour. This process of change is slow and is linked to educational attainment and social class, with the middle class and better educated seemingly more able and willing to negotiate domestic tasks. However, domestic labour, as with paid work, illuminates the inter-weaving worlds of male and female labour. In the home, many women continue to focus on caregiving tasks and this is reflected in the areas of paid work in which they dominate; education, health and social care, the service sector and retail. Men continue to be associated with tasks that are more physical or involve numeracy and computation skills, whether paid or unpaid. Further, the idea of men as the main breadwinners, while diminished, remains strong in the global-wide images and ideas that surround hetero-sexual relationships at the core of many families.

Beck (2000) has argued that antagonism between men and women is evident as tensions mount between the expectations of equality and the continuing inequality of unpaid domestic labour and paid work. Women experience disappointment as a rhetoric of equality does not equate with the daily realities they experience in and out of the home as unpaid and paid work remains gendered. Women may also have to make difficult choices about how and where to engage in paid work; for example, working part-time or in a job that is not suited to their education but is close to home. These choices may facilitate care work as well as generating pay, but in the long run will limit opportunities and lifetime income, including pension entitlements.

> **?**   Do women choose to work part-time? Or does part-time work reflect opportunities and constraints? Explain your answer using examples drawn from what you know of your family.

The lifetime implications of limited opportunities and choices are aptly illustrated by global trends on poverty. Roughly 70% of the world's poor are women and this results from the combination of unpaid and paid work, limited access to jobs, and the gender pay gap. The bulk of workers in the garment industry are women and there are examples, too, of children exploited in this and other industries, including fruit picking, farming and manufacturing. There is a triple disadvantage for many women (concentration in low-paid jobs, care responsibilities, and managing work and home life), especially in the majority world, where opportunities and choices are limited or non-existent. The arguments put forward by Beck (2000) have limited relevance to many people in large parts of the world. This reminds us that our perspectives are driven by the experience of our up-bringing and anticipated lifestyle.

In sum, unpaid domestic labour remains imperative to household management and is generally organized in ways that facilitate participation in employment, education or training, or support for those too young, ill, or old to engage in these activities. Welfare policies and services also assume that a level of unpaid domestic and care labour is available; for example, rehabilitation following hospitalization, parental involvement in homework and school activities, and informal care for sick or vulnerable family members or neighbours (Sevenhuijsen, 1998).

QUANTIFYING AND VALUING UNPAID WORK

The debate about how the value is placed on unpaid work is not a new one. The exclusion of unpaid work from categories of work used by governments began during the nineteenth century with the census survey. While paid domestic work continued to be counted, unpaid domestic labour was excluded (Luxton and Gorman, 2001). In conventional economics one measure of activity is the GDP. GDP is the market value of all goods and services produced within the borders of a country in one year. The GDP of a country is often used to compare the relative health of economies.[4] The greater a country's GDP, the presumption is that the general standard of living will be higher for many people, if not all. This calculation assumes that businesses and markets generate wealth while families and households buy and consume, rather than produce. Unpaid care and domestic work is not included in this calculation. Yet as we have demonstrated throughout this book, families are the major social grouping responsible for the raising of children and for the care of the old or sick, and they support individuals to participate in paid work, education and training. Families are crucial to members and societies most notably through producing and supporting the next generation. In the majority world, women undertake even larger amounts of household and paid work. Family businesses and farms, many of which provide subsistence, depend on the unpaid labour of women and children. Governments and agencies such as the OECD are beginning to recognize the limitations of focusing solely on GDP as is clear from Box 6.2.

Box 6.2   Alternative ways of recognizing determinants of societal progress

Measuring their populations 'general well-being' is increasingly a concern of governments across the world, including those in France, the UK, Ecuador and Bolivia (in the latter two the indigenous concept of 'buen vivir', or 'living well', has been incorporated into their state constitutions). The quality of family life is recognized as being a major contributor to 'general well-being'

(Continued)

---

4   The measure of GDP has been criticized, not least by the OECD. As with any attempt to measure economic activity there are anomalies. However, we draw attention to this as it remains the commonly cited measure and one used by governments and the financial sector (see http://unstats.un.org/unsd/sna1993/toctop.asp).

(Continued)

and the UK Prime Minister, David Cameron, explicitly linked the development of accurate measures by the Office for National Statistics with his Government's agenda to make the country 'family-friendly' (www.number10. gov.uk/news/speeches-and-transcripts/2010/11/pm-speech-on-well-being-57569).

An international commission on the measurement of economic performance and social progress was created at the beginning of 2008, on the initiative of the French government. Current measures of economic performance, in particular those based on GDP, were perceived to be inadequate measures of societal well-being and economic, environmental, and social sustainability.

The commission's work is not focused on France or the minority world but aims to provide a template for every interested country or group of countries. Members of the commission are respected experts from universities, governmental and intergovernmental organizations, in several countries (USA, France, UK and India). Rapporteurs and secretariat are provided by the French National Institute for Statistics and Economic Studies (INSEE), the French Economic Observatory (Observatoire Français des Conjonctures Économiques, OFCE), and OECD (Commission on the Measurement of Economic Performance and Social Progress, 2011). (See: http://www.stiglitz-sen-fitoussi.fr/en/index.htm).

Recognizing and calculating unpaid work is controversial and complex as much of this work is ensnared in cultural and gendered norms. Elson (2006) argues that more should be done by governments and supranational organizations to access the value of unpaid work and to add the relative volume of this to the GDP. One study estimated that the value of unpaid work excluded from the calculation of GDP in the UK is up to 77% of the current total of GDP, and in India it is between 26% and 50%. Calls for taxation and welfare policies to support an unpaid caregiver model through, for example, financial incentives to family members involved in care work, have been met with resistance. Governments assume current levels of service provision will be supported by unpaid work and any change to that equation would incur costs considered unacceptable by most politicians and policy makers (Sevenhuijsen, 1998).

VITAL BUT SUBORDINATE

Industrialization played a major role in the physical separation of home from work and exacerbated ideas about women's association with home life and domestic labour, regardless of time spent in paid work. Women workers became viewed as carers first and foremost, seemingly willing to offer flexibility in addressing domestic and care needs of others.

The development of the term housewife, and more recently the phrase househusband, removed the gender neutral shield of housework and describes who has primary responsibility for undertaking or organizing unpaid work. Individual development, aspirations and economic needs have encouraged and enhanced women's participation in formal labour markets. In the minority world, women's participation in paid work is at a higher proportion than at any other period in capitalism apart from the two world wars. Women are expected to engage in paid work, at least part-time, in conjunction with caring and other unpaid work. Further, technologies, especially information technologies, have opened up the possibility of doing paid work in a range of locations, including home. Through these changes and blurring of boundaries women are spending more hours in all forms of labour albeit that domestic and care work remain vital but subordinate to paid employment.

Despite our dependence on unpaid domestic and care work the low status of the 'job' continues. An early study of housework was undertaken by Lopata (1972), drawing upon data collected from housewives living in Chicago in the 1950s and 1960s. This, and the research by Oakley (1974) with London-based housewives, noted that the route into unpaid domestic work, generally through marriage or cohabitation, combined with the apparent lack of training and no payment, promoted the notion of a labour of love. Further, the increasing dominance of paid work was also a factor in the language surrounding housework; responses to the question 'What do you do?' included 'I'm just a housewife' or 'I stay at home to look after the family'. These statements further emphasize the isolation and alienation many housewives speak of, despite the varied skills and long hours required to keep the family running. Physical separation from extended family members, workplace colleagues and friends can reinforce feelings of loneliness and reduced status. Much of the work is repetitive, with obligations and responsibilities, including the provision of meals to schedule and washing and ironing clothes for particular points in the week (such as school uniforms and work shirts for Monday mornings). Unpaid domestic work has a cyclical quality and varies with the presence of young children and sick or elderly dependants. Regardless of the life stages of family members, household routines get organized around the core activities of employment, education and training. Those responsible for unpaid domestic work often bemoan the restrictions imposed by work–family necessities.

Unpaid labour is also imperative to charities (the not-for-profit sector) with international and national charities dependent on this labour to varying degrees. Historically, volunteering was considered an acceptable pursuit for women from better off families, whose removal from paid work was a key marker of social standing (Veblen, 1970). This gender and social class trend remained evident up to the 1990s, but today both men and women participate in formal volunteering work approximately in equal measure. This contrasts with the gendered patterns of unpaid work in families. That said, like unpaid work, volunteering is not included in national or international statistics (Benn, 1998; Taylor, 2004). Unpaid work, in its varied forms, remains under-researched and generally addressed with a focus on gender and the home. Unpaid domestic work and volunteering underpin human flourishing in numerous and interlocked ways. These include something as personal as childrearing in families as well as more community-orientated activity such as ensuring a youth club or toddlers' play group keeps running.

FAMILY PRACTICES AND WORK

In Chapter 2 we introduced the work of Morgan (1996), and his concept of 'doing families'. This was coined to describe the relationships, activities and practices that take place in families. The 'doing of work', especially paid work, is central to the ways in which families organize. In noting the transformations of work and home life, Glucksmann's (2005) concept of the *total social organization of labour* (TSOL) offers a useful framework (Box 6.3).

Box 6.3   The total social organization of labour

In this model Glucksmann gives equal significance to paid work and to developments in 'non-market and unpaid work, including the proliferation of the modes and extent of care work, the growth of voluntary or community work in the public domain, and shifts in both directions across the commodity/non-commodity divide' (2005: 20). Aspects of care giving and provision and well-being can be found in a range of statutory duties, policies and related activities: health and safety, equality and diversity, maternity and parental leave, religious observance, bullying and harassment, personal development, voluntary redundancy, early retirement, employer pension schemes, grievance procedures, and dismissal.

The 'doing of care' across the world and over time shows many similarities and yet differences. Our understandings, practices and experiences of work and care change over time and space. Unpaid work and care work are vital to human flourishing but are often taken for granted. By this we refer to the manner in which care work is required but at the same time it is assumed and how it is sourced and managed is not readily discussed. Here we draw attention to another framework that may help to explain how families think about and experience care and work – caringscapes (Box 6.4).

Box 6.4   Care and work over the past, present and futures: caringscapes

A *caringscape* perspective notes the complex ways in which people and families think about care and work over time (McKie et al., 2002). It differs from TSOL by positioning care work centre stage and asserting that thoughts about care are never far away from our daily activities and future plans. In assessing care work we draw upon memories, images and evidence.

We may examine the actualities and possibilities of the familial decisions and activities that include the following dimensions of the processes of caring and working (McKie et al., 2002: 915):

> planning, worrying, anticipating, speculation, prioritizing, assessing the quality of care, accessing care, controlling care, paying for care, shifting patterns of work, job (in)security, the potential for promotion, moving home, managing family resources, supporting school work, being involved in the school or care group, and so on.

For example, if we consider the process of becoming a parent and taking maternity or paternity leave, speculating and planning about parenting starts many years prior to pregnancy and the actual experience of parenting. Children and young people will speculate about parenthood; they play 'families' in nursery and school, and participate in social and personal education classes (Gittins, 1997; Prout, 1999). Schools and other societal pressures will promote certain notions of family life and locations of family living (the 'home'). Children grow up in 'their family' in a particular locality and within their family's social network, and will reflect on parenting and what they might do differently when they grow up. In some families children and young people may come into contact with social and legal services as a result of parental abuse or divorce (Daniel and Ivatts, 1998; Charles, 2000).

Thinking about these processes over time and in space alerts us to the possible times and spaces in which policies and services might be relevant to these informal care processes. A number of these issues are considered in the next section in Box 6.5, which introduces a study called WORKCARE. The project reviewed available data on how families combine work and care in various countries in Europe. The impact of welfare policies, services and the pay levels of men and women were all factors in family practices.

POLICY, POLITICS AND FAMILIES

In recent years the EU has devoted a lot of time and effort to developing a common approach to work and care giving across Member States. The emphasis in EU strategies is upon adults actively engaged in paid work; this differs from much of the majority world where children and older people are likely to be engaged in paid work at earlier and later ages, respectively. However, in the EU it is an accepted norm that working life starts in the late teens or 20s and will end in the 60s. While unpaid domestic and care work is recognized, the priority is to have all who are deemed able to be active in education, training or employment. The economic approach which underpins these policy directions is not without its critics, but nevertheless the EU is keenly promoting economic and social policy initiatives aimed at reducing individual and family dependence on welfare benefits and services. By way of an exchange between workers and government, employers are encouraged to use legislation and guidance to offer minimum levels of protection for employees.

The term *flexicurity* was coined within EU circles, derived from the words flexibility and security; flexible job arrangements combined with statutory levels of protection and support, including a written contract and stated rates of pay and of sickness benefits, among other benefits. The idea is that flexibility and security should not be seen as opposites but as complementary. In its broadest interpretation it is about flexible work organizations where people can combine their work and private responsibilities, where they can keep their training up to date and potentially have flexible working hours. It is also about giving both employers and employees a more flexible environment for changing jobs. Security means 'employment security' – to provide people with the training they need to keep their skills up to date and to develop their talent as well as providing them with adequate unemployment and related benefits if they were to lose their job for a period of time.

Widely heralded as a positive step in encouraging employers to address work–life balance issues for employees, has there been a discernable impact? See Box 6.5.

Box 6.5   The WORKCARE project

This three-year EU funded project is one example of research which examined the issues related to work and care in detail. It considered the relationship between EU strategies, governmental policies and services, economies and demographic trends, with the responses of individuals to work and care. The project combined an analysis of policy documents with a range of research methods, including secondary analysis of data from the European Social Survey and the International Social Survey Programme. Further, interviews were conducted in Austria, Denmark, Hungary, Italy, Poland, Portugal and the UK. Findings included:

- Families with both parents in paid work are becoming the norm.

- Fertility rates are higher in countries with policies and services that enable parents to combine paid employment with care for children.

- In the absence of affordable childcare, it continues to be women who take time out of the workforce, often working part-time and in less secure types of work.

- Members of the extended family, especially grandparents, and friends form an important source of support. In those countries without affordable childcare there is a higher reliance on the extended family.

Several types of welfare regimes were identified across Europe. Closest to European policy objectives was the 'extensive family policy' regime that exists in Sweden, Denmark, Belgium and France. Here mothers are back in employment after three months to one year of parental leave and rely to a great extent on state-provided childcare. Surprisingly this scheme was found to be not always the most expensive, and was comparable with the 'long-leave, part-time' model in Germany, Austria and Luxembourg where mothers have parental leave for up to three years.

Overall, the research team suggested that flexicurity reflected and drew upon deeply entrenched gendered attitudes to work and care. The tendency in workplace practices was to provide flexibility and security for men, but often only flexibility with little or no security for women. Individuals and families often make decisions based on the potential for quality child and elder care, as well as on salaries. Flexicurity therefore needs to take into account a gender perspective.

In March 2010, the average gender pay gap – the average difference in gross hourly earnings between women and men across the economy as a whole – stood at 18% for the EU; men continue to earn more than women. The gender pay gap, combined with the limited provision of affordable quality care services in many countries, reinforces discriminatory outcomes. These outcomes are occurring at a time when an ageing population and concerns about fertility rates reinforce contradictory pressures on women regarding care roles and employment. Viewing flexicurity through a 'gendered lens' illuminates how supranational approaches can shield and reinforce inequitable experiences. For more information on the project see: http://ec.europa. eu/social/main.jsp?catId=547

? Refer back to Box 6.3 and Box 6.4. How can the frameworks of TSOL and caringscapes help to explain some of the issues raised in the WORKCARE project on families combing paid work and care responsibilities?

EXPLAINING PREFERENCES AND CHOICES

Sociologists have described and explained the structures in which families form and change, and processes and practices of family life. To aid the exploration of families and work we draw attention to two bodies of thinking: the relationship between structure and agency (Giddens, 1986; Finch, 2007), and opportunities, hurdles and choices in combining the varied types of work (Hakim, 2000; Crompton, 2006; Sullivan, 2006). As Finch points out, 'We cannot understand support in families simply as a matter of individual preferences and choices' (1989: 86). Family members will assist or ignore others in ways that reflect much more than individual choices. Wider economic structures, welfare benefits, and belief systems interweave with social class, gender and ethnic identity, and as Finch continues,

> human action creates and recreates social structures, but at the same
> time social structures make is possible for human beings to interact
> with one another – they facilitate action as well as constrain it.
> (1989: 86)

Here, Finch draws attention to the work of Giddens (1986) and the assertion that explanations of social action must consider both social structure (including opportunities for paid work, welfare benefits and infrastructure) and human agency. The term 'structuration' describes this interaction between structures, actions and norms. In explanations of their past and present, individuals will explain what they have done and why. This narrative constitutes an action in its own right but also infuses conversations and speculation on aspirations, anticipations and choices. Thus the past, present and future for individuals and families interweave, and are moulded by structures and actions.

Feminist perspectives, discussed in the latter half of Chapter 2, on work and family have offered varied and detailed critiques of the creation and reinforcement of gender stereotypes (Tong, 2009). Having worked to promote equal citizenship (Walby, 1990), the reconceptualization of masculine and feminine identities (Jackson and Scott, 2001; Connell, 2009; Hearn and Pringle, 2009) and global connections in economic exploitation (Harley, 2007), contemporary analysis illuminates the subtle, on-going inequalities and tensions in families. Many women continue to be financially dependent on their partners. This dependence is multifaceted. Some couples choose this arrangement to facilitate childrearing in the way they consider best. Generally this starts from pregnancy and childbirth and subsequent involvement in insecure, temporary, casual or part-time work.

As stated in Box 6.5, there remains a gender pay gap between men and women, with women earning on average 15–20% less than men in the equivalent job. The gender pay gap differs according to the calculations adopted and the employment and welfare policies operating in various countries (European Commission, 2009; Fawcett Society, 2010). Women are predominately employed in sectors associated with feminine skills which generate lower levels of pay. This undervaluation, coupled with assumptions about women's pay being necessary but secondary to that of the male partner, ensures that discrimination continues. Welfare policies and services, such as those regarding paid maternity and parental leave, vary widely between countries and also impact on gender differences in work and income. Add to this the choices women may make, namely, to have children, care for others, work part-time, or refuse overtime or promotion, and thus women continue to receive less pay than their male equivalents.

?   In Chapter 2 we explored sociological explanations available to examine families and family life. Have a look again at this chapter and choose three explanations you consider to be relevant. Jot down why you consider these to be of interest and how these aid exploration of family life and work.

The Fairness in Families Index was launched in 2010 and draws upon data from the OECD to rank 21 countries on the basis of family fairness indicators, including parental leave, the ratio of men's to women's time spent caring for children, the proportion of women in management roles, the percentage of men in the part-time workforce and the amount of time spent by men and women doing unpaid domestic work. Over the 10 indicators, Sweden was ranked first and Switzerland last. The USA rated twelfth and the UK eighteenth (The Fatherhood Institute, 2010). This index illustrates how welfare policies and support for families to combine caring and working diverge across these countries. How work and care is managed provides evidence of the nature and content of family policies.

MIGRANT DOMESTIC WORKERS

The outsourcing of domestic work and paying for domestic labour continues to have a notable impact on families and workers in many parts of the world. Better off households that are able and choose to pay for domestic work often do so to enable the adults in the household, including women, ready participation in paid work. The ways in which paid domestic labour may evolve is evidenced by the work of Hochschild (1997; 2003a) on the global economy in women's work. Migrating domestic workers generate income for a notable number of families in the economies of transitional regions and countries. The impact of migrant labour on the families and economy of the Philippines is illustrated in the studies of Parrenas (2005), which describe how traditional gender patterns have been disrupted through the formation of transnational households. Their prevalence 'threatens cultural parameters and institutional norms marked by material inequalities between men and women as well as ideology' (Parrenas, 2005: 5). Hochschild (2003a) notes that at the turn of this century approximately half of the world's 120 million legal and illegal migrants were female, marking a new trend in the mobility and working lives of women in the majority world. As women in the minority world increase their participation in paid work, women from the majority world have been migrating to find paid work as nannies and maids. Some are also travelling or are trafficked for sex work.[5] Hochschild (2003a) comments that there is a transfer of services across and within countries as housewives' traditional unpaid work is undertaken for low wages by women from poor communities. This, the author concludes, is evidence of a care deficit in the minority world met through global transfers of people, labour and pay. By contrast the needs of families and children in the majority world are unlikely to be fully met and thus a care deficit is created which draws upon available extended family members to support dependants. Thus in many poorer nations, parental engagement in the labour market increasingly involves transnational migration where, in order to reconcile paid work and family responsibilities, children may have to be left behind in the care of the extended family. The term 'global care chains' has been used to describe the phenomenon of migrants moving from poor to

---

5 The term trafficked refers to the illegal and often forced movement of mostly women and children to work in the sex industry.

rich worlds specifically to look after other people's children or elderly people while leaving behind those to whom they would normally provide care (Hochschild, 2003c; Lan, 2006).

> ➔ Chapter 4 looks in greater detail at the policy and practice implications of 'global care chains'. These proliferate when minority world caring needs are met by migrants from the majority world and how governments and supranational institutions are compelled to develop policy responses to ensure migrants are protected outside their country of origin and that their dependants who have been 'left behind' have some recourse to state assistance. At a supranational level, the UN International Convention on the Protection of the Rights of All Migrant Workers and Members of their Families 'takes into account the fact that migration is often the cause of serious problems for the members of the families of migrant workers, as well as for the workers themselves, in particular because of the scattering of the family' (UN, 1990). Signing up to its 93 Articles, binds nations to commitments to uphold a comprehensive range of rights and duties towards migrants and their families and provides the convention's subjects with grounds of appeal against host governments' adverse treatment of them.

SUMMARY

In this chapter we have explored a major dimension of family life, namely how paid and unpaid work forms the basis of sustainable households and families. The interdependency of unpaid and paid work is assumed and largely taken for granted by family members, employers and governments as evident in policies and services including education, health and social care. Families depend on the resources generated through paid work to a large degree and on benefits in cash and kind where welfare policies and services exist.

An examination of who works where and when illuminates global, ethnic and gender inequalities. Access to 'decent work' is viewed as fundamental to addressing poverty by a number of supranational organizations including the UN, ILO and EU. Engagement in paid work is now perceived as a human right. Being active in education, training or employment is an obligation for individuals. The generation of money and benefits allows support for individuals, dependants and partners. The pressures to be in paid work are intense and a global phenomenon.

Unpaid work includes varied tasks and requires a range of skills: cleaning, cooking, childcare, shopping, managing budgets and organizing family activities and events. These, among other tasks, are fundamental to family survival and flourishing. While vital to ensuring availability for paid work, unpaid work continues to be subordinated. We proposed two analytical frameworks which seek to map and examine how these types of work and varied tasks are dynamic and fluid. TSOL (Glucksmann, 2005) starts from the activities of work, paid and unpaid: doing work. By contrast, 'doing care' is the focus of caringscapes (McKie et al., 2002). The framework places a focus on the interdependencies of relationships and the physical and emotional tasks – care and caring – that imbue our lives. The term global chains of care draws attention to transnational trends in migration and care work between the majority and minority worlds.

EXPLORE FURTHER

Bowlby, S., McKie, L., Gregory, S. and MacPherson, I. (2010) *Interdependency and Care Over the Lifecourse.* London: Routledge.
Crompton, R. (2006) *Employment and the Family: The Reconfiguration of Work and Family Life in Contemporary Societies.* Cambridge: Cambridge University Press.
Edgell, S. (2006) *The Sociology of Work: Continuity and Change in Paid and Unpaid Work.* London: Sage.

USEFUL WEBSITES

The Alfred P. Sloan Work and Family Research Network offer online information about work and family. This site is hosted by Boston College, USA, and is global in content on work and family research. The network targets the information needs of academics and researchers, workplace practitioners, state public policy makers, and interested individuals offering:

- multidisciplinary, credible teaching resources and access to the world's foremost work–family academics and researchers
- evidence-based information on cutting-edge workforce issues, talent management, and the impact of work and family issues on business outcomes
- unbiased policy data about work and family trends, legislation, and statistics.

See http://wfnetwork.bc.edu/

The ILO is the international organization responsible for drawing up and overseeing international labour standards. It is a 'tripartite' UN agency that brings together representatives of governments, employers and workers to jointly shape policies and programmes promoting 'decent work' for all. The ILO argues that this gives its policies and resources strengths by incorporating 'real world' knowledge about employment and work. See www.ilo.org

The OECD promotes policies to improve the economic and social well-being of people around the world. It has 34 member states and works with governments, businesses, trade unions and other groups. See www.oecd.org

PART IV

CONCLUSIONS

7 Families into the Future

Keywords: futures, change, continuity, longevity, greying population, patriarchy, science, reproductive technologies, policy, politics

INTRODUCTION

In this concluding chapter we build on themes introduced earlier by considering their likely future importance, the extent to which they are commonly expressed across the world and the threats, and opportunities they present to families, wider society, politicians and policy makers. While keeping in mind our underlying concern with implications for family structure and family process and the need to maintain a global perspective, other key interconnected themes we revisit include shifts in demography, gender, relationship formation and working patterns, and how they impact on care. We also consider some of the other influences we expect to see on families as we move deeper in to the twenty-first century, focusing particularly on the possibilities presented by technology such as ART and increasingly sophisticated and accessible means of communications. It is not a new experience for families to be separated by oceans and continents but digital media go some way to attenuate the sense of separation when, for example, instant messaging through texting and tweeting can take place on a daily, if not hourly basis.

The first section of this chapter describes how global trends are likely to impact family life in the future and draws on Chapter 1, while the second section focuses on where and why differences as well as similarities are likely to emerge given the influential role of social structure. In the third section we look more closely at the dangers and opportunities these trends and futures represent for the sustainability of family life and consider how threats can be mitigated and potentialities realized. In many ways families thrive on being able to maintain important traditions and it is important to anticipate likely effects when continuities that enable them to function well are threatened. However, the issue of sustainability also has to be critically examined given that individuals subject to inflexible norms concerning family life can benefit from a loosening of these expectations, notwithstanding the personal difficulties this can present to other family members.

For example, the international fatherhood movement argues that parenting behaviour is shaped less by biology than by social conditioning, that men have strong and innate fathering instincts that are often sabotaged by cultural and social expectations. When mothers assume that men are less suited to caring roles than them, they distrust men's abilities to perform tasks adequately. This can hamper their own ability to integrate working and caring roles and erode men's confidence in their parenting abilities (Burgess, 1998). Resolving such tensions requires change in both women's and men's expectations, thus philosophical and social challenges often also have to be grappled with by the wider society.

The fourth and final section looks again at political and policy implications of the trends and futures discussed throughout the chapter: the challenges and opportunities these present to governments and legal systems among others.

We draw on the content of previous chapters (see Box 7.1 for key recurring points) and on many of the theoretical frameworks which aid understandings of families. To varying degrees these emphasize the importance of social structure, and individual and family choices, and the role these forces play in shaping responses to wider social change.

> ## Box 7.1   Reprising what families are, what they do and how we can understand them
>
> - Families are the oldest and the most important and enduring form of social grouping.
>
> - Most of us, at every age and stage of our lives, think of ourselves as part of one or more families.
>
> - Family arrangements vary across countries and communities, reflecting a range of social and economic arrangements.
>
> - They change all the time; families are formed, dissolved and reconfigured in the light of many factors. Historical research demonstrates that families are in a constant state of flux.
>
> - Comment, debates and policies bring families into the spotlight, and the question of how families can be supported, monitored, adapted and encouraged is repeatedly raised.
>
> - Sociology offers ways (or theories) of examining families and relationships.
>
> - Commentators and researchers may be optimistic, pessimistic or ambivalent about families, family life and the ways they change in response to a range of opportunities and challenges.

In Chapter 2 we explained that sociologists use the term social structure to refer to the relatively stable pattern of relationships between people in families, organizations, neighbourhoods, regions and countries and the structural features of a society provide its framework. At the core of this framework are the expectations and obligations which appear to govern people's actions. People are surrounded by structures which create, reinforce or challenge social roles: families themselves, education, labour markets and political systems. Within these contexts they may choose to act or recognize their constraints. The potential for agency on the part of an individual, or family grouping, is evident in the inequalities between families across the globe. Structures and agency interweave, reflecting belief systems and cultural norms.

Also in Chapter 2 we explained that theories are required to offer explanations and ideas on new, existing and differing combinations of events and activities. So sociological theory on families does not stand still, but like its object of study is constantly evolving, with research centres at universities focusing on developing particular explanations for families' behaviour. At the University of Hull the 'Displaying Families' project seeks to understand better how modern-day families need to make visible 'who belongs' as a result of changes in our social context. A team of psychologists at the University of Denver are studying partnership formation patterns through the development of commitment theory. However, we identified four main strands of theory to provide useful navigational aids to the subject's long and complex history of scholarship, and these are summarized in Box 7.2.

Box 7.2   An overview of sociological theory on families

- Structural approaches (particularly those of Durkheim, Parsons and Merton) emphasizing the 'ties that bind': the ways in which families provide ties that keep people in cohesive groupings that are the basis to ordering societies.

- Social interactions and sociological ideas on how individuals are actors and engage with each other in varied ways which create interdependencies (drawing on the work of Weber and Goffman).

- Conflict theories with the focus upon economic systems and the role of families in supporting and sustaining dominant means of production, focusing upon the work of Marx and Habermas.

- Feminist approaches in which the issues of gender, power and difference were brought to the fore (by Oakley, Lengermann and Niebrugge-Brantley, and Mies among many others).

See Chapter 2 for more detail on how these strands of theory developed and may be compared.

While variations in social structure across the world provide a frame for understanding differences, these differences are to a greater or lesser extent blurred by the process of globalization. The consumption patterns accompanying this process have facilitated a degree of homogenization (Leeder, 2004). The IMF defines globalization as 'the growing economic interdependence of countries worldwide through the increasing volume and variety of cross-border transactions in goods and services and of international capital flows and also through the more rapid and widespread diffusion of technology' (Wolf, 2000: 9).

TRENDS AND FUTURES

When considering how family life is changing across the world it is important to remember that there have always been dynamic forces acting on families and societies, opportunities and challenges have constantly been responded to as demonstrated by the historical studies mentioned in earlier chapters. Similarly, while globalization and global forces do much to create the context for family change and continuity, we do not want to overstate the 'newness' of their influence.

Box 7.3 indicates that globalization (and the homogenization that can accompany it through the blending of cultures) has been a recognized phenomenon since long before the internet, democratized air travel or a plethora of supranational institutions (such as the UN, EU or the World Health Organization). However there are other reasons why we should be cautious about how we think about globalization and particularly about treating today's interconnectedness as new. Firstly, authors point out that the term 'globalization' seeks to capture a package of many different yet interrelated changes, yet it has become a very widely adopted shorthand, a term 'perhaps used rather sloppily as if it was an explanation for changes in itself' (Jamieson, 2010b: 4). Secondly, the idea that the interconnectedness of the world (economically, politically, culturally as well as ecologically) is new is associated with a Eurocentric or Euro-North American-centric perspective, both of which tend to read history as if it began with Europe and treat Europe's modernity as the catalyst for interdependence (Jamieson, 2010b). This, however, ignores the fact that the imperialism, colonialism and slavery that made so-called 'Western modernity' possible, have connected histories (Bhambra, 2007).

Box 7.3   Earlier recognition of the pervasiveness of global influences

In 1936, the anthropologist Ralph Linton described globalization in terms of a typical day in the USA during which one might rise from a bed that came from the Near East via northern Europe, with sheets made of either cotton from India or silk from China. Men's shaving follows an Egyptian tradition and the wearing of neckties comes from seventeenth-century Croatia. Breakfast is eaten from plates invented in China, with knives from southern India, forks from Italy and spoons from the Romans. Our food consumption patterns originate from elsewhere: oranges from the eastern Mediterranean, cantaloupe melons from Persia, coffee from ancient Abyssinia. Cigarettes are Mexican in origin and tobacco itself came from Brazil. Linton ends with the fact that we read newspapers printed in type invented in Germany and 'thank a Hebrew deity in an Indo-European language that we are 100% American' (1936: 327).

In order to avoid a Eurocentric or Euro-North American-centric perspective we have throughout this book used the terms majority world and minority world.

➔ As we said in Chapter 1, what is often referred to as the 'Third World' is the majority world with most of the global population and landmass (Punch, 2003). Those who live in more affluent societies, including North America, Europe, Australia, New Zealand and parts of Latin America are in the statistical minority.

The adoption of the terms minority world and majority world reminds us of the disproportionate impact of the few affluent economies on global economics, health and well-being and climate change.

WORKING PATTERNS, GENDER AND CARE

If we unpack a little of what globalization entails, it becomes clear that the vast expansion of the movement of global capital from one country to another has impacted whole societies and has trickled down to family life. Multinational corporations proliferate and English is now spoken in almost a fifth of the world and continues to spread and undergo adaptations (Leeder, 2004). Some argue that this constitutes a new kind of colonialism, a 'takeover' by technology, language and ideas emerging from minority countries, that will result in cultural genocide or the destruction of culturally specific practices and groups of people (Bennholdt-Thomsen and Mies, 1999).

> **?**   From your own travel and experience, what majority world trades and customs are you aware of that have been displaced by the penetration of minority world technologies and practices? What have been the good and bad impacts on families, culture and society?

Questions arise for families such as who will work for the multinationals, how far are they prepared to travel to do so and how that enables or hinders caregiving in the family. Although women have always worked, in many parts of the majority world, they have done so in a home-based way (Edgell, 2006). Sweatshops are working environments considered to be unacceptably difficult or dangerous where workers often work long hours for unusually low pay in conditions that make few or no concessions to health and safety requirements. These and other settings that provide cheap labour for incoming global companies, require women (and often children) to leave their households, thus significantly and directly impacting on family life.

Women are not only working more but they are also moving into traditionally male-dominated employment and, despite encountering some resistance, for example from religious authorities (particularly when women want to occupy status positions in some religious hierarchies) such changes seem likely to progress further (Leeder, 2004; Peters, 2004). Concomitantly parenting is also likely to undergo (further) transformation. Although historically and internationally women have carried out a disproportionate amount of childcare, often working a 'second shift' after paid labour (Hochschild and Machung, 2003), a degree of change is becoming evident, particularly in the minority world. Shifts are taking place in the domestic division of labour with men increasing the time they spend in household and childrearing tasks (Gershuny, 2000).

The combined effect of these shifts in working, gender and care is likely to be the further waning of patriarchy, although progress on this front is highly patchy in different regions of the world as we discuss below (see Therborn, 2004). Also, when thinking about the relationship between work and care it is vital to look beyond the care of children and to see the particular significance of eldercare, given the demographic challenges already with us and which lie ahead.

➔ The extent to which patriarchy is declining in different societies across the world is also discussed in Chapter 3.

DEMOGRAPHY: FERTILITY, LIFE EXPECTANCY AND CARE

The American demographer Warren Thompson observed changes in birth and death rates in industrialized societies over the previous 200 years and developed a model called the democratic transition (*Encyclopedia of Population*, 2003). This model represents the transition from high to low birth and death rates that a country undergoes as it develops from a pre-industrial to an industrialized economic system (although it should not be assumed that the model applies to all countries and is deterministic of their development). One consequence of such a demographic transition is the ageing of populations in most developed economies. The maturing of the labour market in the EU, for example, in terms of age and therefore experience, has required the development of strategies to encourage those who might otherwise have retired to remain for longer in employment.

➔ Refer to Chapter 3 for more material on the 'greying' of populations which, we explained, presents difficulties as well as opportunities.

Increased longevity, while a success story for many societies in that it reflects significant developments in public health and awareness, overall national and personal prosperity and access to ever more sophisticated healthcare, also has significant implications for families and governments. The requirement for social care noted in Box 7.4 is likely to exceed the capacity that the state can affordably deliver and, regardless of their circumstances, families will be required to play a much greater role. While in many families there is a strong desire to provide eldercare, other social trends militate against this being easy to achieve. In the second topic in Chapter 1 we illustrate 'actual' experiences in Singapore, Japan and China where adherence to the virtue of filial piety is a valued continuity outworked adaptively to changing economic and social conditions.

Box 7.4   The implications of an ageing population for the UK

According to a leading British policy thinktank, the projected rapid increases in the UK's population in the coming years, and, the fact that it is becoming older overall present 'the most serious social policy issue in decades' (Centre for Social Justice, 2010: 18). They describe the significant pressure on age-related public services – such as the state pension and benefit system, healthcare and social care provision – given that, by the year 2024, one in five people will be of pensionable age: a 32% increase. Moreover, many individuals within the pensioner population will be living for much longer by 2033 (Office for National Statistics, 2009b).

Greater prevalence of dual-earning couple families, where both adults work outside the home, sharply decreases the availability of daytime care for older relatives. In societies that have experienced high levels of divorce and separation, spouses are also less frequently available to provide care. Despite a decrease in widowhood, it is not unusual for people to be single in older age.

> ➡ The ways in which working patterns impinge on families' ability to care are explored in greater depth in Chapters 4 and 6.

At the same time however, many grandparents are fit enough to enjoy caring for dependent grandchildren. A pan-European survey shows that 58% of grandmothers and 50% of grandfathers provided regular or occasional childcare in the past year for their grandchildren aged 15 or younger (Hank and Buber, 2009) while in the USA 43% of grandmothers say they provide regular childcare (Fuller-Thomson et al., 1997; Baydar and Brooks-Gunn, 1998). Of course, grandparental care may not just help out working parents. Grandparents are stepping in where families have irremediably broken down due to abuse and violence and this trend is set to continue with many minority world governments looking for family-based ('kinship care') solutions to prevent children from becoming wards of the state. Not only is the care of such children highly expensive but they may suffer highly deleterious outcomes. In many majority world contexts, particularly in countries with high prevalence of AIDS, the care given by the grandparental generation to their dead children's children will remain indispensable.

RELATIONSHIP FORMATION

Cherlin (2004) described the trend towards more individualized couple relationships that is a feature of many minority world societies and how this is a further development of the transition seen in marriage in the mid-twentieth century. Social changes in the wake of the

Second World War placed more emphasis on the emotional satisfaction of spouses for marital success and shifted away from the importance of marriage as a social institution (Burgess and Locke, 1945). The second transition to the individualized marriage expands the emphasis on personal choice, self-development and indeed self-fulfilment as a goal of the relationship.

> ➜ For more detail on changes in the ways many couples are forming long-term relationships please turn to Chapter 5.

The institution of marriage itself has become more dispensable prior to childbearing in many societies. Leeder describes the spread of these shifting norms to other contexts saying that 'many definitions of what are acceptable sexual behaviours are evolving as a result of rapid importation of sexual ideas from minority world countries' (2004: 39).

It is likely therefore that relationships in many countries 'receiving' these ideas will be increasingly subject to significant pressure from the high expectations that tend to accompany 'individualized' marriage and intimate partnerships. Indeed there are now estimated to be 5,000 divorces a day in China (UN Department of Economic and Social Affairs, 2009), and the increase in relationship breakdown in countries such as India is partly attributable to such shifts and also to changes in legislation. This will have implications for the care of dependent children and older family members as mentioned earlier.

Obviously more readily available and socially acceptable divorce can also make it easier for partners, usually but by no means always women, to leave relationships that are abusive or violent. However, rising divorce rates in a country such as Iran (particularly in urban areas) may be rather less advantageous to women. Divorce became simpler after the Islamic Revolution and unilateral rights belonging to the Islamic legal tradition were restored to men (Hutter, 1998). Although the law was modified to provide more protection for women when abuses became apparent (Aghajanian, 1986) wives still have far fewer rights to obtain divorce than husbands.

Authors caution against overemphasizing greater individualism and the decline in traditional ways of conducting relationships on a global canvas not least because polygamy, arranged marriages and other forms of marriage remain acceptable in certain cultures (including some ethnic minority subcultures within Western societies). Jamieson (2010b) refers to the review of studies of families in the last century, a major piece of work undertaken by Goran Therborn (2004), and to smaller qualitative studies reporting on couple relationships and parent–child relationships. Combined, these illuminate that 'continuity balances or outweighs changes that appear to enhance individual freedoms; patriarchy can survive the easing off of some forms of male power' (Jamieson, 2010b: 6).

> **?** Throughout this book we have emphasized and explained changes in family structures and processes. However it is important to reflect also on what has not changed from one generation to another. What aspects of your and your parents' or grandparents' family life are more similar than different? Why do you think they have remained fairly unchanged?

THE IMPACT OF TECHNOLOGY ON FAMILIES

Finally, in this section we reiterate the importance of technological advances to family but widen the discussion beyond improvements in electronic means of communication (referred to in Chapter 5 as 'relational technology') to consider the impact of ART. Not only does widely available technology such as Skype™ allow global families to keep in touch but it also contributes to the worldwide blending or homogenizing of cultures as television and other media facilitate the reaching of large and disparate groups of people (Toffler, quoted in Zwingle and McNally, 1999). Cultures will continue to evolve to meet technological challenges, responding to influences originating across the globe, and bringing families with them on the journey.

The potential for ART to transform our understanding of what it means to be a family is easily overlooked. The world's first successful *in vitro* fertilization took place in 1978, resulting in the birth of Louise Joy Brown in Manchester, UK. Since then, jurisdictions have had to develop legal protocols to regulate what has become the fertility industry, given that scientists now have the ability to initiate life in contexts where this would previously have been impossible. Women are enabled to give birth far later in life: it is now not unheard of to start or continue childbearing in one's sixties. This has implications for those partnering far later in the lifecourse and for children born earlier who are potentially old enough to be their siblings' parents.

Same-sex couples can raise children together who bear the genetic material of one of them and donated gametes. It is not new for children to be raised in same-sex households and early studies of same-sex parents concentrated on families where children were born inside heterosexual partnerships before one of the natural parents subsequently entered a gay or lesbian relationship (Golombok, 2007). However, one trend emerging as a result of the possibilities opened up by assisted reproduction and the legal recognition of same-sex couples is the reframing of parenthood as a socio-legal rather than a biological concept (Bainham, 2008). For example in Canada, provision to replace the term 'natural parent' in national law with the term 'legal parent' accompanied the recent legalization of same-sex marriage and in Spain birth certificates for all children now read 'Progenitor A' and 'Progenitor B' instead of 'mother' and 'father'.

Critics see these changes as fundamentally challenging the two-person, mother-father model of parenthood and argue that the possibility of assisted reproduction for same-sex couples or single people should not change the meaning of parenthood for everybody (Marquardt, 2006). Others contend that this is a welcome erosion of the heteronormative structures underlying many societies. We shall return to this subject later in the chapter when considering political and policy responses to family change.

In this section we have sketched out many broad trends while leaving to one side the unevenness of their impact and spread across the globe, and it is to this that we now turn.

COMMONALITIES AND DIFFERENCES ACROSS THE GLOBE

Notwithstanding the importance of globalization as the common backdrop to social life, most if not all of the changes in family referred to throughout this book continue to be structured by existing family systems which are themselves grounded in regionally specific norms and institutions. Marriage rates may have fluctuated in industrialized countries while remaining relatively stable in Asia and Africa.

> ➜ The unevenness of alterations to family structure receives more detailed attention in Chapter 3.

Fertility and death rates have declined in many countries with wider access to safer forms of contraception and abortion, increased survival rates of children, better health-care and higher levels of familial resources. However, there remain many extremely poor societies which have not seen these gains or have seen a stalling or reversal of improvement due to political unrest or disease epidemics such as AIDS.

The UN and World Health Organization (WHO) estimate that about 1,500 women continue to die every day in childbirth and that for every woman who dies giving birth, around 20 more suffer injury, infection or disease (WHO, 2005, 2007b). Around 11,000 newborns die (four weeks old or less) each day (WHO, 2005). As deficits in availability, accessibility, affordability and quality of care are fundamentally responsible (WHO, 2005), the vast majority of these deaths are avoidable. Large regional differences in maternal mortality rates (MMR) bear out this analysis. In sub-Saharan Africa, for example, a woman has a one in 13 chance of dying in childbirth. In industrialized countries, the risk drops to one in 4,085, reflecting global differences in life chances and choices (UN International Children's Fund (UNICEF), 2003).

When the UN set the Millennium Development Goals (MDG) in 2000, world leaders agreed that maternal deaths should be reduced by 75% by 2015. Billions of dollars of funding was pledged by governments and private foundations in the G8 Muskova Initiative on Maternal, Newborn and Under-Five Child Health in 2010 (Group of 8, 2010). While pressure to deliver on this MDG remains high, monitoring actual progress is vital as the MDG deadline approaches. Moreover, high levels of health and social inequalities within *wealthy* nations are reflected in comparative maternal mortality rates, with the latest UN statistics placing the USA 50th in terms of the rate of maternal deaths, with countries such as Bulgaria, South Korea and Kuwait ranked ahead (Amnesty International, 2010).

BELIEFS AND BEHAVIOURS

Families are also greatly affected by religious trends and movements. We noted above that the 1979 Islamic Revolution in Iran affected divorce procedures, and, in neighbouring Afghanistan during the second half of the 1990s, Taliban rule led to earlier marriage, larger families and strong pressures on women to return to subservient positions. Such developments coexist with the worldwide reach of the Women's Movement, with UN and other international groups counting gender as one of their major focuses. Leeder describes how, in each society, there exists a 'dynamic tension between forces for social change and those desiring maintenance of status quo' (2004: 267), the playing out of which will determine whether global trends are bucked or followed. In this section we shall revisit key themes identified earlier and examine the most relevant similarities and differences between and within countries.

On the subject of work and families, contrasts are made between expectations placed on children and young people in the minority world as opposed to their counterparts in the poorer, majority world. The eradication of exploitative forms of child labour and the universal provision of education are clear goals for many global campaigning organizations and there are strong social justice arguments against the running of sweatshops to fill the shopping malls of the West. However Jamieson (2010b) criticizes those writers who refer to a 'European tradition' in which children are treated as dependants in need of protection rather than recognized as inter-dependants, responsible for and capable of contributing to the family household. She notes the commonplace expectations on working-class children in the UK and elsewhere in Europe in the early twentieth century that they would contribute to household resources, e.g. by foraging for fuel and food, performing domestic work and remitting earned income to their parents when they started paid work in their early teens. It is, she says, within the relatively recent past that working-class children have become so comprehensively viewed as dependants rather than inter-dependants (Jamieson, 1987).

> **?** When reflecting on your own childhood, do you think more or less responsibility is carried by children and young people today?

Many minority world societies are currently experiencing a lengthened period of dependency (Jones, 2002), with what has been termed a 'boomerang generation' of young adults returning home to their parents after tertiary education, or following a short period of solo living or sharing with friends (Berrington et al., 2009). Further, with first marriages, on average, taking place at later ages and more informal partnering in one's early twenties, it is not uncommon for cohabiting couples to live with one set of parents to save money, often to clear student and other debt or to build up funds to buy their own housing. Again, this shows similarities with extended family households in the majority world but also the revisiting of trends from earlier generations when young couples were unable to set up their own homes until later in the lifecourse.

> **?** Think about the social, economic and relational implications for both generations when minority world adult children establish their first households with one of their sets of parents. What are the positive, negative and neutral outcomes? What might prevent or facilitate this becoming a majority practice in countries where it is presently comparatively rare?

Returning to gender, it is important not to overestimate the waning of patriarchy in many African and Asian countries despite gains for equality in Europe and North America and the influence of supranational organizations and declarations discussed in Chapter 3. The birth of boys continues to be favoured for social and economic reasons, and their care and education takes precedence over that of girls in many cultures in various ways. Where a dowry has to be paid to secure a husband, for example in India, girls take money out of the family whereas boys bring resources in. Working patterns for girls may be educationally disadvantageous, for example in Benin, school hours are long and inflexible and do not accommodate girls' domestic responsibilities (Gaba-Afouda, 2004). So-called 'honour-based' violence is commonly perpetrated in these regions to protect the family from disgrace when women do not conform to expected norms of sexually related conduct. (Some ethnic minority families living in Western settings have brought these and other so-called 'honour-based' practices with them from their country of origin and uphold them despite their illegality in their host country.)

Active steps are still taken in many majority world societies to secure male children (for example, China, South Korea, the Balkans and India), such as sex-selective abortion. The shortage of women that this has produced has implications for vulnerable women and children at risk of being trafficked between and within countries to fuel growth in the sex industry. Further, trafficking, particularly from poor to richer nations is also increasing and this is gaining salience as a human rights issue. In the coming years we should expect lobbying and pressure at the national and supranational government level to increase as the human implications of this problem intensify. In the minority world there are concerns that assisted reproduction and screening in pregnancy will produce 'designer babies', where sex and other desirable attributes are chosen. Sperm-sorting services in the USA report that 80% of parents want a girl, indicating that a preference for boys does not apply cross-culturally (Parliamentary Office for Science and Technology, 2003).

In terms of demography, we noted in Chapter 1 that many majority world countries are seeing welcome gains in survival rates of children into adulthood while increased longevity is the success story of the minority world. These differing patterns mean that a significant development in the twenty-first century is the diverging composition of minority and majority world populations. Older people (aged 60 and over) outnumber younger age groups in the former while the latter is characterized by having high percentages of the population below the age of 25. These broadbrush trends should not mask majority world continuities, such as the massive number of early and avoidable deaths due to maternal and infant mortality, infectious and curable diseases, natural disasters and wars (World Health Organization, 2007a, 2007b). AIDS has drastically depleted a generation, leaving millions of children orphaned and wholly dependent on grandparent carers, and will remain an ongoing challenge. Although the overall trend is a decrease in HIV incidence with 33 countries seeing a drop of more than 25% between 2001 and 2009 (22 of which are in sub-Saharan Africa, with the biggest epidemics in Ethiopia, Nigeria, South Africa, Zambia, and Zimbabwe having either stabilized or showing signs of decline), several countries in eastern Europe and Central Asia have seen an HIV incidence increase of more than 25% over the same period (Joint United Nations Programme on AIDS, 2010).

The minority world is facing a shortage of available family carers for an ageing population in a context where the safety net provided by welfare states is contracting, as we noted in Chapter 6. Parents needing to migrate long distances to find work, and AIDS, have both greatly contributed to a similar shortage in the majority world, where there is minimal state assistance. The recent trend we have seen of many grandparents reaching a point in the lifecourse where they might otherwise expect to be looked after by their adult children, but are instead taking on full-time financial and caring responsibilities of their grandchildren (whether due to disease, death or labour migration) looks set to continue.

Finally, when we consider the likely direction of relationship patterns, it is worth noting that empirical work from both the majority and minority worlds reveals the widespread appeal of the notion of more equal and intimate relationships (Padilla et al., 2007). Where this emphasis has been found, it can often coexist with entrenched patterns of hierarchy and inequality. For example, an ethnography by Jennifer Hirsch describes significant generational changes in marital ideals in Mexico: a new emphasis on *confianza* (trust), intimacy and mutually pleasurable sex. Yet a husband can still expect his wife to ask his permission to leave the house or fetch him a glass of water at his command (Hirsch, 2007). Thus while a global (if uneven) shift has been discerned away from 'traditional' notions of family (that emphasize the importance of social obligation) and towards models of family that are 'increasingly based on a "love" that is chosen, deeply felt, "authentic" and profoundly personal' (Padilla et al., 2007; xv), there is a pervasive sense of an uncompleted revolution.

> **?** It has been said that 'Women have run lap after exhausting lap in the long race towards equality. It is up to men to run the last few' (Reeves, 2002: 40). In what ways could it be argued that there has been an uncompleted revolution in family relations in the minority world?

'Traditional' practices *are* evolving. Riphenburg (1997) describes changes in marriage practices among the Shona, the dominant ethnic cluster in Zimbabwe. In this large, extended family system, brideprice is paid to the bride's family by the prospective groom's family. The bride's paternal aunt typically negotiates all the arrangements and exerts strong control over her niece's marriage. However, the process takes a long time, and, in the context of many other social changes, this kind of family has become much less common; despite attracting disapproval, more people are cohabiting without being married (Meekers, 1994).

In summary, the overall picture of persistence as well as change, and the persistence of global diversity (Therborn, 2004) accompanied by a degree of global convergence looks set to continue. Given these dynamics it is important to consider how families might be affected, for good and ill, and what can be done, where necessary, to mitigate harmful influences.

SUSTAINABLE FAMILIES?

We have already explained how, across the world, the family is constantly required to react to changes in the local, national and international economy, and to potential and actual shifts in social and cultural norms. We need to look at the sustainability of families through two different lenses. The first lens assumes a broadly conservative approach and looks at how families can be supported to maintain many of their caring and nurturing functions in the face of significant challenges. The second, more radical, lens is focused on how the changes swirling around families may be fundamentally altering their form and function and also how this might, in some ways, be welcome.

Addressing the more radical perspective first, it is important to assert, as we did in earlier chapters, that changing family forms do not always signal decline. Solo living in the minority world is a case in point: rather than reducing social networks and interaction and being symptomatic of a more individualized approach to family life, it is clear that many women living alone will maintain kin and friendship ties. Men's experience of single living may be more problematic. A British study showed that there has, over the past 30 years, been a dramatic increase in institutional bed occupancy among men aged 25–44 and that they are showing signs of greater propensity to ill-health (Prior and Hayes, 2003). Since 1981 the most vulnerable men are those who have never married and for whom social isolation is a key factor. Earlier in the century many of these men would have left their birth families to marry, as marriage was the marker of entry into adulthood (Mansfield and Collard, 1988), thus exchanging one support system for another.

Solo living is, of course, usually just one of several different household arrangements that will be experienced throughout the lifecourse. As we said in Chapter 2, Beck and Beck-Gernsheim (1995) have written about 'post-familial families' in which people create families, leave them for moments of time or longer periods and then freely choose to return, thus asserting agency. Of course, if dependant children are involved, the 'voyage of self-discovery' that such a trajectory implies (for example if a parent feels trapped and unable to stay within the nuclear family but then reconnects) can be very difficult to understand. Others contend that as the 'nuclear family' of parents and children is often 'not so nuclear' (Hansen, 2005), given that such a configuration works best when it receives care and support from beyond its boundaries, and from both kin and friends, the pain felt due to the departure of a parental figure can be mitigated.

In the majority world, the destabilizing of family norms would arguably be welcome if it allowed women greater agency, for example concerning their own sexuality. Female circumcision is one example of a form of control exerted over female family members by male relatives, particularly brothers, uncles and fathers. Male-dominated professions currently barred to women, not least because of their incompatibility with domestic responsibilities, will not be opened to women until there has been a loosening of socially sanctioned expectations. Men might also be constrained by similarly ascribed roles if expected to work in family businesses or continue a family tradition of entering a particular profession which would not be their chosen occupation.

Bearing these caveats concerning stability of norms in mind, we now consider some of the ways in which the changes identified throughout this book might threaten the sustainability of families in ways that require mitigation. In the last section we focused mainly on differences *between* countries, but *within* countries there may be significant variation that is a cause of concern. In the USA and the UK for example, considerable variability of family types exists between ethnic and religious groups. Among families originating from South Asia in the UK, divorce and lone parenthood are relatively low and cohabitation is almost non-existent. Among Black families, parental separation, lone parenthood and cohabitation are all relatively high (Rowthorn and Webster, 2006). Recent analysis of the UK Millennium Cohort Study found that just over half of mothers who are Black Caribbean are married when the child is born, compared with about 70% of mothers who are white. By contrast, almost all mothers who are Bangladeshi, Pakistani or Indian are married when their child is born (Goodman and Greaves, 2010). In the USA, more than two-thirds of Black births were to unmarried mothers in 2009 (Wilcox, 2010). Poverty and poor employment opportunities as well as cultural factors in many black communities all play a significant role in the choice of family type, but high levels of more informal childbearing are themselves perpetuating these cycles of poverty.

A recent OECD study looking at the effects of lone parenthood across a wide range of member countries points to the need for high levels of state subsidies to level out the economic disadvantages that tend to accompany single childbearing (OECD, 2009b). However, the changes to welfare states which began before the current global recession and the extremely high levels of government borrowing following the global economic crisis are severely constraining public finances. It will become increasingly difficult to support adequately the very high numbers of lone parents whose former partners are unable or unwilling to provide sufficient levels of child maintenance.

Also, challenges to welfare regimes are set to generate greater tensions in all families. A recent evaluation of data on social welfare spending from 15 European countries in the years 1980 to 2005 found that each £70 reduction in social welfare spending per person would increase alcohol-related deaths by about 2.8% and cardiovascular mortality by 1.2%, indicating that even modest budget cuts could have a significant impact on public health (Stuckler, 2010).

THE IMPORTANCE OF CHILDCARE

> ➜ We described in Chapter 1 how childcare deficits strain families in which (all) working-age adults have to work.

The withdrawal of rights to low-cost, full-time daycare in the Russian Federation after 1989 has hit many families hard, especially given the prevailing trend to divorced and widowed single mothers with high rates of full-time employment. Thus current generations of adult women active in the labour market are experiencing greater tensions between employment and care responsibilities than previous generations. The demise of welfare benefits and the growth in insecure and low-paid work has made the financial and practical support of grandparents and friends indispensable. At the same time, over-stretched families are finding it exceptionally difficult to assist elderly relatives themselves facing sharply reduced pension and healthcare provision (Ovcharova and Prokofieva, 2000).

Other families are caught up in 'global care chains' (Hochschild, 2003a) involving the transnational migration of adults from poor to rich countries to look after other people's children or elderly people. Yet they have their own dependants: children and elderly relatives, left in the care of other family members to whom remittances are usually sent.

> ➡ The emotional and practical strains this entails for the migrants, as well as for those left behind (carers and dependants) were discussed in Chapters 4 and 6, and look set to continue given the lack of opportunities to earn money in the sending countries.

Even in minority world contexts where there is adequate and affordable childcare and parents are coming home at the end of the day, the demands of work can undermine their emotional and physical availability for their children and other family members. Global working across time zones can involve the intrusion of work-related activities during times typically required for family activities. Flexible working may mitigate that to some extent, but it is also associated with the porous boundaries of expectations (Bailyn, 2003) with workers under pressure to be available 'whenever necessary' rather than during set hours. Cultural expectations also make it hard to manage the competing demands of work and family life. Many careers today seem to involve and require the internalization of ideals which prioritize the demands of work over those of the family, such as notions of professionalism which 'sustain definitions of selfhood that elevate the workplace over home life' (Kerfoot, 2002: 93).

Hochschild (1997) reveals how workers can collude with these cultural pressures when work is an easier environment to operate in than home. Her research found that few workers applied for family-friendly policies that 'offered more unconflicted time at home' (1997: 22) and ascribed this to the way home has become more like work than work itself. Emotional support and appreciation may be more readily available at work than at home, as work provides many people with their community and their support network. They feel more relaxed there than they do at home – where there are demanding family members and a depressing quantity of domestic chores. She concluded that for many the site for unsatisfying labour has shifted away from the industrial sphere and now finds itself in the domestic context. Research that enables us to go beyond simplistic criticism of employment conditions and looks at the pressures on employees from families themselves is therefore important.

> ? Think about some of the processes that take place in families you know with dependent children. Do parents ever confess to deliberately coming home after infants are asleep to avoid the stress of tired and fractious bedtimes, or talk about going back to work after holidays and weekends 'for a rest'? What enables people to make those choices and in what kinds of work would this attitude be more likely to prevail?

Finally, the separation of occupational and domestic spheres is not always treated as an unlimited good. Some writers argue that a more sustainable future lies in 'integrating' work and family wherever possible rather than trying to 'balance' the demands of each, particularly when both spheres require ever greater flexibility (Rapoport et al., 2002). The notion of 'time sovereignty' (Reeves, 2001), giving more workers control over where and when they work so that work commitments can be met in a way that they will flow smoothly with all the other, previously conflicting, priorities of life, is presented as a solution. However, this will do little to reduce the problems of dependant care or assist the many people who prefer to keep work and leisure completely separate, both spatially and temporally.

In spite of greater explicit recognition from government, employers and wider society of the pressures family members combining work and care are under, it therefore seems likely that old risks (of care deficits and role strain) will continue to present and that new risks will emerge. For example, while it is recognized that very young children need high levels of time and attention from primary caregivers (usually parents) or qualified professional childcare workers, teenage and older children present different challenges. Socialization, boundary setting, and maintenance and nurture continue beyond the early years and values are difficult to impart in the prevailing context of time famine. An analysis of calls to the main parenting helpline in the UK found that the majority of parents are seeking help when their teenage children are displaying physically and verbally aggressive behaviour (Parentline Plus, 2010). Aggressive behaviour is often a symptom of either emotional or mental health problems and prevalence data suggest this is a significant and pervasive problem (Green et al., 2005) that is gaining increasing salience in government policy. The final section of this chapter will consider ways in which other threats to the sustainability of family we have identified are being addressed by governing bodies as we move further into the twenty-first century.

SHAPING POLITICS AND POLICY

The challenge facing all governments, at the most general level, is how to enable the development and maintenance of conditions which will protect and enhance life-enriching family relationships, notwithstanding the potential disruption that can be caused by economic recession, mobility, and migration, epidemics of disease and climate change. This presents political as well as policy challenges. Government rhetoric has to strike the right chord with families, members of which naturally constitute a significant proportion of the electorate in representative democracies.

➔ Chapter 4 looks in detail at family policy challenges facing local and national governments and the political difficulties they encounter when they are considered to be interfering with family practices or commenting on family structures.

Without attempting to cover a wide range of possible issues here, we restrict ourselves to a few general comments then look in more detail at two policy areas of current and future concern to governments: the need to accommodate and address family fragility (particularly in ways that recognize class and ethnic differences) and the need to respond to calls for legal recognition of same-sex partnering and parenting.

Typically, the more individualized in orientation and wealthy a country is, the more social programmes its government provides, in contrast with poorer countries where families traditionally assist needy members (Leeder, 2004). Recently, wealthy nations such as Qatar, which have not in the past developed a body of social policies, are responding to the depth and breadth of social and economic change and its potential and actual effects on families, by developing an 'integrated social policy' prioritizing strong cohesive families (see Box 7.5).

Box 7.5 'Developing an integrated social policy for Qatar'

According to the Qatari government, by 2030 Qatar aims to be an advanced society capable of sustaining its development and providing a high standard of living for all people. Qatar's national vision defines the long-term outcomes for the country and provides a framework within which national strategies and implementation plans can be developed.

The Qatar National Vision 2030 project calls for strong cohesive families, an effective social protection system for all Qataris, effective public institutions, and strong and active civil society organizations. Its purpose is to support the achievement of these social development outcomes through the development of an integrated social policy for Qatar. While it is common for social policies

(Continued)

(Continued)

to be linked to social services, such as education, health, employment and social protection and security, this project extends the definition of social policy beyond the provision of such basic amenities to protection and social justice for all men, women and children.

The rationale for developing such an integrated social policy refers to the rapid modernization, economic growth and social change that Qatar is undergoing, which necessitates the development of effective institutions and mechanisms that will ensure a safe, secure and stable society (General Secretariat for Development Planning, 2010).

At the same time as some countries are developing comprehensive social policies, others are in the process of reconfiguring and, to some extent, dismantling welfare regimes and arrangements that have been in place for half a century or more. In the USA, welfare reform has ended the federal guarantee of financial assistance for poor children, putting in its place a 'workfare' programme that requires parents and others in receipt of welfare payments to work. It is argued that the US government has no comprehensive plan to assist contemporary families (Martin, 1997) although expenditure on the elderly has increased (Chapa et al., 1988), an emphasis that is likely to be maintained given the 'greying' of the population.

?   For what other reasons, beyond the increasing proportion of elderly sections of the population, might governments focus more resources and assistance here rather than on the early years of childhood?

ADDRESSING FAMILY FRAGILITY

As part of its overall welfare reform agenda, the USA has, however, also introduced a programme called the Healthy Marriage Initiative, which aims to address the high levels of single parenthood associated with welfare dependency and poverty. Given the distinct needs of different ethnic minorities, separate but related programmes have been set up such as the Hispanic Healthy Marriage Initiative and the African American Healthy Marriage Initiative (AAHMI). Hispanic minorities have much higher than average teenage birth rates, an upward trend of births outside marriage, and 30% of Hispanic children live in poverty (Administration for Children and Families, 2010). There are similar concerns about the future of African American families, given that between 1940 and 1990 the percentage of Black children living with both parents dropped from 75.8% to 33.2%, largely because of increases in never-married Black mothers. During this period African Americans reported more spousal abuse, singles and couples reported less connection to relatives and Blacks who married (and stay married) increasingly indicated lower marital satisfaction (Malone-Colon, 2007).

While the socioeconomic pressures that increase Black couples' vulnerability to other stressors are acknowledged (Clark-Nichols and Gray-Little, 1991), the AAHMI aims to improve child well-being, foster responsible fatherhood, and build stronger African American families and communities through a focus on strengthening couple relationships. In Chapter 4, we referred to this emphasis as a future growth area for policy, evident in programme developments in Norway (Helskog, 2009), Australia (van Acker, 2009) and the UK, with interest also in many other countries including Singapore (Huang, 2005) and India (Henry, 2010).

The backdrop of globalization presents other new challenges to governments where divorce and separation are concerned, such as when 'international families' are involved. Legislative positions in any one country have to be worked out in collaboration with other jurisdictions given that couples coming from very different countries might otherwise have highly conflicting laws concerning children of their union. International treaties such as the Hague Convention on the Civil Aspects of International Child Abduction aim to protect children internationally from the harmful effects of being wrongfully removed by one of their parents following a custody dispute. The Hague Convention aims to decrease the number of international abductions through judicial remedies (Hague Conference, 1980). This and similar conventions are in force in over 40 countries, including states as diverse as the UK, Argentina, Bosnia-Herzegovina, Chile, Finland, Romania, Zimbabwe and the USA.

National laws concerning the family are also increasingly subject to those passed by supranational institutions such as the EU. The EU Convention on Jurisdiction and the Recognition and Enforcement of Judgments in Matrimonial Matters 1998 sets out rules for determining jurisdiction in matrimonial disputes in all the countries of the EU, including the accession states that joined in 2004 and 2007 (with the exception of Denmark). This convention was subsequently repealed and superseded in November 2003 by Council Regulation (EC) No 2201/2003, Concerning Jurisdiction and the Recognition and Enforcement of Judgments in Matrimonial Matters and Matters of Parental Responsibility (otherwise referred to as 'Brussels II'). Tensions can arise, however, when legal harmonization is sought, for example when national courts are compelled to follow foreign divorce laws through the practice of what is known as 'applicable law' (Centre for Social Justice, 2009).

SAME-SEX RELATIONSHIPS AND ASSISTED REPRODUCTION

Other legal challenges relating to the family and strongly linked with globalization emerge in the area of same-sex relationships. Jurisdictions not permitting the full and equivalized recognition of same-sex marriage are under some pressure to acknowledge the legality of a marriage contracted abroad. A landmark case concerning two female academics, Professors Celia Kitzinger and Sue Wilkinson, who had married in British Columbia, Canada in 2003, shortly after same-sex marriage became legal, was brought before the High Court of England and Wales (Family Division) in 2006 (Probert, 2009).

The couple's relationship had no legal status at all in the UK until two years later when, with the implementation of the Civil Partnership Act 2004, the relationship was automatically converted to a civil partnership. Kitzinger and Wilkinson rejected civil partnership status, believing it to be both symbolically and practically a lesser substitute and unsuccessfully asked the court to recognize their overseas marriage in the same way that it would recognize the marriage of an opposite-sex couple. They argued that a failure to do so breached the European Convention on Human Rights, incorporated into domestic UK law by the Human Rights Act 1998.

These and other international conventions will increasingly be used to argue for changes in domestic laws concerning same-sex partnering and parenting. At the same time, campaigners are concerned that the rights of adults to reproduce are trumping the future rights of children yet to be born, to know both their (genetic) father and mother. They argue that this conflicts with the paramountcy principle in the internationally respected (and much copied) UK Children Act 1989, which requires that when courts determine questions relating to the upbringing of a child, the child's welfare shall be the paramount consideration. This position is, however, countered by those who describe reproductive choice as a basic human right, extending this to cover the right to reproduce in a variety of ways made possible by new reproductive technologies (Harris, 2000). They argue that regulation or constraint is both wrong and unnecessary except in the most extreme of circumstances, because 'unless the child's condition and circumstances can be predicted to be so bad that it would not have had a worthwhile life, a life worth living, then it will always be in that child's interests to be brought into being' (Harris, 2000: 30). Similarly, the assumption that the children's future welfare is a relevant consideration when deciding whether to provide a person with assisted conception services is challenged (Jackson, 2002). The prevailing situation in many jurisdictions has been described as a 'rights see-saw' (Centre for Social Justice, 2008: 21), in which clarity has still to emerge.

SUMMARY

Throughout this chapter and indeed throughout the whole of this introductory textbook, we have attempted to distil and make comprehensible global and national trends in the area of family life. Without unduly simplifying the notion of globalization we have shown how it provides the backdrop to many of the changes, challenges and choices facing families. Yet we have also insisted on the need to be aware of local structures which always mediate to some degree the influences of external forces.

Looking back over all the previous chapters, we have emphasized the importance of family practices and identities and the ongoing need for their careful study as these illuminate a wide range of different professions and inform related academic disciplines. The way people talk about their families and the meanings associated with members of one's kinship network show great diversity while still revealing shared priorities. Ways in which social scientists understand and make sense of these priorities are described by us in terms of the theories they work with and refine in light of empirical data collected either through national surveys and other quantitative means or by observing family life close at hand.

Some of the challenges of researching family life are described. These include shedding preconceptions from our own domestic experiences, ensuring that we are informed by accurate historical material and staying attentive to the extraordinary insights that can come from studying ordinary routines and rituals. We moved on to explain that it is becoming increasingly common for this 'stuff of everyday life' to be the concern of governments. They strive both to demonstrate an understanding of the challenges faced by constituents and subjects, and yet also to avoid encroaching too far and exceeding what is locally deemed to be the appropriate purview of the state. Perhaps delicacy is universally perceived to be most important when considering adult couple relationships and sexuality, an area in which people's expectations can be so high. Yet capacities to sustain these vital links across the lifecourse seem, in many cultures and settings, to be under threat.

We considered the challenges and also the opportunities for families provided by the overlapping and often highly intrusive world of work. Earning a living is usually the key to family survival and a route to self-realization, yet inherently risky when it draws family members ever longer distances away from each other or consumes time that might otherwise have been spent sustaining and developing couple, parental and other family relationships.

In this final chapter our aim was to draw all these threads together and to give a sense of how the past and the present will inform and shape the future. With this in mind we found these words from the sociologist Elaine Leeder, who has also written extensively about global families, an apposite note to draw this book to a close:

> The family has been around since the beginning of humankind and clearly will exist in some form forever. However, what it looks like, what it does and how it operates depends on variables that are complex. The structural arrangements of society affect the family and influence the entity the family becomes. The family does not operate in a vacuum ... one needs to see the family in the context of these structural arrangements and social order ... an appreciation of this complexity is part of education. In a dynamic process the family acts and reacts to the social, political, environmental and economic forces (structural arrangements) around it. The family in the world is in process: resilient, the family copes with the forces acting on it and adapts in an ongoing manner that makes it a highly elastic and changeable form. (2004: 2)

Sociology concerns the study of groups in societies and we noted at the outset of the book and this chapter that families are the oldest and most important and enduring form of social grouping. We also asserted that sociological analysis is imperative to the study of families and relationships. Throughout the preceding chapters we have introduced a range of material on trends in families across the globe as well as theories that offer ways of exploring and understanding these. It is our hope that the sociological perspectives we have introduced will encourage readers to explore and critically reflect on the many ways in which people engage in families and relationships.

EXPLORE FURTHER

Cheal, D. (2008) *Families in Today's World: A Global Perspective*. London: Routledge.

Leeder, E. (2004) *The Family in Global Perspective: A Gendered Journey*. New York: Sage.

Power, A., Willmot, H. and Davidson, R. (2011) *Family Futures: Childhood and Poverty in Urban Neighbourhoods*. Bristol: Policy Press.

Somerville, M. (2007) 'From homo sapiens to techno sapiens: children's human rights to natural human origins', in M. Somerville (ed.), *The Ethical Imagination: Journeys of the Human Spirit*. Melbourne: Melbourne University Press.

Therborn, G. (2004) *Between Sex and Power: Family in the World, 1900–2000*. London: Routledge.

Therborn, G. (2010) *The World: A Beginner's Guide*. Oxford: Polity.

USEFUL WEBSITES

On the subject of ART, there are many articles and information pages on the website of BioCentre, a British thinktank focusing on emerging technologies and their ethical, social and political implications. BioCentre is a cross-disciplinary network of scientists, physicians, ethicists, lawyers, researchers and others, who share a common concern that, in welcoming new developments in technology, the dignity of the individual and the uniqueness of human nature is asserted from a UK, European and global perspective. See www.bioethics.ac.uk/topics/index.php. A similar US-based resource is at http://bioethics.com/

The Millennium Project was founded in 1996 after a three-year feasibility study with the United Nations' University (UNU), Smithsonian Institution, Futures Group International, and the American Council for the UNU. It is now an independent non-profit global participatory futures research thinktank of futurists, scholars, business planners, and policy makers who work for international organizations, governments, corporations, NGOs, and universities. The Millennium Project manages a coherent and cumulative process that collects and assesses judgements from over 2,500 people selected by its 40 nodes around the world. The work is distilled in its annual 'State of the Future' and 'Futures Research Methodology' series, and special studies. See www.millennium-project.org/

Several times throughout this book we have referred to the UN Millennium Development Goals. In 2010 the UN Summit on the Millennium Development Goals concluded with the adoption of a global action plan to achieve the eight anti-poverty goals by their 2015 target date and the announcement of major new commitments for women's and children's health and other initiatives against poverty, hunger and disease. Progress is charted at www.un.org/millenniumgoals/

Glossary

Abuse: Physical, sexual and verbal acts with a high probability of causing long-term harm to the recipient, who may be a child or a partner.

Affinal relationship (or affinity): Refers to people who are related by marriage (or legally recognized partnership) ties. A relative by marriage is an affine. There are three types of affinity. Direct affinity exists when a couple are married or in a legally recognized relationship. Secondary affinity exists between a spouse and the other spouse's relatives by marriage, and collateral affinity is between a spouse and the relatives of the other spouse's relatives.

Bilateral descent: The kinship organizing system in societies where rights and obligations are based on and recognized as existing between relations on the mother's and father's side of the family (in contrast to unilineal descent systems). Bilateral kinship systems are basic to Western culture but from a global perspective are comparatively rare.

Birth rate: Typically expressed as the number of live births per 1,000 women of child-bearing age.

Breadwinner: Any person in the family who earns some or all of the household income on a regular basis.

Bride wealth: A payment in goods or property, or a combination of both, made to the bride's family by the husband's family.

Cohabitation: Living together in a sexual and economic relationship without having undergone a wedding ceremony or a registered marriage.

Cohort: All those persons who were born within a highly limited span of years and who, therefore, from birth to death experience the same national events, moods, and trends at similar ages.

Collateral kinship: Refers to a relative descended from the same biological pool but in a different line on the family tree, for example one's uncle (father's brother, mother's brother, father's/mother's sister's husband) or nephew (sister's son, brother's son, wife's brother's son, wife's sister's son, husband's sister's son).

Community:	A form of social organization that gives people a sense of shared interest in and belonging in some form to a larger group either geographically or as an identity.
Conjugal relationship:	A heterosexual partnership traditionally established through legal marriage, but in many societies cohabitation can now offer a basis to kinship that has some similarities. The conjugal *family* of parents and their dependent children is often referred to now as a **nuclear family**.
Consanguineous relationship (or consanguinity):	Holds where people are biologically or blood related. A consanguine is a relative by birth in contrast to in-laws related by marriage ('affines') and step-relatives. A **consanguineal family** consists of a parent, his or her children, and other people usually related by blood.
Crude divorce rate:	The number of registered divorces in a given year per 1,000 of the population.
Crude marriage rate:	The number of marriages registered during the calendar year per 1,000 of the population.
Demographic changes:	Key changes to the population which impact on the family. For example, changes can include delayed pregnancy and marriage, a declining or burgeoning fertility rate and the ageing of the population.
Demography:	The social scientific study of human populations, which is particularly concerned with births and deaths, marriages/cohabitation and divorce/separation.
Dependent children:	A dependant is someone defined as a child who is sustained by another person, such as his or her parents or guardians.
Development:	The degree of industrialization, health, welfare and education of a nation. Development measures also consider the life expectancy of a nation's citizens and the extent to which they have clean (drinkable) water and an adequate income.
Disability:	A physical or mental inability to do something that most other people would consider normal, or an impairment that substantially limits one or more major life activities.
Divorce:	The formal legal termination of a marriage that has been legally constituted.
Dowry:	Goods or property, or a combination of both, that the bride brings with her, from her family, into the new family she forms on marriage.
Dual-income families:	Both parents are involved in the labour market, as opposed to one assuming childcare and other domestic roles to the exclusion of paid work (typically the mother)

and the other earning all of the household income (typically the father).

Egalitarian: Another word for equality. When used with reference to the family it implies symmetry in roles, status and division of labour for both members of the conjugal couple.

Empirical: The objective measuring and testing of social phenomena leading to the production of statistical and other data.

Endogamy: Marriage between people of the same social category or group and, conversely, the prohibition or strong discouragement of marriage or sexual relations outside one's social group.

Ethnicity: This is a term used to describe a category for describing collective identities. Ethnic groups share a distinct set of beliefs and cultures based on historical or geographical origins.

Exogamy: Marriage between people from different social categories or groups, whether defined by religion, caste or locality.

'Families we live with': Term associated with John Gillis (2004: 989) to describe our daily and actual experiences of family life, in contrast to 'families we live by', which refers to ideals we hold for our family life, however unrealized these might be.

Family: A family is generally based on marriage, intimate partnerships, biological descent, and adoption. It is a small group of people who share a distinct sense of identity and responsibility for each other. Commitment to family members generally outweighs commitments to others.

Family, beanpole: In many minority world societies, where people live longer but have fewer children (so each generation has fewer siblings), and family trees of living relatives are becoming longer and thinner, sometimes extending to four generations.

Family, blended: Similar to but not the same as a step-family – a couple family that contains two or more children, at least one of whom is the natural child of both members of the couple, and at least one is the stepchild of either of the couple.

Family breakdown: When one or more members of the family, generally adults, leave the family relationship and also often the family home.

Family cohesion: Individual activities, and policies and practices that sustain and support members of families to stay together and support each other.

Family, intact: A couple family containing at least one child who is the biological or adopted child of both members of the couple, and no child who is the stepchild of either member of the couple. (*See also* **family, blended** and **family, step**).

Family, matrifocal: A nuclear family without an adult male functioning as a husband/father, who may be missing due to death, separation from the mother, divorce, abandonment or because of the need to migrate to find employment. The mother raises her children more or less alone and subsequently has the major role in their socialization (such families are also referred to as 'matricentric').

Family, nuclear and extended: A family is a group of people sharing close personal relationships that endure across generations and link people in the past, present and future. A household of two generations, generally parents and children is commonly referred to as the nuclear family. An extended family incorporates three or more generations vertically, grandparents, grandchildren and great-grandparents and children, and horizontally, aunts and uncles.

Family of choice: A phrase used to describe a family structure created often but not exclusively by non-heterosexuals, which emphasizes community and mutual support through loving and caring relationships rather than biological connectedness.

Family of origin: The family into which an individual was born. Sometimes also called one's **family of orientation**, although if the birth family breaks down through the end of the parents' couple relationship, or the child is given up for adoption, the new family of which the individual is part becomes the family of orientation.

Family of procreation: The family in which a person has his or her own children, although some family units are formed by couples where there is no intention to raise children either because of voluntary childlessness, infertility or because the family unit is based on a same-sex relationship.

Family policy: Set of policies geared towards supporting or strengthening the functions families carry out. These are, according to the UN Programme on the Family (2009), reproduction, care, emotional support and intergenerational solidarity (the close interpersonal ties seen across two or more generations within families, characterized by interdependence and mutual support).

Family practices: Term developed by David Morgan (1996: 190) which he defined thus: 'practices often little fragments of daily life which are part of the normal taken-for-granted existence of practitioners. Their significance derives from their location in wider systems of meaning.'

Family, processes: The functions carried out by family members, or the dynamics of the relationships in the family structure.

Family, reconstituted: Families where one or both partners has separated or divorced and has formed a new relationship with a second partner, taking with them some or all of their children. (*See also* **families, step**.)

Family, stem: Narrow nuclear family, descended over generations. Similar to **family, beanpole**.

Family, step: A term often used interchangeably with **reconstituted families**. A step-family is a family in which one or both members of the couple have children from a previous relationship.

Family strategies: Term used to refer to how families create and shape their responses to change.

Family structures: This term is used to describe how families are composed or how families are formed.

Family, traditional: Heterosexual couple, married, living with their children in a cohesive and stable family unit.

Family, transnational: A family in which members live in different countries and possibly continents.

Fertility rate: Typically expressed as the number of live births per 1,000 women of childbearing age.

Fictive kinship: Practice of referring to close family friends using terms associated with family membership such as aunts or uncles, sisters or brothers.

Formal care: Care that is regulated by statutory bodies and generally takes place from the recipient's home. The main types of formal care include before and/or after school care, long day care, family day care, occasional care and preschool. It also involves all types of residential care establishments (both public and private) and children placed in formal fostering or under guardianship.

Functionalism: Perspective that dominated sociological thinking until the 1960s which stressed the importance of the 'functional fit' of the institutions that make up society (particularly the family) and held that social events are best explained in terms of the functions they perform – that is, the contributions they make to the continuity of a society. Functionalists viewed society as a complex system whose various parts work in a relationship to each other in a way that needs to be understood.

Functions: The purpose of an aspect or unit of society (such as the family) or the activity it carries out which meets individual or wider social needs. The family as a basic social unit performs essential functions for its members (such as socialization and physical

	care) and for society by reproducing the next generation and thus ensuring continuity.
Gender:	Social expectations surrounding appropriate behaviour for the members of each sex. Gender is often wrongly used to refer to physical differences between men and women (which should correctly be attributed to sex). Gender refers to socially determined traits of what it means to be masculine and feminine. The study of gender relations has become one of the most important areas of sociology in recent years.
Global care chains:	A term developed by Hochschild (2003b) to refer to the links between people across the globe which are based upon paid and unpaid care work. The so-called outsourcing of care and domestic work takes place on national and transnational scales and involves the movement of workers – most often women many of whom leave behind dependants – who migrate from rural to urban, cross border (e.g. Mexico to California) or cross continents (Philippines to USA). Some economies are dependent upon the return of resources from these migrant workers.
Globalization:	Term applied to the process of increasing global interconnectedness and growing interdependence between different peoples, regions and countries in the world as social and economic relationships reach across the world.
Heteronormative:	The cultural bias favouring opposite-sex relationships and opposing same-sex relationships of a sexual nature. To the extent the former are viewed as normal and the latter are not, lesbian and gay relationships are subject to a heteronormative bias.
Heterosexual:	Social and sexual behaviour, practices, and identity based on a primary preference or desire for the opposite sex.
Homosexual:	Social and sexual practices describing sexual attraction towards, and responsiveness to, members of the same sex.
Household:	A group of two or more related or unrelated people who usually reside in the same dwelling and who make common provision for food or other essentials for living; or a person living in a dwelling who makes provision for his or her own food and other essentials for living without combining with any other person.
Household strategies:	Term used to describe how members of a household create and shape their responses to everyday activities and change.
Hypothesis:	An idea, or an educated guess, about a given state of affairs or a relationship between two different variables. A hypothesis is proposed to form the basis for research or empirical testing in order to prove or disprove what it states.

Ideology:	A shared system of beliefs and values defining and justifying a particular way of life as opposed to other ways of living. As these ideas are talked about and become incorporated into debates, policies and activities, over time they become accepted as providing a dominant view. Many argue that ideologies are used as a screen to inequalities and structures that create and justify unequal relationships. Ideologies present differences and inequalities as inevitable and universal.
Individualism:	Broadly speaking this refers to any set of ideas emphasizing the primary importance of the individual and the individual's interests and the value attached to individual freedom and individual choice. The philosophy of individualism is frequently contrasted with collectivism, where the collective rather than the individual good is paramount. Some thinkers express concern that individualism has become excessive to the detriment of strong and stable families.
Industrialization:	Industrialization, one of the main sets of processes influencing the social world over the past two centuries, is said to take place when a culture or a region becomes more economically dependent on factory/manufacturing employment and large-scale production than on farming. It is paralleled by the process of urbanization. The tiny proportion of the population working in agriculture presents a major contrast with pre-industrial countries.
Infant mortality rate:	Typically expressed as the number of deaths of infants in their first year of life per 1,000 population.
Informal care:	Regular and sustained care and assistance provided by a person, such as a family member, friend or neighbour to the person requiring support, usually on an unpaid basis.
Interview:	A research method that involves asking people questions, often on a one-to-one basis. The process of interviewing can be structured where all the questions are written down in advance, or unstructured, where the interview is like a conversation.
Lifecourse:	The series of social and family-oriented positions through which a person moves during the course of his or her life. This can be highly individualized in societies where it has become less common to follow a standard pattern or **lifecycle**, in which a sequence of stages are followed in a particular order.
'Local extended family':	Families with much contact with extended kin facilitated and reinforced by the nearness or geographical proximity of such kin.
Lone person:	A single person who makes provision for him or herself without combining with any other person to form part of a multi-person household. The lone person may live in a

	dwelling alone or share a dwelling with another individual or family.
Longitudinal study:	A study that follows a cohort of people through a number of years of their lives, thus tracking changes in their lives and the effects of early events on later life.
Majority world:	What has often been called the 'Third World' is the majority world with most of the global population and landmass (Punch, 2003). (See also *Minority world*)
Marriage, arranged:	When the marital partner is not chosen by the prospective bride or groom (as in what is often referred to as a 'love' marriage) but by others, usually their parents, although the right to veto or to choose partners with parental agreement is now common.
Marriage, forced:	When individuals are made to marry someone against their will usually under threat of violent and/or abusive consequences or social shunning if they refuse to comply.
Marriage or marital status:	An individual's position in a set of social categories defined in relation to marriage. Such statuses include single (never married), cohabiting (living together without being married), married, separated (from a marriage or other partner), divorced (where the marriage has been legally ended) and widowed (having experienced the death of a marriage partner).
Marxism:	Theoretical perspective linked to the writings of Karl Marx that places a major emphasis upon the conflict that exists between social classes, categories of people divided according to their type of labour and ownership of wealth. In the capitalist system the people who own the means of economic production exploit the people who work for them for wages. Families are also exploited by capitalism as they undertake the reproduction of future workers and sustain current and former workers. (See also *Majority world*)
Matrilineal descent:	The kinship organizing system which traces ancestral descent through the mother's (maternal) line. One of two types of **unilineal descent**.
Minority world:	A term used to describe more affluent societies, including those of North America, Europe, Australia, New Zealand and parts of Latin America, which are in the statistical minority of the world. (See also *Majority world*)
Monogamy:	A form of marriage involving two people. Serial monogamy is becoming a common feature of some societies due to separation and divorce and subsequent re-partnering/remarriage.
Neolocal residence:	A living arrangement in which a newly formed couple, married or otherwise, establishes a residence independent

	of both families of origin. In societies where the couple are expected to live with or very near to the wife's or husband's kin this is known as **matrilocal** and **patrilocal** residence, respectively.
Norms (or normative guidelines):	Rules of behaviour which reflect a culture's values and expectations, either prescribing a given type of behaviour, or forbidding it. Norms are always reinforced by sanctions of one kind or another, varying from informal disapproval to physical punishment or even execution.
One-parent family:	A family led by a single parent with at least one dependent or non-dependent child (regardless of age) who is also usually resident in the same household. A one-parent family may include any number of other dependent children, non-dependent children and other related individuals. Also known as lone-parent family or single-parent family. (*See also* **Family** and **Family, matrifocal**.)
Patriarchy:	The processes of male domination.
Patrilineal descent:	The kinship organizing system which traces ancestral descent through the father's (paternal) line. One of two types of **unilineal descent**.
Politics:	The term politics is generally applied to behaviour within civil governments. Politics is a process by which groups of people make collective decisions. Politics is also evident in other group interactions, including corporate, academic, and religious institutions.
Policy:	A policy is typically described as a deliberate plan of action to guide decisions and achieve (a) rational outcome(s).
Polyandry:	A form of marriage involving simultaneous and socially accepted relations between one woman and two or more men.
Polygamy:	A type of marriage involving three or more people.
Polygyny:	A form of marriage involving simultaneous and socially accepted relations between one man and two or more women.
Population centre:	An area where people are concentrated, such as towns or cities.
Positivism:	The term used for knowledge that is thought to be disciplined, empirical, and scientific. Knowledge that emerges from research based upon positivism is considered to be free from bias that can emerge from organizations and beliefs, for example, political parties and governments, religious groups and or communities.

Post-industrial society: A term to describe the move from economic activity based on the production of goods through manufacturing and heavy industry, to services and knowledge/information businesses.

Pre-modern period: Broad term that refers to agricultural and usually pre-literate societies before they have undergone a period of modernity (industrialization and urbanization).

Principle of stratified diffusion: Term associated with Willmott and Young to describe how traits and characteristics of higher social classes become copied by lower social classes over time.

Purposive sampling: This process is the selection of a particular group of people on purpose. Popular with qualitative research, the variables according to which the sample is chosen are driven by the research questions.

Qualitative: This refers to research that is concerned with meaning and emotions.

Qualitative method: This involves the collection of meanings, collected from interviews, diaries, letters and observation. It is usually richer and more detailed than quantitative data, but difficult to determine how representative it is as there is a danger of subjectivity and samples tend to be small.

Quantifiable: Where findings from research can be measured in statistical form.

Quantitative: This refers to research concerned with numerical and statistical data.

Quantitative method: This involves the collection of numerical data, collected from questionnaires and observation. It generates data that can be manipulated mathematically and statistically. Information generated provides characteristics and trends but will offer limited understanding as to why people act as they do or how they feel about experiences and issues.

Race: The term used to describe the social construction of categories based on observable physical and cultural characteristics. The use of this term is often predicated on supposed biological differences which are thought to lead to social differences.

Random sample: This is a group of people chosen on the basis that everyone in a given population has an equal chance of being selected.

Reductionism: Practice of treating everyone within a social group as having similar characteristics.

Reflexivity: Reflexivity includes both a subjective process of self-consciousness inquiry and the study of social behaviour with reference to theories about social relationships. In sociology it usually refers to the capacity of an individual to recognize their place in social structures and the impact of that on their interpretation and analysis of data and theories.

Relative poverty: Lacking the things that others in your culture expect to be able to afford.

Representativeness: The extent to which a small group can be said to reflect the social characteristics of a larger group from which it is drawn.

Research strategy: The methodological approach to undertaking research.

Rite of passage: A ceremony or significant event marking a milestone in the lifecycle, such as coming of age, graduation, marriage, leaving school.

Ritual: Specific behaviour that has significant meaning.

Same sex: Members of a single sex; often used to describe the partnership of homosexual men or women.

Social: Broad term relating to people and their interaction and engagement with each other

Social cohesion: When there is a strong bonding and sense of belonging within a group of people or society.

Social control: The way in which people's behaviour is affected by the social rules of the cultures in which they live.

Social policy: The guidelines and interventions for the changing, maintenance or creation of living conditions that are conducive to human welfare. Social policies focus on social issues.

Social trend: Term is used to describe an observable pattern occurring within a social context.

Stereotype: A commonly held, public belief about specific social groups, or types of individual.

Stratification, economic: Marxist idea that society is divided in economic terms, based on relationship to the means of production.

Structure, formal: External influences that have established rules and policies, such as government, legal system, etc.

Structure, informal: External influences that are fluid and flexible in their impact, such as peer group, subcultures, etc.

Subculture: A small group of people with different norms and values from mainstream society.

Subsistence: A form of living in poverty where only basic necessities are consumed.

Survey: A study technique involving research of a large number of people.

Survey design: The methodological construction used in undertaking a survey.

Texting: The exchange of brief written messages between mobile phones over cellular networks.

Theory:

A set of ideas, offering an explanation, usually based on reasoned evidence.

Tradition:

Social behaviour that celebrates certain norms and values associated with the past.

Tweeting:

Twitter is a social networking and micro-blogging service that enables its users to send and read messages known as tweets. Tweets are text-based posts of up to 140 characters displayed on the author's profile page and delivered to the author's subscribers, who are known as followers.

Unilineal descent:

Where social group formation and membership recognizes and is based on relations on either the mother's side or the father's side but not both.

References

Administration for Children and Families (2010) The healthy marriage initiative, available at www.acf.hhs. gov/healthymarriage/about/hispanic_hhmi.htm (accessed 27 December 2010).

Aghajanian, A. (1986) 'Some notes on divorce in Iran', *Journal of Marriage and Family*, 48 (4): 749–55.

Allan, G. (1985) *Family Life. Domstic Roles and Social Organisation*. Oxford: Basil Blackwell.

Allan, G. and Crow, G. (2001) *Families, Households and Society*. Basingstoke: Palgrave Macmillan.

Allan, G.A., Hawker, S. and Crow, G. (2011) *Stepfamilies*. Basingstoke: Palgrave Macmillan.

Almond, B. (2006) *The Fragmenting Family*. Oxford: Oxford University Press.

Amato, P.R. and Previti, D. (2003) 'People's reasons for divorcing: gender, social class, the life course, and adjustment', *Journal of Family Issues*, 24(5): 602–26.

American Heritage Dictionary (2000) *Dictionary of the English Language*. Orlando: Houghton Mifflin Company, available at www.thefreedictionary.com/politics (accessed 9 April 2011).

American Psychological Association (2009) 'Report of the APA Task Force on the Sexualization of Girls', available at www.apa.org/pi/wpo/sexualization.html (accessed 5 June 2011).

Amnesty International (2010) *Deadly delivery: the maternal health care crisis in the USA*. London: Amnesty International Publications 2010.

Anderson, M. (1980) *Approaches to the History of the Western Family 1500–1914*. Basingstoke: Macmillan Press.

Antonucci, T.C., Arjouch, K.J. and Janevic, M.R. (2003) 'The effect of social relations with children on the education–health link in men and women aged 40 and over', *Social Science and Medicine*, 56(5): 949–60.

Aos, S., Lieb, R., Mayfield, J., Miller, M. and Pennucci, A. (2004) *Benefits and Costs of Prevention and Early Intervention Programs for Youth*. Olympia, WA: Washington State Institute for Public Policy.

Appleton, L. and Byrne, P. (2003) 'Mapping relations between family policy actors', *Social Policy and Society*, 2(3): 211–19.

Appleton, L. and Hantrais, L. (eds) (2000) *Conceptualizing and Measuring Families and Family Policies*. Loughborough: European Research Centre, University of Loughborough.

Apter, T. (2009) *What Do You Want from Me? Learning to Get Along with In-Laws*. New York, NY: Norton.

Arber, S., Hislop, J., Bote, M. and Meadows, R. (2007) 'Gender roles and women's sleep in mid and later life: a quantitative approach', Sociological Research Online, 12 (5), available at www.socresonline.org. uk/12/5/3.html (accessed 5 June 2011).

Arts, W. and Gelissen, J. (2002) 'Three worlds of welfare capitalism or more? A state-of-the art report', *Journal of European Social Policy*, 12(2): 137–58.

Bailyn, L. (2003) 'Academic careers and gender equity: lessons learned from MIT', *Gender, Work and Organization*, 10(2): 137–53.

Bainham, A. (2008) 'Arguments about Parentage', *Cambridge Law Journal*, 67 (2): 322–51.

Baker, M. (2011) *Choices and Constraints in Family Life*, 2nd edn. Don Mills: Oxford University Press Canada.

Baldassar, L. (2007) 'Transnational families and aged care: the mobility of care and the migrancy of ageing', *Journal of Ethnic and Migration Studies*, 33(2): 275–97.

Banjee, B. (2007) *Corporate Social Responsibility: The Good, the Bad and the Ugly*. Cheltenham: Edward Elgar.

Barefoot, J.C., Gronbaek, M., Jensen, G., Schnohr, P. and Prescott, E. (2005) 'Social network diversity and risks of ischemic heart disease and total mortality: findings from the Copenhagen City Heart Study', *American Journal of Epidemiology*, 161(10): 960–7.

Barnes, M., Chanfreau, J. and Tomaszewski, W. (2010) *Growing up in Scotland: The Circumstances of Persistently Poor Children*. Edinburgh: The Scottish Government.

Bauman, Z. (2003) *Liquid Love: On the Fidelity of Human Bonds*. Cambridge: Polity Press.

Bauman, Z. (2005) *Liquid Life*. Cambridge: Polity Press.

Baydar, N. and Brooks-Gunn, J. (1998) 'Profiles of grandmothers who help care for their grandchildren in the United States', *Family Relations*, 47(4): 385–93.

Beck, U. (2000) *The Brave New World of Work*. Cambridge: Cambridge University Press.

Beck, U. and Beck-Gernsheim, E. (1995) *The Normal Chaos of Love*. Cambridge: Polity Press.

Becker, G.S. (1993) *A Treatise on the Family*. Cambridge: Harvard University Press.

Bengtson, V.L., Acock, A.C., Allen, K.R. and Dilworth-Anderson, P. (eds) (2004) *Sourcebook of Family Theory and Research*. Thousand Oaks, CA: Sage.

Benn, M. (1998) *Madonna and Child: Towards the New Politics of Motherhood*. London: Jonathan Cape.

Bennholdt-Thomsen, V. and Mies, M. (1999) *The Subsistence Perspective: Beyond the Globalized Economy*. London: Zed Books (1st edn 1972).

Benson, H. and Callan, S. (eds) (2009) *What Works in Relationship Education?: Lessons from Academics and Service Deliverers in the United States and Europe*. Doha: Doha International Institute for Family Studies and Development.

Bernard, J. (1982) *The Future of Marriage*, 2nd edn. New Haven: Yale University Press.

Bernardes, J. (1985) 'Family ideology: identification and exploration', *Sociological Review*, 33(2): 275–97.

Bernardes, J. (1997) *Family Studies: An Introduction*. London: Routledge.

Bernhardt, E. (2004) 'Cohabitation or marriage? Preferred living arrangements in Sweden', European Observatory on Social Situation, Demography and Family Paper 04/2004, available at www.oif.ac.at/sdf/sdf04-04-bernhardt.pdf (accessed 16 January 2011).

Berrington, A., Stone, J. and Falkingham, J. (2009) 'The changing living arrangements of young adults in the UK', *Population Trends*, 138: 27–37.

Bhambra, G. (2007) *Rethinking Modernity: Postcolonialism and the Sociological Imagination*. Basingstoke: Palgrave Macmillan.

Bibi, S., Cockburn, J., Fofana, I. and Tiberti, L. (2010) *Impacts of the Global Crisis and Policy Responses on Child Well-Being: A Macro-Micro Simulation Framework*. Italy: UNICEF, Innocenti Working Paper No. 2010–06.

Birkett, D., Johnson, D., Thompson, J. and Oberg, D. (2004) 'Reaching low-income families: focus group results provide direction for a behavioral approach to WIC services', *Journal of the American Dietetics Association*, 104: 1277–80.

Bittman, M., Rice, J. and Wajcman, J. (2004) 'Appliances and their impact: ownership of domestic technology and time spent on household work', *British Journal of Sociology*, 55(3): 401–23.

Blaikie, A. (1998) 'Scottish illegitimacy: social adjustment or moral economy?', *Journal of Interdisciplinary History*, 29: 221–41.

Bloch, M. (1953) *The Historian's Craft*. New York: Vintage.

Bogenschneider, K. (2000) 'Has family policy come of age? A decade review of the state of U.S. Family Policy in the 1990s', *Journal of Marriage and the Family*, 62(4): 1136–59.

Boss, P., Doherty, W.J., LaRossa, R. and Schumm, W.R. (2008) *Sourcebook of Family Theories and Methods: A Contextual Approach*. New York: Plenum.

Bott, E. (1968) *Family and Social Network*. London: Tavistock.

Bourdieu, P. (1996) 'On the family as a realised category', *Theory, Culture and Society*, 13(3): 19–26.

Bowlby, S., McKie, L., Gregory, S. and MacPherson, I. (2010) *Interdependency and Care Over the Lifecourse*. London: Routledge.

Brannen, J. (2003) 'The age of the beanpole family', *Sociology Review*, 13(1): 6–10.

Brannen, J. and Moss, P. (1992) 'Dual earner households after maternity leave in the U.K', in S. Lewis, D. Izraeli, and H. Hootsmans (eds), *Dual Earner Households: International Perspectives*. London: Sage.

Bryman, A. (2008) *Social Research Methods*, 3rd edn. Oxford: Oxford University Press (1st edn 2001).

Bumpass, L.L., Martin, T.C. and Sweet, J.A. (1991) 'The impact of family background and early marital factors on marital disruption', *Journal of Family Issues*, 12: 22–42.

Burgess, A. (1998) *Fatherhood Reclaimed: The Making of the Modern Father*. London: Vermilion.

Burgess, E.W. and Locke, H.J. (1945) *The Family: From Institution to Companionship*. New York: American Books.

Buss, D.M. and Barnes, M. (1986) 'Preferences in human mate selection', *Journal of Personality and Social Psychology*, 50(3): 559–70.

Butler, J. (1990) *Gender Trouble: Feminism and the Subversion of Identity*. London: Routledge.

Centre for Social Justice (2008) *Fathers not Included: A Response to the Human Fertilisation and Embryology Bill*. (Interim Report from the Family Law Review). London: Centre for Social Justice.

Centre for Social Justice (2009) *European Family Law: Faster Divorce and Foreign Law* (Interim Report from the Family Law Review). London: Centre for Social Justice.

Centre for Social Justice (2010) *The Forgotten Age: Understanding poverty and social exclusion in later life* (Interim Report from the Older Age Working Group). London: Centre for Social Justice.

CESifo (2008) '*Bismarck versus Beveridge: Social Insurance Systems in Europe*', CESifo DICE Report, No. 4/2008, available at www.cesifo-group.de/portal/page/portal/DICE_Content/SOCIAL_POLICY/Basic_Protection/SP060_GUARANTEEING_SUFFICIENT_RESSOURCES/bsimarck-beveridge-dicereport408-db6.pdf (accessed 16 January 2011).

Chapa, J., Hayes-Bautista, D. and Schink, W. (1988) *The Burden of Support: Young Latinos in an Aging Society*. Stanford, CA: Stanford University Press.

Charles, N. (2000) *Feminism, the State and Social Policy*. London: Macmillan.

Charles, N. and Kerr, M. (1988) *Women, Food and Families*. Manchester: Manchester University Press.

Cheal, D. (1991) *Family and the State of Theory*. London: Harvester Wheatsheaf.

Cheal, D. (2002) *Sociology of Family Life*. Basingstoke: Palgrave Macmillan.

Chen, X. and He, Y. (2005) 'The family in mainland China: structure, organization, and significance for child development', in J.L. Roopnarine and U.P. Gielen (eds), *Families in Global Perspective*. Boston: Pearson.

Cherlin, A.J. (2004) 'The deinstitutionalization of American marriage', *Journal of Marriage and Family*, 66(4): 848–61.

Cheung, C., Kwan, A. and Ng, S. (2006) 'Impacts of filial piety on preference for kinship versus public care', *Journal of Community Psychology*, 34(5): 617–34.

Clark, A. and Moss, P. (2005) *Listening to Children. The Mosaic Approach*. London: National Children's Bureau and Joseph Rowntree Foundation.

Clark-Nichols, P. and Gray-Little, B. (1991) 'Effect of economic resources on marital quality in black married couples', *Journal of Marriage and Family*, 53(3): 645–55.

Clifford, C. (2010) '*Rebuilding the Lives of Child Soldiers in Sri Lanka*', report available at http://children.foreignpolicyblogs.com/2009/07/20/rebuilding-the-lives-of-child-soldiers-in-sri-lanka/ (accessed 27 June 2010).

Coleman, P.G., Ivani-Chalian, C. and Robinson, M. (1999) 'Self and identity in advanced old age: validation of theory through longitudinal case analysis', *Journal of Personality*, 67(5): 819–49.

Coltrane, A. (1998) *Gender and Families*. Thousand Oaks, CA: Pine Forge.

Connell, R. (1987) *Gender and Power: Society, the Person and Sexual Politics*. Stanford, CA: Stanford University Press.

Connell, R. (2009) *Gender*. Cambridge: Polity Press.

Consortium of Family Organizations (1990) 'What is a family policy perspective and why is it needed? *Family Policy Report*, 1: 1–6.

Coontz, S. (1992) *The Way We Never Were*. New York: Basic Books.

Coontz, S. (2004) 'The world historical transformation of marriage', *Journal of Marriage and Family*, 66(4): 974–9.

Coontz, S. (2005) *Marriage, a History: From Obedience to Intimacy, or How Love Conquered Marriage*. New York: Viking.

Cowan, C.P. and Cowan, P.A. (1992) *When Partners Become Parents: The Big Life Change for Couples*. New York: Basic Books. Republished by Lawrence Erlbaum Associates, Fall, 1999.

Cowan, C.P. and Cowan, P.A. (1995) 'Interventions to ease the transition to parenthood: Why they are needed and what they can do', *Family Relations*, 44: 412–23.

Cowan, P. and Cowan, C.P. (2008) 'Diverging family policies to promote children's well-being in the UK and US: some relevant data from family research and intervention studies', *Journal of Children's Services*, 3(4): 4–16.

Crompton, R. (2001) 'Gender, comparative research and biographical matching', *European Societies*, 3(2): 167–90.

Crompton, R. (2006) *Employment and the Family: The Reconfiguration of Work and Family Life in Contemporary Societies*. Cambridge: Cambridge University Press.

Cunningham-Burley, S. and Jamieson, L. (eds) (2003) *Families and the State: Changing Relationships*. Basingstoke: Palgrave.

Curthoys, A. (1993) 'Identity crisis: colonialism, nation and gender in Australian history', *Gender and History*, 5(2): 165–76.

Cusworth, L. (2009) *The Impact of Parental Employment (Studies in Cash and Care)*. Aldershot: Ashgate.

D'Abbs, P. (1991) *Who Helps? Support Networks and Social Policy in Australia*. Melbourne: Australian Institute of Family Studies.

Daniel, P. and Ivatts, J. (1998) *Children and Social Policy*. London: Macmillan.

Davidoff, L. and Hall, C. (1987) *Family Fortunes*. London: Hutchinson.

Davis, K. (1991) 'Critical sociology and gender relations', in K. Davis, M. Leijenaar and J. Oldersma (eds), *The Gender of Power*. London: Sage.

de Botton, A. (2010) *The Pleasures and Sorrows of Work*. London: Penguin.

de Tocqueville, A. (1945) *Democracy in America*, Vol. 2. New York, NY: Vintage Books.

Delamont, S. (2001) *Changing Women, Unchanged Men: Sociological Perspectives on Gender in a Post-Industrial Society*. Buckingham: Open University Press.

Delphy, C. (1977) *The Main Enemy*. London: Women's Research and Resources Centre.

Demeny, P. and McNicoll, G. (eds) *Encyclopedia of Population* (2003) New York: Macmillan Reference USA, pp. 939–40.

Dench, G. (2000) *Grandmothers of the Revolution*. London: Hera Trust.

Department for Children, Schools and Families (2010) *Support for All: The Families and Relationships Green Paper*. London: The Stationery Office.

Department of Work and Pensions (2010) 'Extra help for families in poverty' (Press Release 23 March 2010) available at http://www.dwp.gov.uk/previous-administration-news/press-releases/2010/march-2010/dwp052-10-230310.shtml (accessed 12 June 2011).

Departments of State and Official Bodies (1915) *Report on the Administration of the National Relief Fund up to 31st March 1915*, Cd 7756, Parliamentary Papers, 1914–16, p.5. London: HMSO.

Dermott, E. and Seymour, J. (2011) *Displaying Families: A New Concept for the Sociology of Family Life*. Basingstoke: Palgrave Macmillan.

Dragon, W. and Duck, S. (eds) (2005) *Understanding Research in Personal Relationships: A Text with Readings*. Thousand Oaks, CA: Sage.

Draper, D. (2009) *Couple Penalty 2008/09*. London: Care.

Duck, S. (2007) *Human Relationships*, 4th edn. Thousand Oaks, CA: Sage (1st edn 1986).

Durkheim, E. (1897) *Suicide: A Study in Sociology*. London: Routledge & Kegan Paul, 1952.

Eagleton, T. (2003) *After Theory*. London: Allen Lane.

Economist (2010) 'Gendercide. The worldwide war on baby girls', *The Economist*, 6 March, pp. 72–5.

Edgell, S. (2006) *The Sociology of Work: Continuity and Change in Paid and Unpaid Work*. London: Sage.

Edin, K. and Kefalas, M.J. (2005) *Promises I Can Keep: Why Poor Women Put Motherhood Before Marriage*. Los Angeles: University of California Press.

Elliott, A. (2009) *Contemporary Social Theory. An Introduction*. London: Routledge.

Elson, D. (2006) 'Women's rights' and engendering development', in E. Kuiper and D. Barker (eds), *Feminist Perspectives on Gender and the World Bank*. London: Routledge.

Eng, D. (2010) *The Feeling of Kinship: Queer Liberalism and the Racialization of Intimacy*. Durham: Duke University Press.

Engels, F. (1845) *The Condition of the Working Class in England in 1844*. London: Harmondsworth Penguin, 1987.

Equality and Human Rights Commission (2010) *How fair is Britain? Equality, Human Rights and Good Relations in 2010*. London: Equality and Human Rights Commission.

Esping-Andersen, G. (1990) *The Three Worlds of Welfare Capitalism*. Cambridge: Polity.

Esping-Andersen, G. (ed.) (2002) *Why We Need a New Welfare State*. Oxford: Oxford University Press.

Esping-Andersen, G. (2009) *Incomplete Revolution: Adapting Welfare States to Women? New Roles*. Oxford: Polity Press.

European Commission (1997) *Promoting the Role of Voluntary Organizations and Foundations in Europe*, COM/97/0241 final. Brussels: European Commission.

European Commission (2009) *EU Campaign on Gender Pay Gap*. Brussels: EUROPA.eu.http://europa.eu/rapid/pressReleasesAction.do?reference=MEMO/09/91&format=HTML&aged=0&language=EN&guiLanguage=en (accessed 24 June 2011).

Eurostat (2007) *Marriage and Divorce Statistics*. Brussels: Eurostat.

Eurostat (2008) *Eurostat Data on the Gender Pay Gap*. Brussels: EU. Available at http://epp.eurostat.ec.europa.eu/tgm/table.do?tab=tableandinit=1andplugin=1andlanguage=enandpcode=tsiem040, (accessed 26 June 2010).

Eurostat (2010) *Marriage and Divorce Statistics*. Brussels: Eurostat.

Fawcett Society (2010) *The Facts*. London: Fawcett Society. Available at www.fawcettsociety.org.uk/index.asp?PageID=981 (accessed 30 December 2010).

Farrington, D.P. and Welsh, B.C. (2007) *Saving Children from a Life of Crime: Early Risk Factors and Effective Interventions*. New York: Oxford University Press.

The Fatherhood Institute (2010) *The Fatherhood Report 2010–11. The Fairness in Families Index*. Abergavenny: The Fatherhood Institute.

Ferge, S. (1997) 'The changed welfare paradigm: The "individualisation of the social"', *Social Policy and Administration*, 31(1): 20–44.

Ferraro, G. (2006) *Cultural Anthropology: An Applied Perspective*. Andover: Cengage Learning.

Fevre, R. and Bancroft, A. (2010) *Dead White Men and Other Important People: Sociology's Big Ideas*. Basingstoke: Palgrave Macmillan.

Finch, J. (1987) 'Family obligations and the life course', in A. Bryman et al. (eds), *Rethinking the Life Cycle*. London: Macmillan.

Finch, J. (1989) *Family Obligations and Social Change*. Cambridge: Polity.

Finch, J. (2007) 'Displaying families', *Sociology*, 41: 65–81.

Finch, J. and Mason, J. (1993) *Negotiating Family Responsibilities*. London: Routledge.

Fine, B. (1992) *Women, Employment and the Capitalist Family*. London: Routledge.

Forrester, D. (2010) 'Hidden harm: Working with serious parental drug misuse', in J. Barlow (ed.), *Substance Misuse. The Implications of Research, Policy and Practice*. London: Jessica Kingsley Publishers.

Fortes, M. (1983) '*Rules and the Emergence of Society*', Royal Anthropological Institute of Great Britain and Ireland Occasional Paper No. 39. London: Royal Anthropological Institute of Great Britain and Ireland.

Foucault, M. (1971) *The Archaeology of Knowledge*. New York: Pantheon.

Fukuyama, F. (1999) *The Great Disruption: Human Nature and the Reconstitution of Social Order*. New York: Free Press.

Fulcher, S. and Scott, S. (2011) *Sociology*, 4th edn. Oxford: Oxford University Press (1st edn 1999).

Fuller-Thomson, E., Minkler, M. and Driver, D. (1997) 'A profile of grandparents raising grandchildren in the United States', *Gerontologist*, 37(3): 406–11.

Future Foundation (2003) *My UK – Redefining Regions: Exploring Regional and Local Identity*. London: The Newspaper Society.

G8 Muskova Initiative on Maternal, Newborn and Under-Five Child Health (2010), 199.

Gaba-Afouda, L. (2004) *Gender Equality in Education in Benin: Summary of Topic*, UN Educational, Scientific and Cultural Organisation, 2004/ED/EFA/MRT/PI/22, available at http://unesdoc.unesco.org/images/0014/001467/146769e.pdf (accessed 27 December 2010).

Gabb, J. (2008) *Researching Intimacy in Families*. Basingstoke: Palgrave Macmillan.

Gaines, S.O. Jr. and Ickes, W. (2000) 'Perspectives on interracial relationships', in W. Ickes, and S. Duck (eds), *The Social Psychology of Personal Relationships*. Chichester: John Wiley & Sons.

Gauthier, A.H. (1999) 'Historical trends in state support for families in Europe (post-1945)', *Children and Youth Services Review*, 21(11/12): 937–65.

General Register Office for Scotland (2008) Increase in Number of Households in Scotland. Edinburgh: Scottish Government. http://www.gro-scotland.gov.uk/press/news2008/increase-in-number-of-households-in-scotland.html (accessed 22 June 2011).

General Secretariat for Development Planning (2010) *Qatar National Vision 2030*. Qatar: Doha Institute for Family Studies and Development, available at www.gsdp.gov.qa/portal/page/portal/GSDP_Vision_Root/GSDP_EN/What%20We%20Do/QNV_2030 (accessed 27 December 2010).

Gergen, K. (1994) *Realities and Relationships: Soundings in Social Construction*. Cambridge: Harvard University Press.

Gershuny, J. (1978) *After Industrial Society: The Emerging Self-Service Economy*. London: Macmillan.

Gershuny, J. (2000) *Changing Times: Work and Leisure in Post-industrial Societies*. Oxford: Oxford University Press.

Giddens, A. (1986) *The Constitution of Society: Outline of the Theory of Structuration*. Berkeley: University of California Press.

Giddens, A. (1992) *The Transformation of Intimacy: Sexuality, Love and Eroticism in Modern Societies*. Cambridge: Polity Press.

Giddens, A. (1998) *The Third Way: The Renewal of Social Democracy*. Cambridge: Polity Press.

Gillies, V. (2003) *Family and Intimate Relationships: A Review of the Sociological Research*. London: Families and Social Capital ESRC Research group, South Bank University.

Gillis, J. (1996) *A World of Their Own Making: A History of Myth and Ritual in Family Life*. Oxford: Oxford University Press.

Gillis, J. (2004) 'Marriages of the mind', *Journal of Marriage and Family*, 66(4): 988–91.

Gittins, D. (1993) *The Family in Question: Changing Households and Familiar Ideologies*. London: Macmillan.

Gittins, D. (1997) *The Child in Question*. Basingstoke: Palgrave Macmillan.

Glaser, K., Montserrat, E.R., Waginger, U., Price, D., Stuchbury, R. and Tinke, A. (2010) *Grandparenting in Europe*. London: Calouste Gulbenkian Foundation.

Global Policy Forum (2008) *Trends in Global Gross Domestic Product*. New York: Global Policy Forum, available at www.globalpolicy.org/ (accessed 27 June 2010).

Glucksmann, M. (2005) 'Shifting boundaries and interconnections: Extending the "total social organisation of labour"', *The Sociological Review*, 53(2): 19–36.

Golombok, S. (2007) 'Research on lesbian and gay parenting: An historical perspective across 30 years', in F. Tasker and J. Bigner (eds), *Gay and Lesbian Parenting: New Directions*. New York: Haworth Press.

González, L. and Viitanen, T.K. (2009) 'The effect of divorce laws on divorce rates in Europe', *European Economic Review*, 53(2): 127–38.

Goodman, A. and Greaves, E. (2010) *Cohabitation, Marriage and Child Outcomes*, IFS Commentary C114, Institute of Fiscal Studies.

Gough, I., Wood, G., Barrientos, A., Bevan, P., Davis P. and Room, G. (2004) *Insecurity and Welfare Regimes in Asia, Africa, and Latin America: Social policy in development contexts*. Cambridge: Cambridge University Press.

Graefe, D.R. and Lichter, D.T. (2008) 'Marriage patterns among unwed mothers: Before and after PRWORA', *Journal of Policy Analysis and Management*, 27(3): 479–97.

Grandin, G. (2010) *Fordlandia: The Rise and Fall of Henry Ford's Forgotten Jungle City*. London: Icon Books.

Green, H., McGinnity, A., Meltzer, H., Ford, T. and Goodman, R. (2005) *Mental Health of Children and Young People 2004*. London: Palgrave Macmillan.

Greenstein, T. (2006) *Methods of Family Research*. New York: Sage. (1st edn 2001).

Grint, K. (2005) *The Sociology of Work: An Introduction*, 3rd edn. Cambridge: Polity Press. (1st edn 1991).

Gupta, N.D., Smith, N. and Verner, M. (2006) *Child Care and Parental Leave in the Nordic Countries: A Model to Aspire to?* Institute for the Study of Labor (IZA) Discussion Paper No. 2014. Bonn: Institute for the Study of Labor.

Gutteridge, R. (2003) *Enduring Relationships: The Evolution of Long-lasting Marriage*. Uunpublished PhD thesis, University of Keele, Keele.

Hagestad, G.O. and Smyer, M.A. (1982) 'Dissolving long-term relationships: Patterns of divorcing in middle age', in S.W. Duck (ed.), *Personal Relationships 4: Dissolving Personal Relationships*. London: Academic Press.

Hague Conference (1980) Convention on the Civil Aspects of Child Abductors. Available at http://hcch.e-vision.nl/upload/conventions/txt28en.pdf (accessed 27 December 2010).

Hakim, C. (2000) *Work–Lifestyle Choices in the 21st Century: Preference Theory*. Oxford: Oxford University Press.

Hall, R., Ogden, P.E. and Hill, C. (1997) 'The pattern and structure of one-person households in England and Wales and France', *International Journal of Population Geography*, 3(2): 161–81.

Hank, K. and Buber, I. (2009) 'Grandparents caring for their grandchildren: findings from the 2004 Survey of Health, Ageing, and Retirement in Europe', *Journal of Family Issues*, 30(1): 53–73.

Hansen, K.V. (2005) *Not-so-nuclear Families: Class, Gender and Networks of Care*. New Brunswick: Rutgers University Press.

Hantrais, L. (2004) *Family Policy Matters: Responding to Family Change in Europe*. Bristol: The Policy Press.

Hantrais, L. (2007) *Social Policy in the European Union*, 3rd edn. Basingstoke: Palgrave Macmillan and St Martin's Press (1st edn 1995).

Harding, P. and Jenkins, R. (1989) *The Myth of the Hidden Economy: Towards a New Understanding of Informal Economic Activity*. Milton Keynes: Open University Press.

Hareven, T. (1994) 'Recent research on the history of the family', in M. Drake (ed.), *Time, Family and Community: Perspectives on Family and Community History*. Buckingham: Open University Press.

Hareven, T. (2000) *Families, History and Social Change. Life-course and Cross-Cultural Perspectives*. Boulder, CO: Westview Press.

Harley, S. (ed.) (2007) *Women's Labor in the Global Economy. Speaking in Multiple Voices*. New Brunswick, NJ: Rutgers University Press.

Harris, J. (2000) 'The welfare of the child', *Health Care Analysis*, 8: 27–34.

Hartman, M. (2004) *The Household and the Making of History: A Subversive View of the Western Past*. Cambridge: Cambridge University Press.

Haskey, J. (2005) 'Living arrangements in contemporary Britain: Having a partner who usually lives elsewhere and living apart together (LAT)', *Population Trends*, 122: 35–45.

Hearn, J. and Pringle, K. (2009) '*European Perspectives on Men and Masculinities: National and Transnational Approaches*. Basingstoke: Palgrave Macmillan.

Helskog, G. (2009) 'The Norwegian State: a relationship educator', in H. Benson and S. Callan (eds), *What Works in Relationship Education? Lessons from Academics and Service Deliverers in the United States and Europe*. Qatar: Doha International Institute for Family Studies and Development.

Hemmings, P. (2007) 'Family policy in Hungary: How to improve the reconciliation between work and family?', *OECD Economics Department Working Papers*, No. 566.

Henning, C. and Lieberg, M. (1996) 'Strong ties or weak ties? Neighbourhood networks in a new perspective', *Scandinavian Housing and Planning Research*, 13(3): 3–26.

Hennon, C. and Wilson, S. (2008) *Families in a Global Context*. London: Rouledge.

Henry, J.A. (2010) 'Protecting our fledgling families: a case for relationship-focused family life education programs', *Indian Journal of Community Medicine*, 35(3): 373–5.

Hiilamo, H. and Kangas, O.E. (2006) *Trap for Women or Freedom to Choose? Political Frames in the Making of Child Home Care Allowance in Finland and Sweden*, Department of Social Policy 15/2006. Turku: University of Turku.

Hilder, P. (2005) 'Neighbourhoods: from hamlets to living together?', in A. Buonfino and G. Mulgan (eds), *Porcupines in Winter*. London: Young Foundation.

Hill, R. (1984) 'Family studies and home economics: towards a theoretical orientation', *Canadian Home Economics Journal*, 34: 9–14.

Hirsch, J.S. (2007) '"Love makes a family": globalization, companionate marriage, and the modenization of gender inequality', in M.B. Padilla, J.S.Hirsch, M. Munoz-Laboy, R. Sember and R.G. Parker (eds), *Love and Globalization: Transformations of Intimacy in the Contemporary World*. Nashville, TN: Vanderbilt University Press.

Hochschild, A. (1983) *The Managed Heart: Commercialization of Human Feeling*. Berkeley, CA: University of California Press.

Hochschild, A. (1997) *The Time Bind: When Work Becomes Home and Home Becomes Work*. New York: Metropolitan Books, Henry Holt and Co.

Hochschild, A. (2003a) *The Commercialization of Intimate Life: Notes from Home and Work*. Berkeley, CA: University of California Press.

Hochschild, A. (2003b) *The Managed Heart: Commercialization of Human Feeling*. Berkeley, CA: University of California Press (1st edn 1983).

Hochschild, A. (2003c) 'Love and gold', in B. Ehrenreich, and A. Hochschild (eds), *Global Woman: Nannies, Maids and Sex Workers in the New Economy*. London: Granta.

Hochschild, A. and Machung, A. (2003) *The Second Shift*, 2nd edn. New York: Penguin (1st edn 2000).

hooks, b. (1984) *Feminist Theory: From Margin to Center*. Boston: South End.

Huang, W.J. (2005) 'An Asian perspective on relationship and marriage education', *Family Process*, 44(2): 161–73.

Hudson, J. and Lowe, S. (2009) *Understanding the Policy Process: Analysing Welfare Policy and Practice*. Bristol: Policy Press.

Hughes, J. (1990) *The Philosophy of Social Research*. Harlow: Longman (1st edn 1980).

Hunt, S. (ed.) (2010) *Family Trends Since 1950*. Bristol: Policy Press.

Huriwai, T., Robertson, P.J., Armstrong, D., Kingi, T.P. and Huata, P. (2001) 'Whanaungatanga – a process in the treatment of Maori with alcohol- and drug-use related problems', *Substance Use and Misuse*, 36(8): 1033–51.

Hurst, C. (2004) *Social Inequality: Forms, Causes and Consequence*. Boston: Pearson.

Hutter, M. (1998) *The Changing Family: Comparative Perspectives*, 3rd edn. New York: Macmillan (1st edn. 1981).

International Labour Organization (2011) *Decent Work Agenda*. Geneva: International Labour Organization. http://www.ilo.org/global/about-the-ilo/decent-work-agenda/lang--en/index.htm (accessed 24 June 2011).

Institute for Family Policies (2008) *Report on the Evolution of the Family in Europe 2008*. Madrid: IPF.

Jackson, E. (2002) 'Conception and the relevance of the Welfare Principle', *Modern Law Review*, 65(2): 176–203.

Jackson, S. and Scott, S. (2001) *Gender: A Sociological Reader*. London: Routledge.

Jamieson, L. (1987) 'Theories of family development and the experience of being brought up', *Sociology*, 21(4): 591–607.

Jamieson, L. (1998) *Intimacy*. Cambridge: Polity.

Jamieson, L. (1999) 'Intimacy transformed? A critical look at the "pure relationship"', *Sociology*, 33(3): 477–94.

Jamieson, L. (2010a) 'Issues facing today's families', paper delivered at Centre for Research on Families and Relationships Conference, 10 Februray 2010. 'Families Today: Where are we now?' Edinburgh: Centre for Research on Families and Relationships.

Jamieson, L. (2010b) 'Changing families and relationships in a changing world', keynote paper presented at the International Conference, 16–18 June 2010. Centre for Research on Families and Relationships. Edinburgh: Centre for Research on Families and Relationships.

Jamieson, L., Morgan, D., Crow, G. and Allan, G. (2006) 'Friends, neighbours and distant partners: extending or decentring family relationships?', Sociological Research Online, 11(3), available at www.socresonline.org.uk/11/3/jamieson.html (accessed 15 January 2011).

Jamieson, L. and Simpson, R. (2010) *Living on Your Own: Social Integration, Quality of Life and Aspirations for the Future*. Edinburgh: Centre for Research on Families and Relationships, University of Edinburgh. Briefing 47.

Jamieson, L. and Toynbee, C. (1990) 'Shifting patterns of parental control', in H. Corr and L. Jamieson (eds), *Politics of Everyday Life*. London: Macmillan.

Jamieson, L., Wasoff, F. and Simpson, R. (2009) 'Solo-living, demographic and family change: the need to know more about men', Sociological Research Online, 14(2/3), available at www.socresonline.org.uk/14/2/5.html (accessed 15 January 2011).

Joint United Nations Programme on HIV/AIDS (2008) *Report on the Global HIV/AIDS Epidemic*, available at http://data.unaids.org/pub/GlobalReport/2008/JC1511_GR08_ExecutiveSummary_en.pdf (accessed 27 June 2010).

Joint United Nations Programme on AIDS (2010) *UNAIDS Report on the Global AIDS epidemic 2010*, available at www.unaids.org/globalreport/Global_report.htm (accessed 27 December 2010).

Jones, G. (2002) *The Youth Divide: Diverging Paths into Adulthood*. York: Joseph Rowntree Foundation.

Jordan, B., Redley, M. and James, S. (1994) *Putting the Family First: Identities, Decisions and Citizenship*. London: UCL Press.

Kamerman, S.B. and Kahn, A.J. (1978) 'Families and the idea of family policy', in S.B. Kamerman and A.J. Kahn (eds), *Family Policy: Government and Families in Fourteen Countries*. New York: Columbia University Press.

Kara, S. (2009) *Sex Trafficking: Inside the Business of Modern Slavery*. New York: Columbia University Press.

Kellerhals, J. (2010) 'Changes in family life – issues for public policy', keynote address at Family Platform Conference, 28 July 2010, available at www.familyplatform.eu/en/home/news/critical-review-conference-lisbon (accessed 30 December 2010).

Kerfoot, D. (2002) 'Managing the "Professional Man"', in M. Dent and S. Whitehead (eds), *Managing Professional Identities: Knowledge, Performativity and the 'New Professional'*. London: Routledge.

Kiernan, K. (2003) *Cohabitation and Divorce Across Nations and Generations*, CASE Paper No. 65. London: London School of Economics.

Kiernan, K. and Estaugh, V. (1993) *Cohabitation*. London: Family Policy Studies Centre.

Kilmer, R., Gil-Rivas, V., Tededchi, R. and Calhoun, L. (eds) (2009) *Helping Families and Communities Recover from Disaster: Lessons Learned from Hurricane Katrina and Its Aftermath (Specific Approaches and Populations)*. Washington: American Psychological Association.

Kimmel, M., Hearn, J. and Connell, R. (eds) (2004) *Handbook of Studies on Men and Masculinities*. London: Sage.

Kraybill, D. (ed.) (2003) *The Amish and the State*. Baltimore, MD: Johns Hopkins University Press.

Kreyenfeld, M., Konietzka, D. and Hornung, A. (2009) 'Family diversity in France, the Russian Federation, and East and West Germany: overview on living arrangements and living conditions', in United

Nations Commission for Europe, *How Generations and Gender Shape Demographic Change: Towards Policies Based on Better Knowledge*. New York/Geneva: United Nations.

Lan, P.C. (2006) *Global Cinderellas: Migrant Domestics and Newly Rich Employers in Taiwan*. Durham: Duke University Press.

Laslett, P. (1965) *The World We Have Lost: England Before the Industrial Age*. London: Methuen.

Laslett, P. (2005) *The World We Have Lost: Further Explored*, 4th edn. London: Routledge (1st edn 1965).

Laswell, H. (1935) *Politics: Who Gets What, When, How*. London: McGraw-Hill.

Laungani, P. (2005) 'Changing patterns of family life in India', in J.L. Roopnarine and U.P. Gielen (eds), *Families in Global Perspective*. Boston: Pearson.

Layard, R., Nickell, S. and Jackman, R. (2005) *Unemployment: Macroeconomic Performance and the Labour Market*. Oxford: Oxford University Press.

Leeder, E. (2004) *The Family in Global Perspective: A Gendered Journey*. New York: Sage.

Lengermann, P. and Niebrugge-Brantley, J. (2000) 'Contemporary feminist theory', in G. Ritzer (ed.), *Sociological Theory*. New York: McGraw-Hill.

Letablier, M.-T., Pennec, S. and Büttner, O. (2003) 'An overview of changing family patterns in Europe', in M.-T. Letablier and S. Pennec (eds), *Changing Family Structure in Europe: New Challenges for Public Policy*. Cross-National Research Papers, Sixth Series, Improving Policy Responses and Outcomes to Socio-Economic Challenges: Changing Family Structures, Policy and Practice. Loughborough: European Research Centre, Loughborough University.

Letkemann, P. (2002) 'Unemployed professionals, stigma management and derived stigmata', *Work, Employment and Society*, 16(3): 511–22.

Levin, I. (2004) 'Living Apart Together: a new family form', *Current Sociology*, 52(2): 223–40.

Lewis, S., Brannen, J. and Nilsen, A. (2009) *Work, Families and Organisations in Transition*. Bristol: Policy Press.

Lindblom, C. (1959) 'The science of "muddling through"', *Public Administration Review*, 19(2): 79–88.

Linton, R. (1936) *The Study of Man: An Introduction*. New York: Appleton Century Crofts, Inc.

Livingstone, S. and Bovill, M. (2001) *Families, Schools and the Internet*. London: Media@LSE, London School of Economics.

Lopata, H.Z. (1972) 'Role changes in widowhood: a world perspective', in D.O. Cowgill, and L.D. Holmes (eds), *Ageing and Modernisation*. New York: Appleton-Century-Crofts.

Love, C. (1999) 'Family group conferencing: cultural origins, sharing, and appropriation: a Maori reflection', in G. Burford and J. Hudson (eds), *Family Group Conferencing: New Directions in Community-centred Child and Family Practice*. New York: Aldine de Gruyter.

Low, B.S. (2005) 'Families: an evolutionary anthropological perspective', in J.L. Roopnarine and U.P. Gielen (eds), *Families in Global Perspective*. Boston: Pearson.

Luxton, M. (1980) *More than a Labor of Love: Three Generations of Women? Work in the Home*. Toronto: Women's Press.

Luxton, M. and Gorman, J. (2001) *Getting by in Hard Times: Gendered Labour at Home and on the Job*. Toronto: University of Toronto Press.

MacLean, A., Harden, J. and Backett-Milburn, K. (2010) 'Financial trajectories: how parents and children discussed the impact of the recession, 21st century society', *Journal of the Academy of Social Sciences*, 5(2): 159–70.

Macpherson, C.B. (1962) *The Political Theory of Possessive Individualism: From Hobbes to Locke*. Oxford: Oxford University Press.

Malone-Colon, L. (2007) '*Responding to the Black Marriage Crisis*', Center for Marriage and Families Research Brief, No. 6, June 2007, available at http://familyscholars.org/ (accessed 16 January 2011).

Mansfield, P. and Collard, J. (1988) *The Beginning of the Rest of Your Life?* Basingstoke: Macmillan Press.

Marquardt, E. (2006) *The Revolution in Parenthood: The Emerging Global Clash Between Adult Rights and Children's Needs*. New York: Institute for American Values.

Marsh, P. and Brennan, E. (2008) 'Family Support Policy: An International Perspective', in J.M. Rosenzweig and E.M. Brennan (eds), *Work, Life and the Mental Health System of Care: A Guide for Professionals Supporting Families of Children with Emotional or Behavioral Disorders*. Baltimore, MD: Brookes.

Martin, G.T. (1997) 'The agenda for family policy in the United States', in T. Arendell (ed.), *Contemporary Parenting: Challenges and Issues*. Thousand Oaks, CA: Sage.

Marx, K. and McLellan, D. (2008) *Capital: An Abridged Edition*. Oxford: Oxford University Press.

Mason, G. (2002) *The Spectacle of Violence: Homophobia, Gender, and Knowledge*. London: Routledge.

Maxwell, J. (1996) 'Social dimensions of economic growth', *Eric John Hanson Memorial Lecture Series*, Vol. 8. Alberta: University of Alberta.

McKie, L. and Cunningham-Burley, S. (eds) (2005) *Families in Society: Boundaries and Relationships*. Bristol: Policy Press.

McKie, L., Gregory, S. and Bowlby, S. (2002) 'Shadow times: the temporal and spatial frameworks and experiences of caring and working', *Sociology*, 36(4): 897–924.

Meekers, D. (1994) 'Combining ethnographic and survey methods: a study of the nuptiality patterns of the Shona of Zimbabwe', *Journal of Comparative Studies*, 25(3): 313–28.

Mies, M. (1999) *Patriarchy and Accumulation On A World Scale: Women in the International Division of Labour*. London: Zed Books (1st edn. 1998).

Milardo, R.M. (1992) 'Comparative methods for delineating social networks', *Journal of Social and Personal Relationships*, 9(3): 447–61.

Millar, J. and Warman, A. (1996) *Family Obligations in Europe*. London: Family Policy Studies Centre.

Mills, C.W. (1959) *The Sociological Imagination*. Oxford: Oxford University Press.

Ministry of Civil Affairs (2009) *Gazette on Civil Affairs*. Beijing: Ministry of Civil Affairs.

Moen, P. and Schorr, A.L. (1987) 'Families and social policy', in M.B. Sussman and S.K. Steinmetz (eds), *Handbook of Marriage and the Family*. New York: Plenum.

Morgan, D. (1975) *Social Theory and the Family*. London: Routledge and Kegan Paul.

Morgan, D. (1996) *Family Connections: An Introduction to family Studies*. Cambridge: Polity Press.

Morris, L. (1997) 'Economic change and domestic life', in R.K. Brown (ed), *The Changing Shape of Work*. London: Macmillan.

Munro, A., Manthei, B. and Small, J. (1989) *Counselling: the Skills of Problem-solving*. London: Routledge.

Murdock, G. (1945) 'The common denominator of cultures', in R. Linton (ed.), *The Science of Man in the World Crisis*. New York: Columbia.

Murdock, G.P. (1981) *Atlas of World Cultures*. Pittsburgh: Pittsburgh University Press.

Murray, C. (2006) *In Our Hands: A Plan to Replace the Welfare State*. Washington: The American Enterprise Institute.

Naito, T. and Gielen, U. (2005) 'The changing Japanese family: a psychological portrait', in: J.L. Roopnarine and U.P. Geilen (eds), *Families in Global Perspective*. Boston: Pearson.

Naldini, M. and Saraceno, C. (2008) 'Social and family policies in Italy: not totally frozen but far from structural reforms', *Social Policy and Administration*, 42(7): 33–48.

Neuliep, J.W. (2008) *Intercultural Communication: A Contextual Approach*. Thousand Oaks, CA: Sage.

Newcastle City Council (2009) *Avoiding Gang Culture: Full Scrutiny Report*, available at www.newcastle.gov.uk/wwwfileroot/cxo/scrutiny/AvoidingGanCulturefullscrutinyreport.pdf (accessed 11 September 2010).

Nixon, P., Burford, G. and Quinn, A. with Edelbaum, J. (2005) *A Survey of International Practices, Policy and Research on Family Group Conferencing and Related Practices*. Englewood: American Humane Association.

Oakley, A. (1974) *The Sociology of Housework*. London: Martin Robertson.

Office for National Statistics (2009a) *Population Trends 138*. available at www.statistics.gov.uk/downloads/theme_population/Pop-trends-winter09.pdf (accessed 5 June 2011).

Office for National Statistics (2009b) *Statistical Bulletin: National Population Projections, 2008-Based*. Newport: Office for National Statistics.

Office for National Statistics (2010) *Households: UK National Statistics*. Newport: Office for National Statistics.

Olson, D.H., Russell, C.S. and Sprengkle, D.H. (1984) 'Circumplex model of marital and family systems: VI theoretical update', in: D.H. Olson and P.M. Miller (eds), *Family Studies Review Yearbook*, Vol. 2. New Delhi: Sage.

Ooms, T. (1990) 'Families and government: Implementing a family perspective in public policy', *Social Thought*, 16(2): 61–78.

Ooms, T. (2002) 'Strengthening couples and marriage in low-income communities', in A. Hawkins, L.D. Wardle and D.O. Coolidge (eds), *Revitalising the Institution of Marriage for the Twenty-First Century*. Westport, CT: Praeger.

Organisation for Economic Co-operation and Development (2009a) *Korea Policy Centre, Society at a Glance Asia/Pacific Edition*, available at www.oecd.org/dataoecd/27/13/43465580.pdf (accessed 11 September 2010).

Organisation for Economic Co-operation and Development (2009b) *Doing Better for Children*. Paris: OECD Publishing.

Organisation for Economic Co-operation and Development (2010) *OECD Family Database*. OECD, Social Policy Division – Directorate of Employment, Labour and Social Affairs, available at www.oecd.org/dataoecd/52/27/41920080.pdf (accessed 11 September 2010).

Ovcharova, L. and Prokofieva, I. (2000) 'Poverty and interfamily solidarity in Russia in the transition period', *Public Opinion Monitoring*. VTSIOM, 4: 29.

Padilla, M.B., Hirsch, J.S., Munoz-Laboy, M., Sember, R. and Parker, R.G. (eds) (2007) *Love and Globalization: Transformations of Intimacy in the Contemporary World*. Nashville, TN: Vanderbilt University Press.

Pahl, R. (1988) 'Some remarks on informal work, social polarization and the social structure', *International Journal of Urban and Regional Research*, 12(2): 247–67.

Pahl, R. (2000) *On Friendship*. Cambridge: Polity Press.

Pahl, R. and Wallace, C. (1985) 'Household work strategies in an economic recession', in: N. Redclift and E. Mingione (eds), *Beyond Employment: Household, Gender and Subsistence*. Oxford: Blackwell.

Pahl, R. and Spencer, L. (2003) *'Personal Communities: Not Simply Families of "Fate" or "Choice"'*, ISER Working Papers, No. 2003–4.

Papini, D., Datan, N. and McCluskey-Fawcett, K. (1988) 'An observational study of affective and assertive family interactions during adolescence', *Journal of Youth and Adolescence*, 17(6): 477–92.

Parentline Plus (2010) *When Family Life Hurts: Family Experience of Aggression in Children*, available at www.parentlineplus.org.uk/files/public/sharedfiles/PplusAggressionOctFinalGL.pdf (accessed 27 December 2010).

Parkinson, P. (2006) 'Keeping in contact: The role of family relationship centres in Australia', *Child and Family Law Quarterly*, 18(2): 157–74.

Parliamentary Office for Science and Technology (2003) '*Sex Selection*', Postnote, July 2003 No. 198, available at www.parliament.uk/documents/post/pn198.pdf (accessed 27 December 2010).

Parrenas, R. (2005) *Children of Global Migration. Transnational Families and Gendered Woes*. Stanford, CA: Stanford University Press.

Parsons, T. (1953) 'A revised analytical approach to the theory of social stratification', in R. Bendix and S. Lipset (eds), *Class, Status, and Power: A Reader in Social Stratification*. Glencoe, IL: Free Press.

Pastorino, E.E. and Doyle-Portillo, S.M. (2008) *What Is Psychology?* Andover: Cengage Learning.

Patterson, C.J. and Friel, L.V. (2000) 'Sexual orientation and fertility', in: G. Bentley and N. Mascie-Taylor (eds), *Infertility in the Modern World: Biosocial Perspectives*. Cambridge: Cambridge University Press.

Peters, T. (2004) *Re-imagine! Business Excellence in a Disruptive Age*. London: Dorling Kindersley.

Phillips, P. (2006) *Censored 2007: The Top 25 Censored Stories*. New York: Seven Stories Press.

Phoenix, A. and Husain, F. (2007) *Parenting and Ethnicity*. York: Joseph Rowntree Foundation.

Plummer, K. (1995) *Telling Sexual Stories: Power, Change and Social Worlds*. London: Routledge.

Prior, P. and Hayes, B. (2003) 'The relationship between marital status and health: an empirical investigation of differences in bed occupancy within health and social care facilities in Britain, 1921–1991', *Journal of Family Issues*, 24(1): 124–48.

Probert, R. (2009) *Cretney and Probert's Family Law*. London: Sweet and Maxwell (1st edn titled *Elements of Family Law* 1987).

Probert, R. and Callan, S. (2011) *History and Family Policy: Examining the Evidence*. London: Centre for Social Justice.

Prodi, R. and Kinnock, N. (2000) 'The Commission and non-governmental organizations: building a stronger partnership', European Commission discussion paper. Brussels: European Commission.

Prout, A. (1999) *The Body, Childhood and Society*. Basingstoke: Palgrave Macmillan.

Punch, S. (2002) 'Research with children. The same or different from research with adults?' *Childhood*, 9(3): 321–41.

Punch, S. (2003) 'Childhoods in the majority world: miniature adults or tribal children?', *Sociology*, 37(2): 277–95.

Quah, S. (2009) *Families in Asia. Home and Kin*. London: Routledge.

Quinton, D. (2004) *Supporting Parents: Messages from Research*. London: Jessica Kingsley Publishers.

Ransome, P. (1999) *Sociology and the Future of Work: Contemporary Discourses and Debates*. Aldershot: Ashgate.

Rapoport, R., Bailyn, L., Fletcher, J.K. and Pruitt, B.H. (2002) *Beyond Work–Family Balance: Advancing Gender Equity and Workplace Performance*. San Francisco: Jossey-Bass.

Reeves, R. (2001) *Happy Mondays: Putting the Pleasure Back into Work*. Harlow: Pearson Education.

Reeves, R. (2002) *Dad's Army: The Case for Father-friendly Workplaces*. London: The Work Foundation.

Reibstein, J. (2006) *The Best Kept Secret: Men and Women's Stories of Lasting Love*. London: Bloomsbury.

Reidel, L. (2008) 'Religious opposition to same-sex marriage in Canada: limits to multiculturalism', *Human Rights Review*, 10(2): 61–81.

Reyes, M.M. (2008) *Migration and Filipino Children Left-Behind: A Literature Review*. Quezon Heights, Philippines: Miriam College.

Ribbens McCarthy, J. and Edwards, R. (2010a) *Key Concepts in Family Studies*. London: Sage.

Ribbens McCarthy, J. and Edwards, R. (2010b) 'Writing the field: key concepts in family studies', paper presented at the International Conference of the Centre for Research on Families and Relationships, 16–18 June 2010, Edinburgh.

Rimashevskaya, N., Vannoi, D. and Malysheva, M. (1999) *A Window to Russian Private Life: Spousal Couples in 1999*. Moscow: Academia Press.

Riphenburg, C. (1997) 'Women, status and cultural expression: changing gender relations and structural adjustment in Zimbabwe', *Africa Today*, 44(1): 33–50.

Ritzen, J. (2000) '*Social Cohesion, Public Policy and Economic Growth: Implications for OECD Countries*', paper presented to OECD/HRDC International Symposium on the Contribution of Human and Social Capital to Sustained Economic Growth and Well-Being, Quebec City, available at www.oecd.org/dataoecd/25/2/1825690.pdf (accessed 14 January 2011).

Robertson, A. (1988) 'Welfare state and welfare society', *Social Policy and Administration*, 22: 222–34.

Rodger, J.J. (2003) 'Family life, moral regulation and the state: social steering and the personal sphere', in S. Cunningham-Burley and L. Jamieson (eds), *Families and the State: Changing Relationships*. Basingstoke: Palgrave.

Roopnarine, J.L. and Gielen, U.P. (2005) 'Families in global perspective: an introduction', in J.L. Roopnarine and U.P. Gielen (eds), *Families in Global Perspective*. Boston: Pearson.

Rosenberg, L. and Bloom, D. (2004) *World Population Prospects 2004*. New York: United Nations.

Roseneil, S. (2005) 'Living and loving beyond the boundaries of the heteronorm: personal relationships in the 21st century', in L. McKie, S. Cunningham-Burley and J. McKendrick (eds), *Families in Society: Boundaries and Relationships*. Bristol: Policy Press.

Roseneil, S. (2006) 'In not living with a partner: unpicking coupledom and cohabitation', Sociological Research Online, 11(3), available at www.socresonline.org.uk/11/3/roseneil.html (accessed 6 September 2010).

Rowlingson, K. (2001) 'The social, demographic and economic profile of lone parents', in J. Millar and K. Rowlingson (eds), *Lone Parents, Employment and Social Policy: Cross-national Comparisons*. Bristol: Policy Press.

Rowthorn, R. and Webster, D. (2006) '*Male Worklessness and the Rise of Lone Parenthood in Britain*', Oxford Centre for Population Research, Working Paper No. 31.

Ruggie, M. (1984) *The State and Working Women*. Princeton, NJ: Princeton University Press.

Sainsbury, D. (1996) *Gender, Equality and Welfare States*. Cambridge: Cambridge University Press.

Sassen, S. (2000) 'Women's burden: counter-geographies of globalization and the feminization of survival', *Journal of International Affairs*, 53, 2: 504–24.

Schneider, D. (1968) *American Kinship: A Cultural Account*. Englewood Cliffs, NJ: Prentice Hall.

Schooler, D. and Ward, L.M. (2006) 'Average Joes: men's relationships with media, real bodies and sexuality', *Psychology of Men and Masculinity*, 7(1): 27–41.

Sevenhuijsen, S. (1998) *Citizenship and the Ethics of Care: Feminist Consideration on Justice, Morality and Politics*. London: Routledge.

Shaw, G.B. (2007) *Getting Married*. Fairfield: First World Publishing.

Silva, E. (2010) *Technology, Culture, Family: Influences on Home Life*. Basingstoke: Palgrave Macmillan.

Silverstein, L.B. and Auerbach, C.F. (2005) '(Post) Modern Families', in J.L. Roopnarine and U.P. Gielen (eds), *Families in Global Perspective*. Boston: Pearson.

Simmel, G. (1950) *The Sociology of Georg Simmel* (compiled and translated by Kurt Wolff). Glencoe, IL: Free Press.

Singapore Department of Statistics (2006) *Annual Review*. Singapore: Department of Statistics.

Smart, C. (1984) *The Ties that Bind: Law, Marriage and the Reproduction of Patriarchal Relations*. London: Routledge and Kegan Paul.

Smart, C. (2007) *Personal Life: New Directions in Sociological Thinking*. Cambridge: Polity Press.

Smart, C. and Neale, B. (1999) *Family Fragments?* Cambridge: Polity Press.

Smart, C. and Stevens, P. (2000) *Cohabitation Breakdown*. London: Family Policy Studies Centre.

Smart, C. and Shipman, B. (2004) 'Visions in Monochrome: families, marriage and the individualization thesis', *British Journal of Sociology*, 55(4): 491–509.

Solesbury, W. (2001) *Evidence Based Policy: Whence it Came and Where it's Going*, ESRC UK Centre for Evidence Based Policy and Practice Working Paper No. 1.

Somerville, M. (2004) 'What about the children?', in: D. Cere and D. Farrow (eds), *Divorcing Marriage*. Montreal: McGill-Queen's University Press.

Spicker, P. (2000) *The Welfare State: A General Theory*. London: Sage.

Stanley, S.M. (2002) 'What is it with men and commitment, anyway?', Keynote address to the 6th Annual Smart Marriages Conference, 9–16 July 2002, Washington D.C.

Stanley, S.M. (2010) 'What is it with men and commitment, anyway?', Working paper to update Stanley (2002), available at www.prepinc.com/main/docs/scotts corner/Men_and_Commitment_Stanley_Update.pdf (accessed 10 November 2010).

Stanley, S.M., Amato, P.R., Johnson, C.A. and Markman, H.J. (2006) 'Premarital education, marital quality, and marital stability: Findings from a large, random, household survey', *Journal of Family Psychology*, 20(1): 117–26.

Statistics Norway (2008) *Statistical Yearbook 2008, Table 47* available at http://www.ssb.no/english/yearbook/2008/tab/tab-047.html (accessed 12 June 2011).

Steenhof, L. and Harmsen, C. (2002) *Same-sex Couples in the Netherlands*, Statistics Netherlands (Division of Social and Spatial Statistics, Department of Statistical Analysis), available at www.cbs.nl/NR/rdonlyres/74975167-2503-43A0-8821-66F88DA2B6B2/0/samesexcouples.pdf (accessed 11 September 2010).

Stone, L. (1977) *The Family, Sex and Marriage in England, 1500–1800*. London: Weidenfeld and Nicolson.

Stuckler, D. (2010) 'Analysis: Budget crises, health, and social welfare programmes', *British Medical Journal*, 340: c3311.

Sugimoto, Y. (2003) *An Introduction to Japanese Society*, 2nd edn. Cambridge: Cambridge University Press (1st edn 1987).

Sullivan, O. (2006) *Changing Gender Relations, Changing Families: Tracing the Pace of Change*. New York: Rowman and Littlefield (Gender Lens Series).

Sullivan, O. (2010) 'Changing differences by educational attainment in fathers' domestic labour and child care', *Sociology*, 44(4): 716–33.

Taran, P.A. and Geronimi, E. (2003) 'Globalization, labour and migration: protection is paramount', in *Perspectives on Labour Migration 3E*. International Migration Programme, International Labour Office, Geneva, available at www.ilo.org/public/english/protection/migrant/download/pom/pom3e.pdf (accessed 27 June 2010).

Taylor, R. (2004) 'Extending conceptual boundaries: work, voluntary work and employment', *Work, Employment and Society*, 18 (1): 29–49.

Thane, P. (2010) *Happy Families? History and Policy*. London: British Academy Policy Centre.

The Millennium Project (2011) *Global Futures Studies and Research*, available at www.millennium-project.org/millennium/demographicsregional.html (accessed 11 March 2011).

Therborn, G. (2004) *Between Sex and Power: Family in the World, 1900–2000*. London: Routledge.

Thompson, M.G. and Heller, K. (1990) 'Facets of support related to well-being: Quantitative social isolation and perceived family support in a sample of elderly women', *Psychology and Aging*, 5(4): 535–44.

Thompson, R. and Amato, P. (1999) 'The postdivorce family: an introduction to the issues', in: R. Thompson and P. Amato (eds), *The Postdivorce family*. Thousand Oaks, CA: Sage.

Times of India (2008) 'Divorces for every 5 knots in Mumbai', 25 January, available at http://timesofindia.indiatimes.com/2_divorces_for_every_5_marriages_in_Mumbai/articleshow/2729438.cms (accessed 11 September 2010).

Tong, R. (2009) *Feminist Thought*. Boulder, CO: Westview (1st edn 1989).

Tough, P. (2009) *Whatever it Takes*. New York: First Mariner Books.

Trades Union Congress (2009) *Women and Recession. How will this Recession Affect Women?* London: Trades Union Congress.

Tyyska, V. (2000) '"Cohabitation" entry', in C. Kramarae and D. Spender (eds), *Routledge International Encyclopedia of Women: Global Women's Issues and Knowledge*, Vol. 1. London: Routledge.

United Nations (1990) *International Convention on the Protection of the Rights of All Migrant Workers and Members of Their Families*, available at www2.ohchr.org/english/law/cmw.htm (accessed 27 June 2010).

United Nations (2004) United Nations General Assembley 59th session Agenda Item 94 A/59/592, available at www.undemocracy.com/A-59-592.pdf (accessed 11 September 2011).

United Nations Department of Economic and Social Affairs, Population Division (2009) *Annual Number of Divorces and Crude Divorce Rates (2009)*, available at www.un.org/esa/population/publications/WMD2008/Data/UNPD_WMD_2008_DIVORCES.xls (accessed 27 December 2010).

United Nations Educational Scientific and Cultural Organization (2009) *Parent Empowerment for Family Literacy Project (PEFaL) Report*, available at www.unesco.org/uil/litbase/?menu=4andprogramme=53 (accessed 27 June 2010).

United Nations International Children's Fund (2003) *Press Release for International Women's Day*, available at www.unicef.org/media/media_7594.html (accessed 28 December 2010).

United Nations Programme on the Family (2009) *Family Policy in a Changing World: Promoting Social Protection and Intergenerational Solidarity*. Report of the Expert Group Meeting Doha, Qatar 14–16 April

2009, available at www.un.org/esa/socdev/family/meetings/egmreportdoha09.pdf (accessed 27 June 2010).

van Acker, E. (2009) 'Service delivery of relationship support programs in Australia: implications for the "community sector"', *Politics and Policy*, 37(6): 1307–29.

Vanek, J. (1974) 'Time spent on housework', *Scientific American*, 237: 116–20.

Veblen, T. (1970) *The Theory of the Leisure Class: An Economic Study of Institutions*. London: Unwin.

Voicu, M., Voicu, B. and Strapcova, K. (2007) 'Housework and gender inequality in European countries', *European Sociological Review*, 25(3): 365–77.

Walby, S. (1990) *Theorising Patriarchy*. London: Wiley-Blackwell.

Walker, J. (2006) 'Supporting families in democratic societies: public concerns and private realities', keynote paper at 53rd ICCFR International Conference 'Families and Democracy: Compatibility, Incompatibility, Opportunity or Challenge?', 7–19 June 2006, Lyon, France.

Wallace, C. (2002) 'Household strategies: their conceptual relevance and analytical scope in social research', *Sociology*, 36(2): 275–92.

Warde, A. (1990) 'Household work strategies and forms of labour: conceptual and empirical issues', *Work, Employment and Society*, 44(4): 495–515.

Weeks, J. (1991) *Sexuality and its Discontents: Meanings, Myths, and Modern Sexualities*. London: Routledge.

Weeks, J., Donovan, M. and Heaphy, B. (2001) *Same Sex Intimacies: Families of Choice and Other Life Experiments*. New York: Routledge.

Whitehead, S. (2002) *Men and Masculinities*. Oxford: Blackwell Press.

Wilcox, W.B. (ed.) (2010) *The State of Our Unions: Marriage in America 2010*. University of Virginia National Marriage Project/Institute for American Values. Charlottesville: University of Virginia.

Williams, F. (2004) *Rethinking Families*. London: Calouste Gulbenkian Foundation.

Williams, M. and May, T. (1996) *An Introduction to the Philosophy of Social Research*. London: Routledge.

Windebank, J. (2001) 'Dual-earner couples in Britain and France: gender divisions of domestic labour and parenting work in different welfare states', *Work, Employment and Society*, 15(2): 262–90.

Wolf, M. (2000) 'Why this hatred of the market', in: J. Lechner and J. Boli (eds), *The Globalisation Reader*. Malden: Blackwell Publishers.

World Bank (2008) *Data on World Economies*. Washington: World Bank. www.worldbank.org (accessed 22 June 2011).

Woodward, K. and Woodward, S. (2009) *Why Feminism Matters: Feminism Lost and Found*. London: Palgrave Macmillan.

World Health Organization (2005) *The World Health Report 2005: Make Every Mother and Child Count*. Geneva: WHO.

World Health Organization (2007a) *The World Health Report 2007 – A Safer Future: Global Public Health Security in the 21st Century*. Geneva: WHO.

World Health Organization (2007b) *Maternal Mortality in 2005: Estimates Developed by WHO, UNICEF, UNFPA, and the World Bank*. Geneva: WHO.

Yi, Z. (2002) 'A demographics analysis of family households in China, 1982–1995', *Journal of Comparative Family Studies*, 33(1): 15–34.

Young, M. (1954) 'The planners and the planned: the family', *Journal of Town Planning Institute*, 60: 134–42.

Young, M. and Wilmott, P. (1957) *Family and Kinship in East London*. London: Routledge and Kegan Paul.

Zinn, M.B. and Eitzen, D.S. (1990) *Diversity in Families*. New York: Harper and Row.

Zwingle, E. and McNally, J. (1999). A world together. *National Geographic*, 196(2): 6–33.

Index